Mediating Business:
The Expansion
of Business Journalism

Peter Kjær & Tore Slaatta (Editors)

Mediating Business:
The Expansion
of Business Journalism

Copenhagen Business School Press

Mediating Business: The Expansion of Business Journalism

© Copenhagen Business School Press, 2007
Printed in Denmark by Narayana Press, Gylling
Cover design by BUSTO | Graphic Design

First edition 2007

ISBN 978-87-630-0199-1

Distribution:

Scandinavia
DJOEF/DBK, Mimersvej 4
DK-4600 Køge, Denmark
Tel +45 3269 7788
Fax +45 3269 7789

North America
International Specialized Book Services
920 NE 58th Ave., Suite 300
Portland, OR 97213, USA
Tel +1 800 944 6190
Fax +1 503 280 8832
Email: orders@isbs.com

Rest of the World
Marston Book Services, P.O. Box 269
Abingdon, Oxfordshire, OX14 4YN, UK
Tel +44 (0) 1235 465500, fax +44 (0) 1235 4656555
E-mail Direct Customers: direct.order@marston.co.uk
E-mail Booksellers: trade.order@marston.co.uk

Table of Contents

List of Contributors 7

Preface 11

CHAPTER 1 13
Mediating Business
Toward a Relational Perspective
Peter Kjær & Tore Slaatta

PART I: BUSINESS NEWS AND MEDIA ORDERS

CHAPTER 2 35
The Nordic Business Press and the New Field of
Business Journalism (1960-2005)
Tore Slaatta with Peter Kjær, Maria Grafström & Niina Erkama

CHAPTER 3 73
The Professionalization of Business Journalism in Finland
Antti Ainamo, Janne Tienari & Eero Vaara

CHAPTER 4 101
Expansion of the Nordic Business Press
Äripäev in Estonia as a Carrier of Western Discourses
Annette Risberg & Antti Ainamo

PART II: BUSINESS NEWS, PUBLIC KNOWLEDGE AND
           MEANING

CHAPTER 5 131
Transforming Business News Content
A Comparative Analysis
Peter Kjær, Niina Erkama & Maria Grafström

CHAPTER 6 159
Changing Constructions of Business and Society in the News
Peter Kjær

CHAPTER 7 187
The Gospel According to the Global Market
How Journalists Frame Ownership in the Case of Nokia in Finland
Janne Tienari, Eero Vaara & Niina Erkama

**PART III: BUSINESS NEWS AND ORGANIZATIONAL
          CHANGE**

CHAPTER 8 217
The Negotiation of Business News
Maria Grafström & Josef Pallas

CHAPTER 9 235
Dressing Up Hospitals as Enterprises?
*The Expansion and Managerialization of
Communication in Norwegian Hospitals*
Haldor Byrkjeflot & Svein Ivar Angell

CHAPTER 10 265
Corporate Governance and the Media
From Agency Theory to Edited Corporations
Lars Engwall & Kerstin Sahlin

CHAPTER 11 285
Media Transparency as an Institutional Practice
Peter Kjær & Kerstin Sahlin

List of Contributors

Antti Ainamo (PhD, Helsinki School of Economics 1996) is Professor of Innovation, Technology and Science policy at the University of Turku. His research interests include: design, fashion, media and, more generally, knowledge intermediation, as well as new and strategic forms of organization. His publications include articles in *Organization Science*, *Research in the Sociology of Organizations*, and *Human Relations*. He also edited *Handbook of Service and Product Development in Communication and Information Technology* (Kluwer Academic Publishers 2003, with T. Korhonen).

Svein Ivar Angell (Dr. art., University of Bergen 2002) is a historian and researcher at the Stein Rokkan Center for Social Research, University of Bergen. His research interests include: Strategic communication in public institutions presently and historically, political history and national identity. He has published several books and articles on these topics, e.g. in *Scandinavian Journal of History*. Currently he is working on a research project on strategic communication in the Norwegian hospital sector.

Haldor Byrkjeflot (PhD, University of Bergen 1998) is a senior researcher at the Stein Rokkan Center for Interdisciplinary Research, University of Bergen. He has done comparative research on healthcare reforms, management systems, business schools and organization of knowledge production and is currently involved in projects on strategic communication in public sector organizations. His publications include Byrkjeflot H. et al. (eds.) *The Democratic Challenge to Capitalism. Management and Democracy in the Nordic Countries* (Fakbokforlaget 2001) as well as articles in *Higher Education* and in Engwall, L. and Sahlin-Anderson, K. (eds.) *The Expansion of Management Knowledge: Carriers, Flows and Sources* (2002).

Lars Engwall is Professor of Business Administration at Uppsala University since 1981. He has also held visiting positions in Belgium, France and the United States. His research has been directed towards structural analyses of industries and organizations as well as the creation and diffusion of management knowledge. He has published a number of books and a large number of articles within the field of management. Among his books related to the present volume are *Management Consulting: The Emergence and Dynamics of A Knowl-*

edge Industry (Oxford University Press, 2002, co-editor Matthias Kipping), and *The Expansion of Management Knowledge. Carriers, Flows and Sources* (Stanford Business Books, 2002, co-editor Kerstin Sahlin-Andersson).

Niina Erkama is a doctoral candidate in the Department of International Business at the Helsinki School of Economics. At the moment she is finalizing her doctoral thesis. Her research interests include: organizational restructuring, shutdowns, in particular legitimation and resistance in organizational settings and in the media. She has previously published in *The Finnish Journal of Business Economics*.

Maria Grafström (PhD, Uppsala University, 2006) is a researcher and lecturer at Uppsala University's Department of Business Studies. Her main research interests concern the relationship between media and corporations and how media participate in creating conditions for corporations. More specifically, she has studied the development and organisation of business newspapers, content and production of business news, and how management models, such as CSR, are created and spread via the media. Maria has published several book chapters and reports within the area.

Peter Kjær (PhD, Stockholm University, 1996) is Associate Professor in the Department of Organization at the Copenhagen Business School. His research interests include: business journalism, management knowledge and institutions, and strategic communication. He has published articles in *Journal of Economic Issues, Scandinavian Journal of Management*, and *Business History*, and has also written a number of book chapters on these topics. In 2001-2006 he directed the research project "The Rise of the Nordic Business Press". In 2003-2007 he participated in the Danish media research project "PRO-Media". Currently he is Director of the Center for Health Management at the Copenhagen Business School.

Josef Pallas is a PhD-candidate at the Department of Business Studies at Uppsala University. His research interests include corporate media and public communication, business journalism, and organizational perspectives on the production of media content. His upcoming thesis investigates corporate media activities involved the in co-creating and co-shaping of institutional settings.

Annette Risberg (PhD, Lund University, 1999) is Associate Professor in the Department of Intercultural Communication and Management at the Copenhagen Business School. In recent years she has focused her research interests on media discourses and the expansion of the media industry, mergers and acquisitions as well as diversity in organisations. She has, for example, published in *Journal of World Business, Culture and Organisations*, and various book chapters in these topics. In 2003 – 2007 Annette was part of the Danish media research project "PRO-Media".

Kerstin Sahlin is Professor of management at Uppsala University. Her research interests include: transnational governance, corporate social responsibility and changes in public-private relations, changed forms of governance in health care and universities, organizing in the mediatized society and the travels of management ideas. She recently edited *Transnational Governance: Institutional Dynamics of Regulation* (Cambridge University Press 2006, with Marie-Laure Djelic), *The Expansion of Management Knowledge: Carriers, Flows and Sources* (Stanford University Press 2002, with Lars Engwall) and *Beyond Project Management: New Perspectives on the temporary-permanent dilemma* (Liber 2002, with Anders Söderholm). Currently she is the deputy vice-chancellor of Uppsala University.

Tore Slaatta (Dr. Polit., University of Oslo, 1998) is Professor in the Department of Media and Communication at the University of Oslo and writes about issues related to European culture and media, the relationship between the economic field and journalism, EU journalism, cultural policies, urban development, design, art and architecture. Slaatta was responsible for the media research in the Norwegian Research Program on Power and Democracy (1998-2003) and director of the research project "Symbolic Power in the Economic and the Political fields", published in *Den norske medieorden (The Norwegian Media Order)* (2003) and *Digital makt (Digital Power)* (2002).

Janne Tienari (PhD, Helsinki School of Economics, 1999) is Professor of Management and Organizations at Lappeenranta University of Technology, Finland, and the Editor of the *Scandinavian Journal of Management*. Tienari's research interests include managing multinational corporations, cross-cultural studies of gender and organizing, and media discourse. He has published in leading international journals such as *Organization, Organization Studies, Journal of Management*

Studies, Gender, Work and Organization, British Journal of Management, Human Relations, Journal of Management Inquiry, and the *International Journal of Human Resource Management.*

Eero Vaara (PhD, Helsinki School of Economics, 1999) is Professor of Management and Organization at Swedish School of Economics and Business Administration in Helsinki, Finland, and a permanent Visiting Professor at Ecole de Management de Lyon, France. His research interests focus on organizational change, strategy and strategizing, multinational corporations and globalization, and the role of the media in organizing and management. He has lately worked especially on narrative and discursive perspectives. His work has been published in leading academic journals such as *Organization, Organization Studies, Journal of Management Studies, Gender, Work and Organization, British Journal of Management, Human Relations, Journal of Management Inquiry,* and the *International Journal of Human Resource Management.*

Preface

In this book we analyze the expansion of business news and the way in which this has transformed the relations between media, business and public discourse in the Nordic countries.

The idea for the book emerged from a conference held in Barcelona in December 2000, where the role of mass media in the consumption of management knowledge was discussed. At the conference it became clear – particularly to a group of Nordic participants – that business knowledge was being increasingly "mediated" i.e. more dependent on being communicated via newspapers, business magazines and other mass media outlets. This mediation of business and management knowledge was associated with an unprecedented expansion of business news that had begun during the 1960s and 1970s but that had remained virtually unnoticed in both media and management studies.

Immediately after the conference we established a joint research project entitled "The Rise of the Nordic Business Press" with the idea of mapping what we regarded as a significant innovative phase in the history of the business press in the Nordic countries. Our first discussions concentrated primarily on historical trends in news content, media organization and journalism in the individual countries. However, as the project evolved, we became increasingly interested in the wider implications of the expansion of business news: how did it alter relations between journalists and business sources, what were the organizational consequences of growing media coverage, how did the expansion of business journalism affect other fields of knowledge, and so on?

In the book we address these concerns by analyzing the expansion of business news in the national media landscapes of Denmark, Finland, Norway and Sweden, and by exploring some of its organizational and societal consequences.

In the course of the project we have received invaluable support from many people and organizations. We wish to thank *NOS-HS (The Joint Committee for Nordic Research Councils for the Humanities and the Social Sciences)* for sponsoring the project. We also wish to express our gratitude to Professor *Roy Langer* of Roskilde University, who helped us to launch the project and served as a constructive force throughout its execution. Further, we would like to acknowledge the valuable contributions of Guðbjörg Hildur Kolbeins and Hilmar Thor

Bjarnason of Reykjavik in the early stages of the project. And finally, we would like to thank Marianne Risberg, who has handled the administration of the project with great efficiency, Nancy Adler who provided excellent linguistic assistance to the authors, and Hanne Tranberg who assisted during the final editing of the book.

Copenhagen and Oslo, May 2007

Peter Kjær and Tore Slaatta

CHAPTER 1

Mediating Business
Toward a Relational Perspective

PETER KJÆR & TORE SLAATTA

Today it seems quite natural that much of the news in our daily news-papers and on our televisions is concerned with business and finance, or that the 12 o'clock news on the radio should automatically include several stories about the financial statements of big companies or the latest developments on the national or international stock exchange. To inside market observers, the extensive media coverage of business and economy just mirrors what they understand as the increasing impor-tance of economic affairs in our daily lives. For better or for worse, economic considerations have become a key factor in all kinds of deci-sions, private as well as public, and the news media's extensive moni-toring of the economic sphere is therefore only natural.

However, the idea of the 'natural' importance of business news in Western, capitalist societies is a fairly recent phenomenon, and a criti-cal look at the changing role of business news journalism is much needed. Over a period of only 30 - 40 years business news has been subject to expansion on a grand scale. The proportion of business news compared to other news in general news media has increased, new out-lets for business information and news have appeared, and new tech-nology has transformed the context for production, mediation and con-sumption of business news. To regard this expansion as a natural re-sponse to changes in the economy obscures its broader significance as part of wider social transformations that seem to take place simultane-ously in different regions of the world.

This book analyzes the expansion of business news in the Nordic region in the period between 1960 and 2005. Although the changing role and power of the financial press and business journalism must be seen as a global phenomenon, we will argue that the Nordic context, characterized among other things by distinct conceptions of the rela-tion between public and private, business and society, etc., provides us with a particularly interesting case for analyzing the changing connections between business journalism, economic organization and public knowledge.

Like virtually all other capitalist economies, those of the Nordic countries have experienced a dramatic expansion in business news production over the last 20-30 years. A detailed study of the Nordic countries allows us to consider some of the basic patterns and dynamics involved in this general development of business news. At the same time, however, the expansion of business news represents a particularly complex challenge to the Nordic countries, where it is occurring in national contexts with relatively weak commercial mass media, highly developed awareness of social welfare and national economic policies, and economic institutions characterized by early internationalization and strong traditions of economic regulation.

Our approach to this transformation will be an *institutional* one, thus entailing an interest in the way concrete fields are regulated and organized, how particular positions, roles and activities are legitimized and how particular norms and worldviews become stabilized and taken for granted. We are interested in the way in which the expansion of business news transforms not only the institutional context of news production, but also the institutional context of the production of shared meaning and knowledge in society and the institutional context within which economic organizations operate today. How has a modern business press emerged, how does it relate to and affect the media context of which it is a part, how does it contribute to the production of economic and business knowledge in society, and how does it transform relations between business organizations and their surroundings?

The collection of articles in this book aims to describe the actors, institutions and dynamics involved in expansion of business as well as some of the implications of the process of expansion. While the chapters represent different theoretical and methodological points of departure, they all share an interest in institutional change observed in three basic dimensions:

In Part I (Chapters 2, 3 and 4), we particularly approach the expansion of business news in terms of a series of changes within and between national or regional *media orders*. Business news is mediated via a great variety of media platforms. Thus, fundamentally, expansion simply means more or larger platforms, or bigger circulation for business news. The concept of media order refers to the way in which the news media construct their own public communicative space, as well as the particular ways of disseminating information in a given society.

Issues to be considered include how business news has expanded in connection with particular technological platforms (print, audiovisual media, Internet), within particular positions or points of departure (general-interest or niche, internal or external, critical or supportive, etc.), and whether the expansion occurs within a national, regional or even a global media order. The expansion of business news does not refer only to particular media platforms, products or outlets. It also implies a transformation of the position of business journalists in the overall field of journalism because business journalism emerges as a distinct and legitimate sub-field of its own (Bourdieu 1993, Benson & Neveu 2005, Slaatta 2002).

In Part II (Chapters 5, 6 and 7), we approach the expansion of business news in terms of a reconfiguration of the *public knowledge and meaning* in society. News production can be seen as a discursive practice that frames public conceptions of social reality and social action while also drawing upon other forms of discourse in society. In this context business news can thus be analyzed in terms of its role as a particular way of framing public conceptions of economic reality and action (Emmison 1983, Parsons 1989, Fairclough 1995, Gavin (Ed.) 1998), and as an important locus for the production of social discourse.

In Part III (Chapters 8-11), we approach the expansion of business news in terms of *organizational change*, since the expansion of business news also transforms organizational environments as well as organizations as such. Economic organizations operate in complex technical and institutional environments. From the perspective of the economic organization, business news can be seen as relevant for the management of an organization's relations with key actors in the environment such as customers or suppliers, and as a source of information about the market or the society in which it operates (Pfeffer & Salancik 1978). In this context the expansion of business news entails an increase in the intensity and complexity of the environmental relations that affect the way organizations can influence their environments – for example by managing media relations and media visibility in particular ways – and, in turn, the way organizations are shaped by their environmental relations, for instance in their perceptions of themselves, of their roles in society or of their future potentials in the market.

The book thus represents three points of entry for empirical research: via the media orders, via public knowledge and meaning, and via economic organizations.

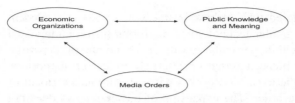

Figure 1.1 Empirical Points of Entry

Below, using these three points of entry, we briefly review earlier re-search on business news and show how the phenomenon of business news has been explored to date, and where we hope this collection of articles will make a contribution to the field.

Business News Research – a Field in the Making

The research literature on business news and business journalism is not voluminous, and most contributions in our view tend to emphasize one side of the business-media-discourse triangle, i.e. they approach busi-ness news either from the point of view of journalism or of public opinion and discourse, or from the point of view of business, manage-ment and organization. As will be clear, research that tries to connect all three approaches is rare.

In media and journalism studies two general types of analysis have been applied to the business press and business news. Scholars with a historical orientation have described the history of key business news-papers or magazines or the emergence of national business press sys-tems. Their work includes studies of the early business press (Forsyth 1964), the development of the specialized business press (Endres 1988), the expansion of business and economy news on television (Mosettig 1985), the changing relationship between business media and the stock market (Quirt 1993), and the history of individual busi-ness news outlets (Rosenberg 1982, Read 1992, Reilly 1999). All these studies concentrate on the innovative role and early professionalization of the business journalist profession, especially in the United States. A number of scholars have analyzed the current status of business jour-nalism. In such cases the emphasis is usually on the role of the press as a countervailing power in society, and it is argued that our first con-cern should be with the quality and professional standards of business journalism. Henriques (2000a) sees the press as 'the last stand' in a so-ciety that has become almost totally dominated by business. At the heart of the matter is the struggle for control or the negotiation of con-trol over the production of meaning between journalists and their sources (e.g. Ericson, Baranek & Chan 1989, Hollifield 1997). Here, several contributors suggest that professional communicators seem to have the upper hand when it comes to getting their views and news across to the general public (e.g. Glasgow University Media Group 1980, L'Etang & Pieczka 1996, Mundy 1995, Davis 2000). This chimes in with Doyle's recent claim that business journalists generally regard themselves as professionals in the business community, where standards of reporting and criticism are set within a business frame of reference (Doyle 2006). Studies emanating from media and journalism research focus primarily on media organizations and the professional norms commonly associated with news journalism (see also Welles 2001, Roush 2004). These studies have much in common with our present interest in the expansion of business journalism within particular media orders, although they tend to evaluate change exclusively from the perspective of the media, rather than considering the relation between changes in journalism and changes in economic organizations and the wider public and political discourses.

A related strand of research emphasizes the effect of the expansion of business news journalism on *public opinion and public knowledge*. Here we find one of the most comprehensive analyses of the history of the business press and its relation to public knowledge, namely Wayne Parsons' *The Power of the Financial Press. Journalism and Economic Opinion in Britain and America* (Parsons 1989). Parsons combines an historical account of the British and American tradition in business journalism with a discussion of the changing relations between business journalism and the expert field of economic commentary. He successfully combines an analysis of changes in business journalism with an analysis of shifts in knowledge orientation and political ideology in society as a whole. However, his claim that the rise of neo-liberalism in the 1970s and 1980s can be explained by, or reflected in, changes in business journalism ignores the fact that business and management also changed during the same period. Parsons' argument must be taken further. Not only has the expansion of business news journalism furthered the flow of economic and business knowledge and promoted its legitimization; it has also transformed the field of business and management. Thus, it remains an important task for research to study how the expansion of business news relate to changes in the economic field, and to consider the potential of business journalism to make a political, organizational and cultural impact also in the economic sphere.

The same criticism can be directed at other important recent research contributions. In an approach that is less historically oriented and more preoccupied with media content, Gavin and associates (Gavin (Ed.) 1998) claim that economic news is constitutive of popular perceptions of the economy and particular ideas about relevance, action, etc., and that by way of various narrative and discursive means it constructs certain entities as pre-given and real. According to this view, business coverage typically entails a strong implicit selectivity as regards themes and actors that may have serious implications for the formation of public opinion and economic policymaking (see also Lindhoff & Mårtensson 1996, Slaatta 2003, Goozner 2000, Poole 2000). Similarly, Neuman, Just & Crigler (1992, see also Parker 1998, Haller & Norporth 1998) argue that common knowledge about the economy is continually being constructed and mediated by the news media through the practice of news production and the professional use of news frames. However, the authors also find that audiences actively participate in the construction and negotiation of the meaning of news. Several other studies maintain that business news as a particular form of discourse has important ideological underpinnings and is characterized by nationalistic, ethnic and gender biases (e.g. Krefting 2002, Vaara & Tienari 2002, Hellgren et al. 2002, Tienari, Vaara & Björkman 2003) which in turn influence the selection, definition and interpretation of news events and actors. We share the emphasis that these studies give to the socially constructed nature of economic knowledge. However, research on public opinion and public knowledge is often more preoccupied with media content and less with relations between the mass media and other knowledge-producers or the concrete relationship between 'economic opinion' and economic actors and institutions. As Parsons, Slaatta and others have suggested, the power and the role of mediated business news discourse can hardly be determined separately from the particular institutional context in which it appears. However, how these connections should be expressed theoretically and studied empirically has not yet been satisfactorily developed.

Research on economic organization suffers from a similar imbalance, so that many concrete aspects of business news production are often neglected. Among studies of the effects of news coverage on markets or 'the economy' in general, Kindleberger's (1989) seminal study of the relationship between economic crisis and news coverage stands out, although the author's explanation of panics and crashes focuses on the market more than on the media. He claims that although the timing of events - their postponement or their speeding up - may be affected by the news coverage, the role of the news media is generally exaggerated (Kindleberger 1989, see also Warner & Moloch 1993).

Studies, geared more toward the micro-level, usually come up with hypotheses about the media's involvement in and effects on the stock market. Thompson, Olsen and Dietrich (1987), focusing on news about firms included in the Wall Street Journal is an example of this, while Becker, Finnerty and Friedman (1995), with its focus on particular financial markets, is another. But little is said in these studies about the specific role of the media or about differences between media platforms or contexts.

A particularly useful line of research is developing within the field of business and management. In this literature it is suggested that media reporting plays an important part in disseminating and popularizing particular models of management and organization (Abrahamson 1996, Alvarez 1996, Mazza 1997, Mazza & Alvarez 2000), and that it affects both individual and collective sensemaking as regards organizational and managerial performance (Meindl, Ehrlich & Dukerich 1985, Chen & Meindl 1991, Hayward et al. 2004, Rindova et al. 2006). A dominant strand of research here has been concerned with the influence of the media on organizational image or reputation (Elsbach & Sutton 1992, Elsbach 1994, Deephouse 1996, 2000, Pollock & Rindova 2003, Carroll & McCombs 2003), identity (Dutton & Dukerich 1991, Elsbach & Kramer 1996, Morsing 1999) and innovation (Nordfors et al. 2006). Recently, a comprehensive literature on public relations, strategic issues management and so on has also appeared, often adopting a critical and historical approach to the communications industry and its implications (e.g. Ewen 1996, Mayhew 1997, Marchand 1998, Kounalikis, Banks & Daus 1999).

Most researchers correctly note the importance of the mass media in this context, but they also emphasize that organizations are becoming increasingly engaged in attempts to manage legitimacy, reputation or identity and, further, that reputations and identities are both constructed in continuous interaction between organizational members, management, the mass media and other important external stakeholders. One or two researchers have begun to look in more detail at the sociology of the mass media (e.g. Deephouse 2000, Carroll & McCombs 2003, see also Nordfors et al. 2006), but few of the other studies mentioned above subject the media itself to empirical investigation, since they are interested primarily in the effects of media coverage in general, often regarding the media as one among several carriers of management knowledge (Sahlin-Andersson & Engwall 2002) or as an influence on organizational identity and legitimacy (Hatch & Schultz 2000).

Lastly, among the studies that have begun to explore more fully the interaction between media development and economic organization, mention should be made of research concerned with the role of new technology and the Internet in the expansion of financial market institutions and trade beyond the boundaries of the nation state (Castells 2000, Everard 2000, Sassen 2000). Here a number of recent studies have examined the development of electronic platforms whose combined purpose is to mediate information, news, analyses and real-time market transactions. According to Palmer (1999), the new technology combining new hardware and software was developed by Reuters during the 1970s and 1980s in order to suit the logic of a new, expansive global market economy (see also Boyd-Barrett & Rantanen 1998, Seidman 1997, Barnes 1998). The new technology, which was an immediate success among traders and brokers, not only provided opportunities for the real-time global trading of international financial products such as currencies (Forex) and futures (Globex) and for all kinds of derivatives, but as the value of trading reached astonishing peaks, it also produced a highly volatile and vulnerable global economy. Claims have been made that the real-time economy has become a threat to itself, and that is has become so difficult to monitor and control how it threatens stability and global governability (Hutton & Giddens 2000, Schiller 1999).

This review of the existing literature and current research suggests that there is a need to transcend the boundaries of what one usually regarded as separate research fields. Although written by scholars from different research traditions, we thus hope that the present volume manages to bring together insights gleaned from media sociology, from public opinion and discourse research, and from studies of management and organization to analyze not only media change, discursive change or organizational change – but also changes in the *interrelationship* of media, public knowledge and organization.

In contrast to many other studies that discuss the news media from a media-centered point of view, or explore business organizations from a management point of view, or look at developments in knowledge and meaning from a discursive point of view, our ambition is to begin to consider the relations between these three aspects. We believe that the adoption of a more relational approach allows us to raise a number of pertinent issues connected with social and economic knowledge, media power and economic governance, and thus contribute to the construction of a future research agenda at the intersection of media studies on the one hand and business and management studies on the other (see also Tsoukas 1999, Christensen 2002, Slaatta 2003).

Figure 1.2 offers an elaborated version of the empirical points of entry, where we also identify the changing relationships that the articles in this book are attempting to consider:

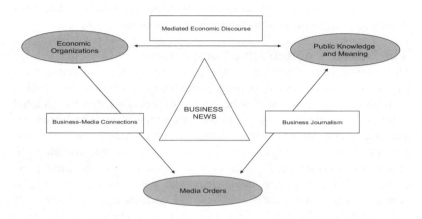

Figure 1.2 Empirical Points of Entry and Analytical Relations

In the three corners of the outer triangle our three points of entry to empirical research on business news expansion - economic organizations; media orders; public knowledge and meaning – are positioned. On the lines between these are the relational aspects that we seek to develop further in this volume: 1) Business-media connections, referring to the way in which media actors engage with their organizational sources and the way in which economic organizations are 'embedded' (Granovetter 1985, Zukin & DiMaggio 1990) in a web of relationships with the media; 2) Business journalism, referring to the way in which public knowledge and meaning are produced by business journalists, while journalists at the same time assume particular relations with imagined (business-oriented) publics and their interests; and 3) Mediated economic discourse, concerning the way in which public discourse becomes dependent on economic or business-oriented frames of meaning, and the way in which business organizations increasingly find themselves being represented or scrutinized by particular forms of such mediated knowledge. The inner triangle links the three relational

21

aspects together, indicating that the expansion, the roles and the functions of business news are connected with all three of them.

Our ambition in this book is thus two-fold. One aim is to describe the expansion of business news, approaching it from the perspective of the media order, public knowledge and meaning and economic organization. Our second aim is to begin to consider the implications of business news expansion in terms of the changing relations between news media, public discourse and economic organization.

The Nordic Comparative Perspective

Our empirical focus is on the development of the business press, business journalism and business news in the Nordic countries since 1960.

With our focus on the Nordic region we acknowledge the situated nature of our empirical study, but we are convinced that the Nordic region represents an interesting alternative research site, where several hypotheses about the expansion of business news can be generated and tested. As noted above, most debates on business news, business journalism and the business media focus on the American or Anglo-American experience. Early contributions such as those in Hiebert & Reuss (1985, 1988, 1995), Thompson, Olsen & Dietrich (1987), and Endres (1988), and more recent ones such as Quirt (1993) Hollifield (1997), Haller & Norpoth (1997), Parker (1997), Barnes (1998), Reilly (1999), Henriques (2000a, 2000b), and Deephouse (2000) have inspired and instructed our thinking, but in terms of their scope of argument and regional focus they deal almost exclusively with the American case. Equally important and with a historical perspective has been Wayne Parsons' study of the power of the financial press (1989), which expands the perspective to include the British business press.

However, we believe that the Nordic region differs from the Anglo-American and British experience. Recently a body of research has emerged outside the Anglo-Saxon countries which support our move towards a regional, comparative study of business news expansion (for a comprehensive bibliography, see Schuster 2002; for an overview of Scandinavian research, see Grafström 2004). This research indicates that there are important institutional differences between North America and the rest of the world that need to be explored more systematically, for instance in economic institutions (Whitley 1994), in media systems (Hallin & Mancini 2003) and in the production of social discourse (Wagner, Wittrock & Whitley 1991, Guillen 1994, Engwall & Sahlin-Andersson 2002).

Most of the studies that have been carried out outside North America emphasize single national cases or particular industries, firms or events (e.g. Lindhoff 1998, Grolin 1998, Davis 2000, Slaatta 2003, Kjær & Langer 2005). There is thus a need to develop a comparative understanding of the interplay of media institutions, discourse and economic organization in a context other than the Anglo-American (see also Gavin 1998, Mazza & Pedersen 2004). We believe that a study of the Nordic countries or the Nordic region provides an opportunity for a move in that direction.

The book is not intended to provide a detailed historical account of key events in Denmark, Finland, Norway and Sweden, nor is it only a story of progress or decline in the practice of journalism in the Nordic region. Rather the chapters explore a number of specific institutional changes in the relationship between business, the media and society during a period of spectacular expansion. The Nordic countries stand out as a fairly homogenous region both economically, culturally, politically and even in terms of the mass media (Byrkjeflot et al. (Eds.) 2001, Hallin & Mancini 2003). The countries are all highly developed capitalist economies, characterized by rather uniform national cultures and systems of parliamentary democracy, characterized by well-established welfare-state regimes and corporatist policy-making. Further they are all characterized by a high level of literacy and newspaper circulation. Admittedly, there are also important institutional differences and divisions within 'Norden' (The North), but on the whole the Nordic countries are sufficiently similar to offer a 'laboratory' in which we can investigate the characteristics of the expansion of business news production under a set of institutional conditions significantly different from those of the Anglo-American model.

Our analysis is thus both comparative and historical. Historically speaking we have chosen 1960 as our starting-point, since that year marks the beginning of an era of innovation in the field of business journalism. In most countries, early attempts to reshape business news date back to the mid-1960's, and it therefore seemed natural to start our formal analysis from 1960, although any analysis with a historical-institutional perspective must naturally consider longer trajectories when describing institutional contexts as they develop. Most of the empirical data collected within the project, in particular the substantial data base concerned with newspaper content used in the second section of the book, has been organized from the 1960 starting point. Further, for practical reasons, 2000 or 2005 have been chosen to represent the 'present' time at which the analysis ends.

An Overview of the Book

Given our theoretical approach and empirical focus, three aspects of the expansion of business news have been of particular interest here: I) how particular media platforms develop within and across particular national media orders; II) how business news comes to represent a particular form of business or economic discourse, thereby affecting the role of the 'economic' as part of the social reality of late modern societies, and III) how business news is being produced, distributed and utilized in institutionalized relations between the media and the business worlds, which in turn has special consequences for economic organizations. These three concerns inform the overall structure of the book.

Part I (Chapters 2-4) considers changes in and across national media orders. In Chapter 2 Slaatta describes, in collaboration with Grafström, Erkama and Kjær, the modernization of the Nordic business press, tracing the development of the main print media platforms for the mediation of business news between 1960 and 2005, from the early innovation phase in the later 1960s to the current challenge from internet platforms operating on a global scale. In Chapter 3 Ainamo, Tienari and Vaara describe how business journalism was transformed and professionalized in the Finnish context, where changes in the media order were closely related to changes in Finland's geo-political position and its general economic strategy for modernization. In Chapter 4 Risberg and Ainamo analyze the way in which, from the late 1980s, the Swedish business newspaper *Dagens Industry* pursued a strategy of internationalization resulting among other things in the launching in Estonia of a business newspaper that became a vehicle for the diffusion of Western market ideas in a post-communist setting.

Part II (Chapters 5-7) is concerned with changes in news content and the way business is represented in the news. Chapter 5 builds on a comparative study of economic news content in the Nordic countries between 1960 and 2000. Here Kjær, Erkama and Grafström describe the general expansion of business-oriented news in all the four Nordic countries, and the way in which, since the 1980s, business news has been popularized and 'corporatized'. In Chapter 6 Kjær studies Danish business news content, and seeks to show how a financial news frame has evolved and has come to dominate the way in which economic activity is represented in the news and how, as a result, the relationship between business and society has been reconfigured in discursive terms. In Chapter 7 Tienari, Vaara and Erkama examine the way in which business journalists become promoters of neo-liberalism. In an analysis of discursive framing in news reports and commentaries on Nokia in Finland, the authors show how the discursive practices of business journalists promote particular versions of social reality while marginalizing and excluding others.

Part III (Chapters 8-11) is concerned with the changing relationship between the media and business. Pallas and Grafström, in Chapter 8, regard the relationship between journalists and their business sources as a negotiated relationship and examine it as such. Starting from a study of interactions between journalist and corporate communicators in Sweden, they illustrate a number of dimensions appertaining to negotiation processes and highlight some of the implicit rules of the game in the field. In Chapter 9 Byrkjeflot and Angell demonstrate how increased media attention leads to the development of communication functions, policies and so on even in a public-sector setting. Thus in a study of communication strategies in Norwegian hospitals, the authors show how the development of such strategies is associated with changes in the media and with an influx of market and management ideas into the public sector. In Chapter 10 Engwall and Sahlin argue that the time has come for a reconsideration of theories of corporate governance, and so they start by including the media as a key governance actor. They claim that the media assume a governance role, directly by monitoring and scrutinizing corporate activity, and indirectly by popularizing and disseminating particular models of management and organization. In Chapter 11 Kjær and Sahlin take this argument further. They see the expansion of the business press as part of a wider quest for transparency that involves new transparency-enhancing technologies, organizations and ideas. The authors hypothesize that media-enhanced transparency may have important organizational effects –in terms of organizational structure and identity and the way organizations are governed.

The contributions to this book describe what amounts to a series of dramatic changes in the relationship between national media orders, social discourses and economic organizations. At the same time, as a first attempt to examine the field of business news, each contribution is also an invitation to engage in further research in the field. While the early chapters discuss important changes in media platforms and journalistic practices, fascinating stories remain to be told about the cross-national innovation of business journalism that has involved institutional entrepreneurs in a dual battle against the political climate of the day and against entrenched beliefs about the status of business and business news coverage. Similarly, while the chapters on business-news content and discourse examine important transformations in the way business is represented in the news, there remains an urgent need to explore some of the important sub-genres of the field, such as stock market commentary or CEO portraits, and to look at some of the new or emerging platforms such as televised or web-based business news. Finally, we have only begun to scratch the surface when it comes to organizational engagement with the media and to the way in which intensified media coverage generates structural and cultural change in individual organizations as well as transforming their relationship with the broader environment.

Against this background we invite our readers to use the material presented above as a jumping board for further exploration of business news, the business media, and the mediation of business.

Bibliography

Abrahamson, E. (1996) Management Fashion. *Academy of Management Review* Vol. 21 (1): 254-285.

Alvarez, J. L. (1996) The International Popularization of Entrepreneurial Ideas. In Clegg, S. R. & G. Palmer (Eds.) *The Politics of Management Knowledge*. London: Sage Publications.

Barnes, F. (1998) The State of U.S. Financial Journalism. *International Economy* Vol. 12 (4): 12-17.

Becker, K. G., J. E. Finnerty & J. Friedman (1995) Economic News and Equity Market Linkages Between the U.S. and U.K. *Journal of Banking and Finance* Vol. 19 (7): 1191-1210.

Benson, R. & E. Neveu (2005) *Bourdieu and the Journalistic Field*. Cambridge: Polity Press.

Bourdieu, P. (1993) *The Field of Cultural Production*. Cambridge: Polity Press.

Boyd-Barrett, O. & T. Rantanen (Eds.) (1998) *The Globalization of News*. London: Sage.

Byrkjeflot, H., S. Myklebust, C. Myrvang & F. Sejersted (Eds.) (2001) *The Democratic Challenge to Capitalism. Management and Democracy in the Nordic Countries*. Oslo: Fakbokforlaget.

Carrol, C. E. & M. McCombs (2003) Agenda-setting effects of business news on the public's images and opinions about major corporations. *Corporation Reputation Review* Vol. 6 (1): 36-46.

Castells, M. (2000) Information Technology and Global Capitalism. In Hutton, W. & A. Giddens (Eds.) *On the Edge. Living with Global Capitalism*. London: Jontahan Cape.

Chen, C. C. & J. R. Meindl (1991) The Construction of Leadership Images in the Popular Press: The Case of Donald Burr and People Express. *Administrative Science Quarterly* Vol. 36 (4): 521-551.

Christensen, L. T. (2002) Corporate Communication: The Challenge of Transparency. *Corporate Communication: An International Journal* Vol. 7 (3): 162-168.

Davis, A. (2000) Public Relations, Business News and the Reproduction of Corporate Elite Power. *Journalism* Vol. 1 (3): 282-304.

Deephouse, D. L. (1996) Does Isomorphism Legitimate? *Academy of Management Journal* Vol. 39 (4): 1024-1039.

Deephouse, D. L. (2000) Media Reputation as a Strategic Resource: An Integration of Mass Communication and Resource-Based Theories. *Journal of Management* Vol. 26 (6): 1091-1112.

Doyle, G. (2006) Financial News Journalism: A Post-Enron Analysis of Approaches towards Economics and Financial News Production in the UK. *Journalism: Theory, Practice & Criticism* Vol. 7 (4): 433-452.

Dutton, J. E. & J. M. Dukerich (1991) Keeping an Eye on the Mirror: Image and Identity in Organizational Adaptation. *Academy of Management Journal* Vol. 34 (3): 517-554.

Elsbach, K. D. & R. I. Sutton (1992) Acquiring Organizational Legitimacy through Illegitimate Actions: A Marriage of Institutional and Impression Management Theories. *Academy of Management Journal* Vol. 35 (4): 699-738.

Elsbach, K. D. (1994) Managing Organizational Legitimacy in the California Cattle Industry: The Construction and Effectiveness of Verbal Accounts. *Administrative Science Quarterly* Vol. 39 (1): 57-88.

Elsbach, K. D. & R. M. Kramer (1996) Members' Responses to Organizational Identity Threats: Encountering and Countering the Business Week Rankings. *Administrative Science Quarterly* Vol. 41 (3): 442-476.

Emmison, M. (1983) Economy. Its Emergence in Media Discourse. In Davis, H. & P. Walton (Eds.) *Language, Image, Media*. Oxford: Blackwell.

Endres, K. L. (1988) Ownership and Employment in the Specialized *Business Press*. *Journalism Quarterly* Vol. 65: 996-998.

Ericson, R. V., P. M. Baranek & J. B. L. Chan (1989) *Negotiating Control: A Study of News Sources*. Milton Keynes: Open University Press.

Everard, J. (2000) *Virtual States*. London: Routledge.

Ewen, S. (1996) *PR! A Social History of Spin*. New York: Basic Books.

Fairclough, N. (1995) *Media Discourse*. London: Edward Arnold.

Forsyth, D. P. (1964) *The Business Press in the United States 1750-1865*. Philadelphia: Chilton Books.

Gavin, N. (Ed.) (1998) *The Economy, Media and Public Knowledge*. London: Leicester University Press.

Glasgow University Media Group (1980) *Getting the Message. News, Truth and Power*. London: Routledge.

Goozner, M. (2000) Blinded by the Boom. What's Missing in the Coverage of the New Economy? *Columbia Journalism Review* Vol. 39 November-December: 23-27.

Grafström, M. (2004) Ekonomijournalistikens mångfald – en forskningsöversikt. Stockholm: SNS Medieforum.

Granovetter, M. (1985) Economic Action and Social Structure. The Problem of Embeddedness. *American Journal of Sociology* Vol. 91(3): 481-510.

Grolin, J. (1998) Corporate Legitimacy in Risk Society. The Case of Brent Spar. *Business Strategy and the Environment* Vol. 7: 213-222.

Guillen, M. (1994) *Models of Management. Work, Authority and Organization in a Comparative Perspective.* Chicago: Chicago University Press.

Haller, B. H. & H. Norporth (1997) Reality Bites. News Exposure and Economic Opinion. *Public Opinion Quarterly* Vol 61 (4): 555-575.

Hallin, D. D. & P. Mancini (2003) *Comparing Media Systems. Three Models of Media and Politics.* Cambridge: Cambridge University Press.

Hatch, M. J. & M. Schultz (2000) Scaling the Tower of Babel: Relational Differences between Identity, Image, and Culture in Organizations. In Schultz, M., M. J. Hatch & M. H. Larsen (Eds.) *The Expressive Organization. Linking Identity, Reputation and the Corporate Brand.* Oxford: Oxford University Press.

Hayward, M. L. A., V. P. Rindova & T. G. Pollock (2004) Believing One's Own Press: The Causes and Consequences of CEO Celebrity. *Strategic Management Journal* Vol. 25: 637-653.

Hellgren, B., J. Löwstedt, L. Puttonen, J. Tienari, E. Vaara, & A. Werr (2002) How Issues Become (Re)constructed in the Media: Discursive Practices in the AstraZeneca Merger. *British Journal of Management* Vol. 13 (2): 123-140.

Henriques, D. B. (2000a) What Journalists Should Be Doing about Business Coverage-But Aren't. *The Harvard International Journal of Press/Politics* Vol. 5 (2): 118-121.

Henriques, D. B. (2000b) Business reporting. Behind the Curve. *Columbia Journalism Review* Vol. 39 (4): 18-21.

Hiebert, R. E. & C. Reuss (1985) *Impact of Mass Media* (First Edition). New York: Longman.

Hiebert, R. E. & C. Reuss (1988) *Impact of Mass Media* (Second Edition). New York: Longman.

Hiebert, R. E. & C. Reuss (1995) *Impact of Mass Media* (Third Edition). New York: Longman.

Hollifield, C. A. (1997) The Specialized Business Press and Industry-Related Political Communication: A Comparative Study. *Journalism and Mass Communication Quarterly* Vol. 74 (4): 757-772.

Hutton, W. & A. Giddens (2000) *On the Edge. Living with Global Capitalism.* London: Jontahan Cape.

Kindleberger, C. P. (1989) *Manias, Panics and Crashes. A History of Financial Crisis.* Houndsmith: Macmillian.

Kjær, P. & R. Langer (2005) Infused with news value: Management, managerial knowledge and the institutionalization of business news. *Scandinavian Journal of Management* Vol. 21 (2): 209-233.

Kounalikis, M., D. Banks & K. Daus (1999) *Beyond Spin. The Power of Strategic Corporate Journalism.* San Francisco: Jossey-Bass Publishers.

Krefting, L. (2002) Re-presenting women executives: valorization and devalorization in US business press. *Women in Management Review* Vol. 17 (3/4): 104-119.

L'Etang, J & M. Peiczka (1996) *Critical Persepctives in Public Relations.* London: Thompson Business Press.

Lindhoff, H. & B. Mårtensson (1996) Dagens ekonomi: Går Persson stiger räntan. In Becker K., J. Ekecrantz, E. Frid & T. Olsson (Eds.) *Medie rummet*. Stockholm: Carlssons.

Lindhoff, H. (1998) Economic Journalism in the 1990s - the Crisis Discourse in Sweden. In Gavin, N.T. (Ed.) *The Economy, Media and Public Knowledge*. Leicester: Leicester University Press.

Marchand, R. (1998) *Creating the Corporate Soul*. Berkeley: University of California Press.

Mayhew, L. H. (1997) *The New Public. Professional communication and the means of social influence*. Cambridge: Cambridge University Press.

Mazza, C. (1997) The Popularization of Business Knowledge Diffusion: From Academic Knowledge to Popular Culture. In Alvarez, J. L. (Ed.) *The Diffusion and Consumption of Business Knowledge*. Basingstoke: Macmillan.

Mazza, C. & J. L. Alvarez (2000) Haute Couture and Prêt-à-Porter: The Popular Press and the Diffusion of Management Practices. *Organization Studies* Vol. 21 (3): 567-588.

Mazza, C. & J. S. Pedersen (2004) From press to E-media? The transformation of an organizational field. *Organization Studies* Vol. 25 (6): 875-895.

Meindl, J. R., S. B. Ehrlich, & J. M. Dukerich (1985) The Romance of Leadership. *Administrative Science Quarterly* Vol. 30 (3): 78-102.

Morsing, M. (1999) The Media Boomerang: The Media's Role in Changing Identity by Changing Image. *Corporate Reputation Review* Vol. 2 (2): 116-136.

Mosettig, M. D. (1985) Ninety Seconds Over the Economy. In Hiebert, R.E. & C. Reuss (Eds.) *Impact of Mass Media* (First Edition). New York: Longman

Mundy, A. (1995) Is the Press Any Match for Powerhouse PR. In Hiebert, R. E. & C. Reuss (Eds.) *Impact of Mass Media* (Third Edition). New York: Longman.

Neumann, W. R., M. R. Just & A. N. Crigler (1992) *Common Knowledge. News and the Construction of Political Meaning*. Chicago: Chicago University Press.

Nordfors, D. et al. (2006) Innovation Journalism: Towards Research on the Interplay of Journalism in Innovation Ecosystems. *Innovation Journalism* Vol. 3 (2) (www.innovationjournalism.org).

Palmer, M. (1998) Global Financial News. In Boyd-Barrett, O. & T. Rantanen (Eds.) *The Globalization of News*. London: Sage.

Parker, R. (1998) The Public, the Press, and Economic News. *Harvard International Journal of Press/Politics* Vol. 2 (2): 127-131.

Parsons, W. D. (1989) *The Power of the Financial Press. Journalism and Economic Opinion in Britain and America*. Aldershot: Edward Elgar Press.

Pfeffer, J. & G. R. Salancik (1978) *The external control of organizations*. New York, NY: Harper & Row.

Pollock, T. G. & V. P. Rindova (2003) Media Legitimation Effects in the Market for Initial Public Offerings. *Academy of Management Journal* Vol. 46 (5): 631-642.

Poole, G. A. (2000) Wealth Porn' And Beyond. *Columbia Journalism Review* Vol. 39 (4): 22-23.

Quirt, J. (1993) *The Press and the World of Money. How the News Media Cover Business and Finance, Panic and Prosperity, and the Pursuit of the American Dream.* Byron, Calif: Anton/California-Courier.

Read, D. (1992) *The Power of News. The History of Reuters.* Oxford: Oxford University Press.

Reilly, K. S. (1999) Dilettantes at the Gate: Fortune Magazine and the Cultural Politics of Business Journalism in the 1930s. *Business and Economic History* Vol. 28 (2): 213-222.

Rindova, V. P., T. G. Pollock & M. L. A. Hayward (2006) Celebrity Firms: The Social Construction of Market Popularity. *Academy of Management Review* Vol. 31 (1): 50-71.

Rosenberg, J. M. (1982) *Inside the Wall Street Journal. The History and the Power of Dow Jones and Company and America's Most Influential Newspaper.* New York: MacMillan.

Roush, C. (2004) *Show me the Money. Writing Business and Economic Stories for Mass Communication.* Mahwah: Lawrence Erlbaum Associates Inc.

Sahlin-Andersson, K. & Engwall, L. (2002) *The expansion of management knowledge. Carriers, flows and sources.* Palo Alto: Stanford University Press.

Sassen, S. (2000) Embedding the global in the national: implications for the role of the state. In Smith, D.A., D.J. Solinger, & S.C. Topik (Eds.) *States and Sovereignty in the Global Economy.* London: Routledge.

Schiller, D. (1999) *Digital Capitalism. Networking the Global Market System.* Cambridge: MIT Press.

Schuster, T. (2002) *International Bibliography Business and Financial Media.* Leipzig: Institut für Kommunikations- und Medienwissenschaft, Universität Leipzig.

Seidman, W. L. (1997) The Future of Financial Journalism. *International Economy* Vol. 11 (2): 39-41.

Slaatta, T. (2002) Med Bourdieu som utgangspunkt: Medienes makt. *Sosiologi idag* Vol. 32 (1-2): 93-126.

Slaatta, T. (2003) *Den norske medieorden. Posisjoner og privilegier.* Oslo: Gyldendal Akademisk.

Thompson, R. B., C. Olsen & J. R. Dietrich (1987) Attributes of News About Firms. An Analysis of Firm Specific News Reported in the Wall Street Journal Index. *Journal of Accounting Research* Vol. 25 (2): 245-274.

Tienari, J., E. Vaara & I. Björkman (2003) Global Capitalism Meets National Spirit: Discourses in Media Texts on a Cross-Border Acquisition. *Journal of Management Inquiry* Vol. 12 (4): 377-393.

Tsoukas, H. (1999) David and Goliath in the Risk Society. Making Sense of the Conflict Between Shell and Greenpeace in the North Sea. *Organization* Vol. 6 (1): 499-528.

Tuchman, G. (1978) *Making News.* New York: The Free Press.

Vaara, E. & J. Tienari (2002) Justification, Legitimization and Naturalization of Mergers and Acquisitions: A Critical Discourse Analysis of Media Texts. *Organization* Vol. 9 (2): 275-303.

Wagner, P., B. Wittrock & R. Whitley (1991) *Discourses on society. The shaping of the social science disciplines*. Dordrecht: Kluwer Academic Publishers.

Warner, K. & H. Moloch (1993) Information in the Marketplace. Media Explanations of '87 Crash. *Social Problems* Vol. 40 (2): 167-188.

Welles, C. (2001) Writing about Business and the Economy. In Thompson, T. (Ed.) *Writing About Business*. Colombia: Colombia University Press.

Whitley, R. (1994) *Business systems in East Asia: Firms, markets and societies*. London: Sage.

Zukin, S. & P. J. DiMaggio (1990) *Structures of Capital. The Social Organisation of the Economy*. Cambridge: Cambridge University Press.

PART I

BUSINESS NEWS
AND MEDIA ORDERS

CHAPTER 2

The Nordic Business Press and the New Field of Business Journalism (1960-2005)

TORE SLAATTA with PETER KJÆR, MARIA GRAFSTRÖM & NIINA ERKAMA[1]

The 1960s and 1970s are most famous for their music, the rise of popular culture, the educational revolution and the student revolt. At the same time however, a veritable revolution was also taking place in modern business news reporting in the Nordic region. In the four Nordic countries (Denmark, Finland, Norway and Sweden),[2] new magazines and journals specializing in business news and business information were making their appearance. To the surprise of many, the new platforms were a success, both journalistically and commercially, with expanding sales and revenues that indicated a connection with deeper social, cultural and political changes in society as a whole. The period between 1960 and 2005 is thus characterized by the prolific and steady rise to power and prestige of the Nordic business press. By our own day, these changes in journalistic practice and in the mediation of eco-

---

[1] The historical data and material for this chapter has been gathered collectively by its authors. Additionally, important interviews with central sources in the history of the business press have been held: In Denmark by Peter Kjær and Roy Langer, in Finland by Antti Ainamo and Janne Tienari, in Norway by Tore Slaatta, and in Sweden by Maria Grafström. An earlier systematic study of the Norwegian business press was undertaken by Tore Slaatta in the book *Den norske medieorden* (The Norwegian Media Order), published within the research project on "Power and Democracy in Norway" (1998-2003) (Slaatta 2003). The systematic study of the Swedish business press has been undertaken by Maria Grafström in her Ph.D. dissertation on the development of Swedish business journalism as an organizational field (Grafström 2006). In Denmark, Kjær & Langer (2005) constitutes a first attempt to chart the development of Danish business journalism, while in Finland the development of Finnish business journalism has been studied systematically by Ainamo et al. (2006), and earlier also by Herkman (2005) and Jyrkiäinen (1994).

[2] Iceland is also included in the geographical area known as the Nordic Countries, but has been excluded here for practical reasons. The Nordic region is presently negotiating its borders towards the east and the Baltic region.

nomic discourse have acquired important economic, political and cultural ramifications and need to be studied as a major element in the recent history of the Nordic countries.

In this chapter we will seek to identify the trajectories of the main print media outlets for the mediation of business news in the Nordic countries in the years between 1960 and 2005. The outlets are analyzed within their respective national media orders, and we look particularly at major variations between the Nordic countries with regard to national contextual background factors. Interestingly, however, what emerges from our comparative approach are the many similarities in the way the new print media outlets were conceived and set up at more or less the same time in all the Nordic countries. This is an indication of the complex relationships that exist within the Nordic region: although the Nordic countries represent separate economies, democracies and societies, all of them nationally organized, and although media orders are historically linked to the formation of nation states, the emergence and early expansion of today's Nordic business press can nevertheless be regarded as the national response of the countries involved to shared cultural, economic, political and social changes in an increasingly global society.[3]

We will argue that the dynamic evolution of business news platforms in the Nordic between 1960 and 2005 can be said to have passed through four phases. The four phases are analytical constructs embracing 1) diachronic variations in the trajectories of established and new platform positions within the national media orders, and 2) synchronic correspondences within each phase across the national media orders.

In the first phase, we note that new business news platforms emerge in the shape of weekly magazines on the margins of the prevailing media orders. These magazines were intended for new audiences addressed in new ways, and they challenged the established positions of the traditional national business newspapers. In the second phase, further platforms for business news emerged in the shape of daily newspapers. These occupied more central and dominant positions, either renewing old outlets (e.g. established business papers turned 'pink'), or as new entrants on the market (either as weekly or monthly magazines or niche newspapers). In the third phase, the expansion reached other

---

[3] The rise of the Nordic business press in this period shows similarities with other European countries; see for instance Wayne Parsons (1989) for the developments within the Anglo-American sphere, and the French case documented by Julien Duval (2004). However, as will be clear in the following pages, because of its post-war history and geopolitical position Finland's case deviates somewhat from the general regional and transnational picture, particularly in the early phases (Ainamo et al. 2006).

platforms in the national media orders, first the general-interest or omnibus press, and later also television news. The last phase brings us to the present period, in which digital communication technology is currently changing the relationship between professional journalism and the production of business news in other, more fragmented and mixed (e.g. public, semi-public and private) circuits of information in an expanding and increasingly globally organized, economic field.

It is important to remember, that although we sometimes refer to 'the Nordic region' as a whole, there are in fact important differences and variations between the media orders of the individual countries. In this chapter we thus emphasize similarities and differences among these countries and seek to avoid a mythical or simplistic, symbolic construction of 'the Nordic region' as such.

In our mapping of the development of business news platforms in the national media orders, we draw on a variety of sources, including historical information on media outlets, sales and revenues, and biographical information about the most significant actors. In addition, interviews have been held with a wide range of editors and journalists with a view to charting the differences in editorial and journalistic strategies regarding such things as the hiring and training of journalists, the choice of formats and journalistic styles, the content mix, advertisements, and the relation between commentary/analytical content and numerical market information. Against this background we attempt to define the positions occupied by the media platforms at different times compared to other news media platforms within the respective national media orders.

Although the level of detail varies between different parts of the historical analysis, we aim essentially to link the narrative of the development of media platforms to the creation and development of a subfield of business journalism within the professional field of news production and journalism within each Nordic country. Thus, whenever possible, we have tried to concentrate on information on the social background and career paths of core business journalists as related to for example family background, education, political affiliations and sources of inspiration. We argue that the emergence of a subfield of business journalism should be seen as the result of changes within the general field of journalism as well as of changes in the external environment (see also Slaatta 2003, Duval 2004). Thus, within the wider journalistic field, we seek to explore how the subfield of business journalism positions itself in relation to other journalistic subfields (political, cultural, sports, etc). We have also looked for changes and tensions, at the time of business news innovation and expansion, in the external relations between the emerging subfield of business journalism and the established and dominant practice of news production in the general field of journalism. In this respect, the changing relationship between the journalistic and the economic field also becomes important to study. The rise of the Nordic business press is obviously connected with the changing relations between these two fields during the period studied. In the economic field, we are thus interested in the way in which economic infrastructure and the regulation of business information have changed, and the way that new elite fractions have emerged within the economic field, more or less corresponding to the flow of new generations of management candidates from the new educational programs in business and management.

Technological change plays an important role in changing the structures and logics in the field of news production. Particularly this becomes important during the latest phase, as interactive information technology has become a powerful new factor as regards to stock exchange information and real-time transactions within the economic field. New technology in turn changes the relations among the established media technologies (print, audiovisual, etc) in the media order. It would be interesting to consider possible future developments in this context, for instance in the increasingly dominant production and mediation of business information on digital news media platforms. Here, however, we are mainly concerned with the recent changes from a historical and sociological point of view. We will not be looking in any great detail at the nature of technological changes, but will consider in more general terms the way in which such changes are currently affecting the production and reproduction of media platforms for business news.

We expect that the Nordic countries will develop along more or less similar lines, but that the timing and the order of events will be different. Generally speaking, these countries have a lot in common when it comes to newspaper consumption, and the role of the print media within the media order as a whole is indisputably important. All four are categorized as belonging to the 'democratic corporatist' category in a recent survey of media systems by Hallin and Mancini (2004: 70). Two important, defining elements of the category are the high level of literacy and the nationwide diffusion of newspapers in the 19th century. Individual idiosyncrasies among Nordic, national media orders will allow to a varying extent for new entrants and the reproduction of old patterns, which means that the trajectories of similar outlets will change at different times and will refer to different platforms in the respective media orders. However, we expect that, as the expansion of business journalism gathers momentum, many pronounced differences among the countries at one particular stage may become less visible at a later stage. Still, we would expect the composition of the national media orders to prevail as a structuring factor as regards business news platforms, particularly in the print and audiovisual media. In particular, we expect that journalistic style, design and cultural and social approach as regards money, finance and economic issues will vary, in line with differences in national cultures (Stråth 1992, Lamont 1992). The latest period studied shows signs of the emergence of a joint Nordic media market, and that ownership is becoming increasingly trans- and cross-national (Harrie 2003). However, differences in language and culture still prevail and although the Nordic region is increasingly becoming part of a globalized, economic world order, the individual countries still define the social and cultural borders within which the national economies are embedded and are socially constructed and legitimized. Public discourse in the separate national media orders on business and economy still focuses on stock markets indexes and business agents that can be defined — still predominantly, albeit changing — as *national* stock markets, indexes and agents. But as we shall see, this applies in increasingly complex and contradictory ways.[4]

The Prophets of the New Economy (1960 - 1975)

The term 'the new economy' was introduced by Pierre Bourdieu in *Distinction (1984)* to describe the changes that occurred in the relationship between the economy, business education and popular culture at the beginning of the 1960s. One of the prolific cultural expressions of this social change was the emergence of new magazines (weekly, biweekly or monthly) focusing on business, management and financial capital and appearing on the periphery of the prevailing national media orders (Bourdieu, 1984). In the mid-1960s and early 1970s, and all within a 5 - 10 years span, a new generation of business oriented,

---

[4] The structures of the national media orders and the positions and powers of the various technologies (radio, print media, and television channels) are generally influenced by national media regulatory politics and national media cultures. But with some exceptions, particularly as regards private television channels and the regulations on advertising in audiovisual media, regulatory regimes have been fairly similar across the Nordic countries, and in any case have not hindered the general expansion of business journalism over time in all the Nordic countries. However, the particular sequence and exact timing of events may have been influenced by national idiosyncrasies concerning media regulation, business education, differences as regards industrial strengths, size of population, urban concentration, language, membership of the European Union, etc.

young men appeared in the Nordic countries. With publicist ambitions and entrepreneurial skills they started to address the business community in new journalistic ways. The colorful and bold front pages of their publications bore original and no-nonsense titles: Capital (*Kapital*) or The Business Week (*Veckans Affärer*).[5] The editors were clearly seeking to address new audiences in new ways.

In Sweden, something was obviously beginning to happen with the merger in 1964 of two old specialized platforms for business journalism, namely *Affärsvärlden* (going back to 1901) and *Finanstidningen* (going back to 1922). However, the resulting publication only achieved a circulation of 4-5,000 copies (Fagerfjäll 1991). One year later in 1965, the modern business weekly *Veckans Affärer* appeared and sold approximately 25,000 copies per issue during its first year. It was thus this newcomer that signaled the real revolution in business journalism in Sweden (Grafström 2006). Similarly, in Denmark the old newspaper *Børsen* (daily, going back to 1896) was reintroduced as a modern business daily in 1970, inspired partly by the success of *Veckans Affärer* in Sweden. *Veckans Affärer* and other international business journals also inspired the introduction of *Kapital* in Norway in 1971, which immediately represented a complete contrast to the old-fashioned traditional shipping daily, *Handels og Sjøfartstidende* (going back to 1912) and the distinguished business magazine *Farmand* (weekly, going back to 1891). In Finland, the journal of commerce *Kauppalehti* (going back to 1898 and published as a daily since 1919) and the weekly *Talouselämä* (going back to 1937) continued to be the dominant platforms for business journalism. In this early period it was thus the main daily, *Helsingin Sanomat* (going back to 1889 and 1904) that was the first to develop Finland's business journalism (Ainamo, Tienari & Vaara 2002). However, *Helsingin Sanomat* retained its character as a traditional newspaper, and no really radical change in business reporting occurred until *Kauppalehti* altered its style of reporting in 1977 (Ainamo, Tienari & Vaara 2006).

The emergence of these new (or reinvented) platforms for business journalism must be considered in relation to a number of significant social and political changes in the Nordic societies at the time. First, the steady growth in their GNP in the postwar period depended to a large extent on the slow but steady success of a few, key industries in the individual countries. Shipbuilding, shipping, fishing and forestry played a central role, particularly in the Norwegian, Swedish and Fin-

---

[5] There is no equivalent new magazine in Finland. Rather, there is an unbroken tradition of business news reporting which is transforming itself within the Finnish media order.

nish economies, while in Denmark and Sweden manufacturing and agriculture were also important. In Finland the metal industry flourished since the Soviet Union demanded various kinds of metal and engineering products as war indemnity immediately after the war. Finland continued to produce these products for the Soviet Union until the mid-1950s. The country's metal industry consequently became an important source of economic growth.

Second, changes were made in the Nordic countries in the legislation and regulation of accounting practice and in the governmentally organized and publicly accessible records and registers of private business information in the early 1970s. Business journalists thus acquired access to important information. Until then, business news had to be acquired mainly from company press releases and exclusive interviews with top managers, leaving journalists with few independent sources and little room for investigative reporting. The new sources allowed a journalist trained in accounting to check management statements more critically against economic results and shareholder revenues.

Third, a major generational shift was taking place in the managerial class in the national industries. Nordic business enterprises had been managed to a great extent by production-oriented managers, many of whom were engineers with specialized knowledge in specific fields of production. In the late 1950s and early 1960s, however, a new generation of students began to appear in the schools and colleges for business education. In due course, the traditionally dominant role of the technical universities and engineering colleges was to be challenged as the main source of recruitment for management positions in the private sector (Engwall & Zamagni 1998, Engwall 1992).[6] These social and generational changes were connected with changes in the nature of academic economic knowledge. As the business schools proliferated in the Nordic countries, a new academic field emerged with an orientation towards the microeconomics of the business firm.

All these changes had cultural and political consequences. In the course of the 1960s and 1970s, the Nordic interventionist model, in which state ownership or subsidization of the key industrial companies was the preferred strategy, was facing increasing doubt and criticism on the part of a growing neo-liberal movement, often referred to as the

---

[6] Engwall argues that the early Nordic business schools became elite institutions, particularly in Sweden. However, the cultural influence of modern management knowledge on all business elites may have been more important than the actual power connected with the distribution of managerial positions. Clearly, there has been a big increase in candidates with business degrees in the Nordic countries, although most of them have, of course, become middle managers, consultants, analysts, etc., rather than top managers.

new right movement (e.g. Bjørklund & Hagtvet 1981, Ainamo, Tienari & Vaara, in the present volume, Boréus 1997, 1994). There was a feeling among the industrial elites that business interests were being threatened by radical political movements on the left, and new platforms for business journalism were being regarded as an important new means of communication in the moulding of public opinion.

Together, these social, political and ideological changes served to intensify divisions and conflicts concerning the control of national economies, in both the economic and the political fields. The postwar consensus in the Scandinavian welfare states, arising from the dominance of the social democratic parties, began to disintegrate. A new economic discourse emerged, propagating supply-side microeconomics rather than traditional Keynesian thinking, and a new, neo-liberal and microeconomic spirit began to challenge the beliefs, visions and traditional base of socio-economic knowledge.

Various private media entrepreneurs and innovators in Sweden, Denmark and Norway took action separately, but they were aware of each other and they drew inspiration from the same range of international journals and publishing trends.[7] The Swedish journal *Veckans Affärer* became the first modern Nordic business weekly, setting an important example and standard for the other countries. Since the late 1950s, the dominant Swedish newspaper and publishing group Bonnier had been nursing plans for a new weekly business newspaper,[8] inspired in part by the steady position of Finland's *Kauppalehti*. Bonnier even considered a Nordic market for business dailies that could link up to provide a coherent advertising market.[9] However, Bonnier encountered ownership restrictions and the decision to publish was never finalized. Instead, the weekly *Veckans Affärer* was launched by the Bonnier-owned company Åhlén and Åkerlund, a magazine and book publisher, under its first editors-in-chief Erik Westerberg and Bertil Torekull. The weekly became an immediate success (Grafström 2006).[10]

---

[7] The international magazines usually referred to are *Fortune* and *Business Week*. Also *The Economist* and *Vanity Fair* are mentioned as general models for elite magazines addressing the new managerial class within the business elites.

[8] The name suggested was Dagens Affärer. For details on Bonnier and the history of *Dagens Industri*, see Bringert & Torekull (1995).

[9] Plans for a daily had existed since the second half of the 1960s. Dagens Affärer was the name of the prototype to Dagens Industri developed by Gustaf von Platen during the early 1970s (Grafström 2006).

[10] It soon increased to a steady circulation to ca. 40,000 that remains today, peaking at 48,000 in 1990 (see Grafström 2006).

Despite the success of *Veckans Affärer* uncertainty remained as regards the market potential for a nationwide business daily in Sweden. The Gothenburg-based newspaper *Göteborgs Handels- och Sjöfartstidning* seized the opportunity in 1970. This old and well-established regional newspaper had traditionally been the most specialized business daily in Sweden, focusing particularly on the trade and shipping industry in the Gothenburg area. Its staff included the 'grand old man' of stock market commentators, Carl Robert Pokorny (Sundqvist 1989: 407). However, the step from a regional to a national audience did not work; rather, it settled the fate of this old and well-established newspaper (see further in Jonsson 2000). In September 1973 it closed down, and the position on a national market was empty again. At this point, and in the same year, Sweden's second largest daily, *Svenska Dagbladet* (dating from 1884) recruited Gustaf von Platen, the former editor-in-chief of *Veckans Affärer,* to direct the build-up of a more focused type of business reporting.

This was regarded not only as a strategy for establishing *Svenska Dagbladet* in competition with the other large national daily, *Dagens Nyheter*; it was also meant to hinder the Bonnier from launching a new business daily (Gustafsson 2002: 267).[11] Well-informed naturally about Bonnier's old idea for a business daily since he had developed a prototype at Bonnier himself, von Platen instead set about strengthening the business journalism element in 'Svenskan'. However, by a strategic maneuver that involved buying and closing down existing technical and professional magazines in business-related magazine markets, Bonnier achieved the leeway for a new journalistic publication. It was Torekull, former news editor of *Veckans Affärer*, who became the first successful editor-in-chief of this nationwide and specialized business newspaper. *Dagens Industri* was launched in 1976 (Bringert & Torekull 1995).

A similar pattern of development can be seen in Denmark, where Bonnier again became an important actor. As in Sweden, the old newspapers had been trying to combat falling sales with new journalistic strategies. In 1966 a young journalist, Erik Rasmussen, was hired by the ailing Copenhagen daily *Berlingske Aftenavis (BA)* to boost the paper's business coverage. This he managed to do with some success, and two years later, together with the young lawyer Christian Lille-

---

[11] The history of *Dagens Nyheter* was written by Stig Hadenius in 2002, but contains no information on the newspapers thinking about economics and business news. As with most historical accounts of newspapers, Hadenius describes the power of *Dagens Nyheter* solely in its capacity to influence on parliamentary politics (Hadenius 2002).

lund, Rasmussen was asked to develop an even more comprehensive plan for *BA*, with an emphasis on business journalism. But their new plans failed to find support with the *BA's* board, and Rasmussen and Lillelund offered their services instead to the business daily, *Børsen*. This was an old, well-established business newspaper as well as being the only Danish business daily at the time. *Børsen* enjoyed close connections with Copenhagen's financial circles, but its circulation had remained stagnant for decades and its economic base was weak. In 1968 *Børsen* was approached by Bonnier, who was interested in investing in the paper. Now Rasmussen and Lillelund, and the *Børsen* board made a deal with Bonnier, who purchased 49% of the newspaper's stock, and who helped to build up a new, editorial team with the assistance of the Swedes (Westerberg, Torekull and von Platen). Rasmussen became editor-in-chief, while Lillelund became managing director, and the new *Børsen* was successfully introduced in 1970. Obviously inspired by *Veckans Affärer*, Rasmussen and Lillelund made changes in *Børsen*'s business news coverage, making it more relevant for a growing audience of 'business people'. At the same time, however, it became more critical of business and management. *Børsen* was intended to be 'an active and modern daily' engaging in an open debate about business issues (Fonsmark 1996: 191).

In Norway the young economist, Trygve Hegnar established *Kapital* as a biweekly in 1971. Hegnar was an energetic sportsman educated in Mannheim, who became interested in introducing journalistic ideas and publication designs from *Der Spiegel* and *Veckans Affärer* into Norwegian business reporting. Hegnar's family background was particularly relevant: his father was a legal adviser to the Norwegian Shipping magnate Fred Olsen, the dominant owner of the major business newspaper in Norway at the time, *Norges Handels og Sjøfarts Tidende (NHST)*. From an early age Hegnar was an enthusiastic writer of letters and comments to newspapers and magazines, occasionally working later as a sports journalist for *Dagbladet*, then Norway's largest newspaper. It was during the years of study in Mannheim that his ideas developed for a modern business publication in Norway. On his return from Mannheim, Hegnar started writing columns for *Farmand*, the well-established Norwegian business weekly. However, he realized that his more radical journalistic ideas could not be pursued there. As a result, while working full-time as a public transport researcher, he produced the first issue of *Kapital* from his office in the kitchen of a small apartment in Oslo.[12] It was to appear twice a week, and was on sale at newspaper stands and kiosks. The early years were hard. In order to survive financially, Hegnar also started publishing books, among them his own highly successful *How to escape taxation* (Hegnar 1973). After a few years of financial uncertainty, the magazine started paying off as sales increased and its reputation grew.[13]

As already noted, developments in Finland took a slightly different course. More markedly than in the other Nordic countries, positions in the Finnish media order continued to be associated with a rhetoric combining national sentiment with liberalism and progress. In addition, as a result of the former union with Sweden, newspapers belonged to two language cultures, which came to define two economies and two power blocks in Finnish society. Within the Swedish-speaking community, *Hofudstadsbladet*, the most important daily (dating back to 1864), also served as the main platform for business news. A few magazine titles appeared during the 20th century (*Mercator* in 1906, *Finansbladet* in 1923 and *Handels och Finansbladet* in 1946). But most importantly for our period, *Forum för Ekonomi och Teknik* was launched in 1968. In the Finnish-speaking community the changes in business reporting were led by Helsingin Sanomat and Uusi Suomi, the two major dailies. Under the leadership of Aatos Erkko, Helsingin Sanomat steadily increased its coverage of business news, managing to take over the exclusive rights to Dow Jones from their competitor *Uusi Suomi* and launching a special business section *Taloustiistai* (Economy/Business Tuesday) in 1972. Uusi Suomi also tried to boost its business coverage, and several eminent business journalists became public figures during this period (e.g. Jaakko Kahma, Rauno Larsio (*Talouselämä*) and Pentti Poukka (*Kauppalehti* and *Uusi Suomi*). Like *Børsen* in Denmark, the established business newspaper *Kauppalehti*, owned by Uusi Suomi Oy, had been a daily for some time (since 1922). In contrast to *Børsen* in the 1960s, *Kauppalehti* managed to keep up its sales well into the 1960s, and had no great incentive to change its journalistic strategies. The new line in business coverage was thus developed in the major dailies, *Helsingin Sanomat* and *Uusi Suomi*. However, for trying to maintain a capitalist and liberalist stronghold against the threat of increasing 'Finlandization' with the influence and pressure from the Soviet Union that this involved during

---

[12] See Geelmuyden (2002).
[13] According Geelmuyden (2002), Hegnar turned down an offer from Torekull and Bonnier in 1974, which he also has called the best decision he has ever made. Hegnar personally made a fortune on the magazine's rapidly increasing sales.

the 1970s, the *Kauppalehti* was effectively blacklisted and, politically, was effectively sidelined. The paper tried to extend its coverage of the increasing bilateral trade between Finland and the Soviet Union, but the two major politically oriented dailies, *Helsingin Sanomat* and *Uusi Suomi*, dominated the field (Ainamo et al. 2006).

The early innovators in the Nordic countries were inspired by their chosen journalistic models, often building on the journalistic ideals of several international magazines, particularly the *Fortune, Forbes* and *Business Week* in the US. The early success of *Veckans Affärer* also played an important part in the understanding of market potentials in the respective countries. The young editors all found that they had to train journalists from scratch. There were few business journalists around, if any, and to be able to write about business and finance, some of the editors felt that they needed people with academic training in business and economics. 'They have to know how to read budgets and accounts' was a frequent comment. Young economists were thus sometimes preferred to trained journalists in the hiring processes. As founders and/or owners, the entrepreneurs more or less invented the journalistic style of the new business journalism in their respective national contexts. The news they published often created a considerable stir and was criticized for being much too harsh and sensational (e.g. Fonsmark 1996: 191). Editors felt that managers had been expecting a supportive parrot, but got a barking watchdog. Thus the editors not only trained their own journalists: even their sources and the business community in general were set for a lesson. An important feature of the new outlets was the editorial. In contrast to the declining importance of editorials in the regular, general-interest press during the 1970s and 1980s, the editorials in the new or reinvented business magazines and newspapers were essential, both for the editorial staff themselves and for their readers. The editors saw themselves as educators of the public with the task of influencing public opinion. Editorials also defined journalistic priorities and ethical rules in a new public sphere. Quite frequently, too, editors had to fight off accusations of lying, damaging criticism, and even industrial espionage. Trygve Hegnar's professional auto-biography for instance, is a continuous documentation of legal actions and trials.

As regards design and layout, the new outlets required attention. Sales had to come mainly from kiosks and newsstands, and since striking colors provided a way of increasing visibility, these were preferred. As the magazines could be read on the shelves, the cover headlines were thought to be extremely important. To a great extent, then, certain journalistic principles for front page stories that were later to become common in tabloid journalism were actually developed in these early, financial magazines. *Kapital* in Norway, for instance, became renowned for its striking orange color and its rather crude homemade-looking design. It was widely believed that the editor did most of the layout himself on his kitchen table. Although the layout now has a more professional look, *Kapital*'s colors and basic design principles have remained essentially the same.

The biographies of the innovators and entrepreneurs of this phase (e.g. Rasmussen, Lillelund, Westerberg, Torekull, von Platen and Hegnar) give us a striking picture of those times, testifying to the social dynamics in journalism and the economic world as a whole. Some of these entrepreneurs began by working for an established newspaper or a firm in the media business. Many of them combined a journalistic instinct with a politically and economically motivated interest in the publicist side of business news. They worked as journalists and had a talent for writing. Their innovative role also benefited from their slightly ambivalent social role as 'inside-outsiders', with little formal or family ties with business organizations or business elites. As a result of their social background and educational training, they stood well with young, middle management people within the economic world. This did not prevent them from being critical in their journalistic style. These young editors and journalists often came to be regarded as strong critics of business practices — even as veritable 'management killers'. There was a journalistic and a commercial strategy behind this: sales were often boosted by repeated attacks and scandalous news stories about politicians, public administrators, officials and managers in the state-owned industries.

The invention of a modern style of business journalism in the Nordic countries coincided with other changes in the media order. The long tradition of the party press system was coming to an end: television had introduced 'visibility' and a visual culture on quite a new scale; journalism had become more autonomous, more independent and more critical. But as the ownership and control from the political parties retreated, the presence of business, microeconomics and professionalized sources became increasingly important for the production of news. Thus, while the new media outlets can be regarded as innovators in the field of journalism, they were also early pioneers in their neo-liberalist criticism of the welfare state, and their opposition to traditional interventionist policies in the Nordic countries. To the economic world, these editors and journalists might have seemed untrustworthy and cynical. But outside this world, and in a more political perspective their editorial writings were accepted as part and parcel of the neo-conservative and neo-liberal movements that were emerging in the Nordic countries at the end of the 1970s (see e.g. Bjørklund & Hagtvet 1981).[14]

Rivals, Copies and Spin-Offs (1975 - 1985)

The second phase in the evolution of media platforms for business journalism differs slightly among the Nordic countries, depending on what had gone before, and what opportunities remained for further expansion in the national media orders. As so often in cultural markets, success can be imitated. The logic of market expansion for cultural goods differs from the logic of other markets: successful markets tend to reproduce themselves and to go on expanding beyond the normal limit of market saturation. In other words, if the markets could absorb the magazines of the early 1970s, there would be a market for later magazines and newspapers as well. Thus, the second phase must be described and explained in part by the internal dynamics of the media orders.

The explanation for this second phase in the expansion of business journalism also has to be sought in the economic and political fields. During the 1970s, the Nordic countries were undergoing important changes on the industrial and economic front. In this respect the economic histories of the Nordic countries were not identical. There are great differences in the timing when their economies boomed and when they faced crisis. Nevertheless they did share certain elements in their histories: The core industries in their state-interventionist economies were no longer the spearhead they had once been, while the tradition of counter-cyclical fiscal policy-making was being increasingly called into question during the 1970s and early 1980s. It became difficult to maintain the state subsidies on grounds of economic efficiency or political legitimacy; inflation and interest rates soared, and there was a growing sense of economic and political crisis surrounding the Nordic welfare state model. At the same time the political movements on the right were gaining momentum, while the ideological conflict between the supporters of a neo-liberal or populist new right movement and the protagonists of the old order (i.e. the social democratic and socialist parties and the labor movements) was intensifying. How-

---

[14] However, Hegnar's experience as a transport economist and researcher probably made him more aware of public administration and collective solutions to social problems than many of his contemporary and more fundamentalist micro-business economists.

ever, the 1970s and 1980s also saw a general rise in private welfare arrangements and a more dynamic private sector in the service industries. Consumption was more or less steadily on the rise, and the early 1980s saw an international trend for economies to boom, in all the Nordic countries referred to as the Yuppie-period, after which a recession period generally set in.

During the booming years the new 'pink press' became the popular social marker for an allegedly 'new' generation of investors and speculators who were bidding for companies with the backing of generous banks and loans. The conspicuous consumption patterns among the new, rich, urban elites and their spectacular investment strategies made good news — but perhaps not very good journalism. The lack of expertise and knowledge among ordinary journalists and the increasing dependence on professionalized source information meant that independent business journalism was a scarce resource.

We have already noted that the relations between the media and the political field had long represented a 'political press system', which structured the media order in homology with the order of political parties. The formal ties between political owners and editors more or less broke down during the 1970s (Grafström 2006, Engblom 2002: 132, Høyer 1995, Salokangas 1999) but informal relations endured into the 1980s. However, other important changes laid the foundations for an increasingly independent and autonomous journalistic field in the Nordic countries. More attention was paid to the education of journalists, and here was a general increase in professionalization, whereby journalistic ideals became less selective and referential and more autonomous and investigative (e.g. Schultz 2006). The transformation of professional standards and ideals occurred at the same time as two other important changes took place in the Nordic media orders. First, the audiovisual media were being deregulated, making way for the private radio and television channels of subsequent years. Except in Finland, where private channels and broadcast advertising had existed since 1957, this meant that Nordic public service broadcasting was facing a totally new competitive environment. Secondly, there was a marked change in the way the popular print media positioned themselves within the media order. According to Høst (1999), the rise of the popular tabloid newspapers in Norway during the 1970s and 1980s shows that active strategies for assimilation and adaptation vis-à-vis competition from television entertainment were succeeding. The tabloid print media introduced a new style of reporting into all kinds of journalism. A personal, close-up, photo-based news story concentrated on the private and the human, arousing emotional identification and personal engagement on the part of the audience. Thus television and tabloid news production promoted new forms of journalism, characterized by more informal styles and codes and giving more importance to visibility in the media order as a whole. Certain parts of the press that did not adapt, particularly local and regional newspapers, went into decline.

However, new monthly, biweekly and weekly outlets for business journalism continued to appear. They focused not only on management, microeconomics and the business firm, but also increasingly on the handling of personal economy, investment strategies, banking and insurance. The first wave of magazines and journals had shown that the market was there, and the market for economic information and services was now expected to expand even more. The success of the first phase was spreading to other niche markets as well: lifestyle magazines, fashion magazines, magazines for the young and others addressing the new audience for financial investments and real estate speculation in the young, urban, upper-middle class. Titles such as 'Your money' (*Dine Penger*) and 'Money and the Private Economy' (*Penge & Privatøkonomi*) were typical here. At the same time the marketing departments of the booming banking industry were busy producing pamphlets, magazines and information about how to get loans, how to invest, and how to spend money.

In Norway, the success of *Kapital* aroused competition. *Økonomisk Rapport* (established in 1974) was a slightly less sensational and more management-oriented magazine than *Kapital* with its microeconomic and obviously political editorial slant. The newcomer soon achieved high sales too, and after a time was reported as surpassing *Kapital* in copies sold. Arguments about sale figures started, and the competition between the two publications also triggered more radical forms of news-hunting, marketing and distribution. Thus instead of simply stealing some of *Kapital's* readers, the newcomer increased overall media consumption. Both publications still exist and their readership remains more or less steady.[15]

While the magazine market continued to expand, attempts were also being made to change the role of business journalism in the daily newspaper market. In Sweden and Norway this resulted in the emergence of new dailies for business journalism and in Denmark and Finland to new editorial strategies in the existing, general-interest

---

[15] However, the old, well established and conservative weekly, *Farmand* could not stand competition. After being sold to the publisher company Cappelen in 1986 (which just had been taken over by Bonnier) it totally flopped and went out of business.

newspapers. The appearance of new sections and more clearly profiled layout with an element of critical business news reporting showed that any serious newspaper was having to address the growing business community with serious information and news coverage.

In Sweden *Dagens Industri (DI)* proved to be the first still surviving attempt at producing a national daily business newspaper. Bonnier and Torekull started cautiously with two issues per week up to 1981. In 1977 *Dagens Industri* consisted of three parts: one for economic and industrial information, one for production and technical news, and a third for human interest stories (Grafström 2006). It made a calculated and cautious entry into the Swedish media order: The paper carried no stock market coverage until 1979, because Bonnier wanted to avoid competition with *Veckans Affärer* (Bringert & Torekull 1995: 100, 130). But in 1981 Hasse Olsson, a journalist from the evening boule-vard newspaper *Expressen,* became editor-in-chief of *DI.* Under Olsson, more radical ideas about journalistic principles and layout were introduced. In 1983 *Dagens Industri* became a daily, becoming known for its focus on business personalities, conflicts, ventures and power struggles, and for business-world gossip presented in a spicy, aggressive and emotive journalistic style.[16] Since then *Dagens Industri*'s sales have been an impressive demonstration of the way business news has expanded (see Risberg & Ainamo, in this present volume). It started slowly in the early 1980s, rising to an average of 30,000 copies a day in 1983.

Kauppalehti in Finland was finally getting its awkward situation under control. In 1977, with the appointment of Arto Tuominen as editor-in-chief, the paper entered upon a period of radical change and relaunching. Tuominen had experience as a television journalist, and had a highly developed sense of news values and a feeling for public debate. His idea was to build up the paper's independent flow of news. These changes inspired a similar change in both *Talouselämä* and *Helsingin Sanomat*. In particular Lauri Helve at *Helsingin Sanomat* developed new styles of journalism, incorporating colorful commentary on the business and management of specific companies and personalities involved, with a view to getting ordinary people interested in business issues (Ainamo, Tienari & Vaara 2002).

---

[16] This according to Thomas Peterssohn, a former employee and the later founder of the Internet based business platform *Ekonomi 24* and editor-in-chief of *Affärsvärlden.* Today Peterssohn is CEO and editor-in-chief of *Tidningarnas Telegrambyrå* (TT, The Swedish news agency) (Grafström 2006).

In Denmark, the monthly business magazine *Erhvervsbladet*, established in 1964 by Bertel Bernhard, was relaunched as a daily in 1974, and it soon gained a foothold in the business news niche, being financed almost exclusively by advertisements and distributed free to firms and private subscribers. Compared to *Børsen*, *Erhvervsbladet* developed a more uncritical and service-oriented news profile in relation to the business community, offering detailed information about small local firms and their managers. *Børsens Nyhedsmagasin* appeared in 1985 as a successor of *Månedsbørsen*, a monthly business magazine published since 1978. *Børsens Nyhedsmagasin* was created by Erik Rasmussen, the editor-in-chief at *Børsen* up to 1974. Rasmussen had started a new publishing house in an ambitious attempt to complement the daily business coverage with publications with special focus on in-depth comment and background information on business and economic issues. A group of distinguished business journalists came together for the purpose. After a tumultuous start, which ended in Rasmussen departure from the magazine, *Børsens Nyhedsmagasin* managed to carve out a niche for itself.

In Norway, the idea of transforming the traditional *Norges Handels og Sjøfarts Tidende (NHST)* assumed concrete form in the mid-1970s. Like *GHS* in Sweden, *NHST* had been its country's traditional, well-established shipping and trade newspaper. The editors were replaced and new strategies were attempted, but the really radical changes appeared when Kåre Valebrokk, a journalist and former businessman was headhunted from the tabloid *Verdens Gang (VG)*. In 1987, a completely new version of *NHST* came out, now under the name *Dagens Næringsliv*. It assumed the Berliner-format (slightly taller than the tabloid format) and it was printed on orange/pink, like the *Financial Times*. To many people's surprise, the journalists were recruited among young academics and economists and among radical journalists from the tabloids or the surviving left wing press. *Dagens Næringsliv* hit the market towards the end of the yuppie-period, and many people thought that both phenomena would disappear together. But instead the paper was a journalistic and a commercial success. *Dagens Næringsliv* came to be regarded as an ambitious business newspaper offering serious investigative journalism and professional comment on international and national business developments. Complaints were soon heard that the paper had become too hostile to business interests. To boost sales, *Dagens Næringsliv* launched a Saturday edition directed more towards culture and feature news, intended for family reading rather than office use (Slaatta 2003). A special new section 'Etter Børs' was introduced, devoted mainly to news and comments on culture, the fine arts and the more exclusive type of consumption goods.

Gradually the field of business journalism became more clearly defined, but it still lacked the prestige of the political press. The business journalist in the general-interest newspapers often remained an in-house expert to whom political journalists could turn, but not one expected to dig out the front page stories. But the founding fathers of the early business magazines continued to enjoy heroic status in business journalism. In Sweden, Torekull moved on to become editor-in-chief of *Svenska Dagbladet* and continues to this day to be an influential and well-reputed publicist and author.[17] In Norway, Trygve Hegnar's rise to personal fame as an investigative economist and publicist was also associated with the rise of television journalism. During the 1970s and 1980s, Hegnar was often featured in news programs, political debates and talk shows. He became renowned for his definite opinions on public issues and his willingness and ability to argue and debate in public. As an experienced publisher, editor and journalist he also set an inspiring example for other journalists who wanted to report on economy and business elites in a more investigative and critical manner. For a while, Hegnar was on the board of the radical tabloid *Dagbladet*, as well as owning a number of local newspapers. During the 1980s, Hegnar's media empire expanded and his personal capital grew. One of his dreams was to publish a newspaper, and in 1980 he made a bid for the shares in *NHST*. His bid was opposed, and he ended up with 10% of the total. He sold these in 1990 to a profit of 25 million Norwegian kroners.

In Denmark the general-interest newspapers were also experimenting with new sections and strategies for producing business news. In 1980 *Jyllands-Posten* launched a supplement on pink paper entitled 'Erhverv & Økonomi' (Business and the Economy). *Berlingske Tidende* followed suit with a similar supplement in 1982. *Berlingske Aftenavis* on the other hand became a weekly newspaper in 1971 under the title *Weekendavisen* and ceased to focus specially on business. *Jyllands-Posten* was based in Aarhus, Denmark's second largest city and aimed to become a genuinely national general-interest newspaper. Its renewed emphasis on business and the economy coverage indicated an attempt to find new readers (as a national newspaper) and to capture advertisement revenues. In both these aims *Jyllands-Posten* proved successful, thus becoming a direct challenge to *Berlingske Tidende*. In

[17] http://www.wwd.se/forfattare/torekull.htm.

1982 after a long period of stagnation and labor conflict, *Berlingske* reconstructed itself and embarked on a long period of relative economic stability. The paper had always enjoyed a reputation for reporting on economic issues and now, with its reconstruction, particular emphasis was also given to business news.

In Norway, *Aftenposten* had traditionally been the most prominent national general-interest newspaper. At the time when *Kapital* appeared, *Aftenposten* still maintained its critical attitude towards the new sensational forms of business journalism, providing the business community instead with pro-business articles and comments and little or no criticism. The newspaper was more active on the political front, where it continued to be a staunch supporter of the conservative party, Høyre. Looking back, it seems strange that at the time when *Dagens Næringsliv* appeared and went from strength to strength, the *Aftenposten* editors did little to improve their business reporting. They maintained their political focus on parliamentary rather than corporate institutions, and because of its dominant position in the Oslo region, it was easy for the paper to retain its position and its advertising revenues without much incentive to make editorial changes. It was not until 1992 that *Aftenposten* made any attempt to counter the challenge from *Dagens Næringsliv.*

Turbulence and Further Expansion (1985 - 1995)

The third phase was heralded by horizontal expansion within the media order in association with the unprecedented infiltration of business news into all kinds of news platforms. Sales of the specialized business newspapers and most prominent magazines continued to grow at a time when many newspapers were having to struggle. It was also now that a new sense of insecurity about the future of the newspaper business began to be felt. Many newspaper owners and editors became unsure of their relations with their readers. It was not as easy as before to attract a young readership, and the old editorial strategies no longer seemed so reliable. At the same time, though, technological changes in production and design were making it possible for many newspapers and magazines to reinvent themselves. Color and photography were more easily accessible for news stories, and the news was increasingly embellished with striking images and portraits of politicians, movie stars and business personalities. All this made it possible to offer the readers something fresh. After their two innovative phases of expansion, the specialized business media now seemed to be consolidating their social and cultural contacts with an extended business community. They tried to keep up with the expansion, but often found themselves in a position where maintenance rather than change was preferred. In this third period thus, editorial changes are more visible within the established general-interest newspapers, who now hired more specialists, increased the number of pages dedicated to business news, and moved business sections and business news stories further towards the front under new titles and given a more attractive design.

The expansion of business news during this period coincided with a major transformation in the logics and hierarchies of the field of journalism as a whole, particularly in connection with the increasingly prominent role of television and various popular forms of presentation in the tabloid press (Bourdieu 1996). Television technology changed the culture and norms of news production by making both the journalists and their sources more visible in the story-telling, thus indicating more clearly than before the autonomy of those constructing the news narratives. Journalists assumed the more participative role of those whose mission was to interrogate and investigate in searching for the truth below the surface. This period was also characterized by the emergence of a public relations profession in the Nordic countries, in part as a response to the developments within the journalistic field as a whole. New companies were appearing offering not so much in 'business' as such, but rather production and handling of company information and the professional design of company communications and public relations. The role of television as a news provider addressing general audiences became more marked during the period. In all the Nordic countries, the public and private channels both started debate and discussion programs on a weekly or even daily basis, alongside other 'infotainment'-programs for a general audience, which again served to increase the visibility of business personalities, investors and managers, the wealthy and the super-rich.

Another quality of television journalism that was reinforced during this period was the particular emphasis on the consumer, which in turn altered the predominant idea of the role of the news media. From being regarded as a critical fourth-estate institution, the news media came to be seen as a service and information provider. In the Nordic societies the deregulatory notions of the 1980s and early 1990s gave way to a new concept of citizen-consumers who required an increasing amount of information about quality, prices and products in order to be able to operate as rational consumers. The media played a dual role in producing this. On the one hand they were cultivating the consumer as the ideal recipient of their own journalistic output. On the other hand they were cultivating their own output to include a stronger element of lifestyle journalism, better suited to selling space and slots to the advertising industry. These editorial and professional changes were made just as ownership in the Nordic news media industry was becoming increasingly concentrated and controlled according to the 'media company model'. The ownership of many private media companies was losing its association with long standing national cultural traditions and its dedicated local or family roots, and was coming to be regarded as a strategic investment in a Nordic (or, increasingly, a European) media industry.

All over Europe, neo-liberal winds could be felt. The neo-liberal economist Milton Friedman's documentaries were shown on public television all over Europe (Parsons 1989) and the Nordic business community seemed to be stronger than ever. However, the fluctuations and crises in the Nordic economies, largely the result of global economic recession between 1986 and 1992, made many people critical of the neo-liberal economists' claims about freedom, progress and prosperity. There were also signs of a revival on the political left, with a new 'alternative' focus on environmental issues and international peace movements. The concept of civil society was becoming popular in democratic theory, and the Solidarity movement in Poland was signaling the coming changes in Eastern Europe and the breakdown of the Soviet empire. Europe was obviously changing, and the Nordic countries that were still outside the European Union (EU) were preparing to become full members of the EU. How political change would be followed by cultural change, and how this could eventually affect regulation of the media and cross-national ownership structures were among the topics discussed in the boardrooms of the Nordic media companies. The national markets were becoming too small to meet the challenge of economic growth and expansion, and the competition among the Nordic media companies was growing more intense.[18]

The national media orders still operated as separate linguistic markets. It was still possible to develop new products on the model of other Nordic successes. In 1989 *Finanstidningen* entered the Swedish market with a view to presenting financial news more 'seriously' than *Dagens Industri* was doing at the time. In the first issue of this new paper Raoul Grünthal, its editor-in-chief, declared his intention of making it the first daily in Sweden with a genuinely financial focus (*Finanstidningen* 1989:1). *Finanstidningen* was modeled after *The*

---

[18] Egmont, Bonnier, Sanoma, Schibsted, Berlingske, Modern Times Group, Alma Media, Orkla and others, see recent publications on The Nordic Media Market, Nordicom.

Wall Street Journal and tried to create a niche for a more exclusive, economically and financially interested public. The readers were expected to be few in number, but financially strong, and it looked good at first with early sales at 4,-5,000 copies. Trygve Hegnar was just as successful with the start-up of *Finansavisen* in 1992. As noted above, Hegnar had been wanting to launch a business daily for a long time. And on 1 October 1992, *Finansavisen* appeared on the Norwegian newspaper market as a business daily. The newspaper started with small resources and a tight budget: a mere 15 employees had to compete with the 240 at *Dagens Næringsliv*. *Finansavisen* was expected to have a short life, but a year later it still existed with a circulation of 9,200 copies, which in principle gave the editor/owner the right to receive a press-subsidy. With his growing personal capital, Hegnar had also become a major capitalist and personal investor in Norway. He invested primarily in hotels and shipping, and for a time was head of the cruise shipping company Kloster Cruise (Vard). This did not prevent him from remaining as editor and weekly commentator for *Kapital* as well as writing a daily editorial comment for *Finansavisen*. *Dagens Næringsliv* maintained its basic focus on business. Like other specialist newspapers, it had no sport or crime coverage. Beside these obvious signs of a 'serious business' image, the success of these two papers in this period can be explained by the appeal they had to readers in the public administration and in bureaucratic organizations. The so-called mixed public/private system of governance in the Nordic countries had over time produced a large composite audience of business news readers.[19]

In Finland, *Helsingin Sanomat* had become the unrivalled major general-interest newspaper when the other main contestant, *Uusi Suomi*, was liquidated in 1992 after first being taken over by the newly established Alma Media Group in 1991. This helped *Kauppalehti* to increase its readership in the general-interest readers' market. Otherwise, the Finnish business press remained much in the same position as it had before.

In Denmark the established niche and general-interest newspaper market continued to expand. Beginning with the centrist-liberal general-interest daily *Politiken* and, successively several other national and regional dailies as well, more newspapers were beginning to hire business journalists to launch dedicated business pages and supplements. One major impetus behind this wave of expansion was a series

[19] The sociologist Gudmund Hernes coined the term "mixed governance" in his book *Blandingsadministrasjon og Forhandlingsøkonomi* (Hernes 1978).

of scandals in the financial sector around 1990, for example what became known as the Hafnia-scandal. These, together with a growing interest in private pension schemes generated a much wider popular interest in business issues as a whole. In addition, a few very specialized newsletters began to appear, for instance *Ugebrevet Mandag Morgen* which was started by the ever active Erik Rasmussen in 1989. Another publication, *Økonomisk Ugebrev,* was established in 1994, with a stronger financial thrust and markedly analytical approach to business news reporting.

In all the Nordic countries during this period, several big news stories connected with business, money and/or finance broke with an aura of scandal and crisis. They involved the revelations of personal fraud, corruption and conspicuous consumption among the nouveau riche, or as company scandals, poor deals, bad management, misdirected bids and spectacular company takeovers.

The Business News Revolution (1995-2005)

The last period in our survey can be described as a revolution on two specific counts: First, business news in this period became a prestigious, journalist beat, with well-paid journalists, a steady flow of big news stories (scandals, crises, fraud, corruption, defeats and victories) and a strong belief in the essential role of business news in society on the part of editors, journalists, advertisers and readers. Secondly, the distinguishing feature of the period was the emergence of new media technology that evolved a strong relationship with the economic field in general and with business news production in particular. Not only have the digital media had a profound effect on the overall structures of the national media orders, but it has a special significance for the role and position of the individual business news platforms within those orders.

The new digital communication technology gradually altered the relationship between the economic field and the media order. The launch of the World Wide Web in 1993 was an important turning point, creating a more or less open and non-hierarchical space for accurate and immediate communication across distance, borders, cultures, countries and economies. The new technology had already transformed the routines of business news production in the economic field. For instance, various providers of cable and satellite services competed in the field of international television news regarding business and finance. Reuters moved its operations into the international television news services by acquiring Visnews (Paterson 1998), but faced competition in the specialized field of business news from Bloomberg and Telerate among others. Later, the combination of traditional news agency work with digital networks transformed the character of international trade and finance, placing the agencies involved at the very heart of international capitalism and globalization (Palmer et al. 1998: 65). Companies, old and new such as AP, Dow Jones, Knight Ridder, AFX and Telerate entered into competition with Reuters, the dominant player in the field overall, selling financial and economic data, news and analyses, and providing platforms, software and hardware for interactive analysis and transactions. By the end of the 1990s, Reuters' position seemed 'a little less overwhelming than it had been at the start of the decade', as Palmer, Boyd-Barrett and Rantanen put it (Palmer et al. 1998: 77).

At least four elements of change in the position and role of business news in the media orders can be said to have derived from these technological and industrial developments. First, the new technology altered the speed and the temporal logic of the news media order, transferring the print media platforms to the commentator and contextualizing level with a role secondary to that of the speed-based agency news services. Second, the new technology has expanded the scope of the information services, making it possible for a growing number of platforms to combine information services with transaction services, analysis, product information and stock-exchange trading. Third, the expansion has paved the way for more specialized platforms and products and a more general and socially expanding platforms and formats for business news. Within many professional fields, Internet platforms of a specialized and more restricted kind (in terms of general accessibility) have taken over as specialized business media and news channels. Fourth, information and transaction services have been offered more often as global products in a global market, thus adding to a general globalization effect and increasing the accessibility of the national media orders. As a result of all this, media organizations and information brokers of a completely new kind have emerged, with little or no journalistic understanding of their own work. On the Internet today there appears to be an anarchistic and non-hierarchical supply of news brokers, analysts, consultancies, e-business specialists, information providers, etc., all functioning outside the traditional field of journalism.

Again, the changes in business news production and the media order need to be considered in association with changes in the economic field as well. The deregulation of the international financial markets in the early 1990s has had a profound effect. New financial products appeared, and real-time markets abounded globally. One important intra-organizational change has been the shift in power and control within business organizations, often described as a transition from management to shareholder control (Byrkjeflot 2001) and has involved attempts by owners to bring out 'real' values and to capitalize on old companies by pushing through mergers and acquisitions on a grand scale. This obviously creates new markets for business information and information services of all kinds; investment strategies, investor relations, public relations-consulting, legal assistance and so on.

In the midst of all this, a new consensus seems to have appeared across political and economic elites about the efficiency and necessity of the market. This consensus is also the result of changes in the way 'citizens' increasingly are supposed to be integrated into an economy, rather than in a society and a welfare state. Subsequently, the citizen-consumer also becomes a citizen-investor, with strong incentives to invest in private pension funds and privately owned shares. Thus today, the economy and the market probably define the most important social bond or relationship between citizens and between them and their societal institutions. The consensus lives on, although the representations and visions of the economy as a natural and a priori legitimized institution of social control are more often contested.

The period has seen the emergence of the information economy as a separate economic field, with its own logics and positions, its own knowledge, values and hierarchies — and of course, its own magazines and news outlets. The 'new economy' was accompanied by a variety of international magazines about new products and innovations on software and hardware within ICT, aimed at the avant-garde of the new economy. The international magazines and their national equivalents soon appeared in the Nordic countries. The magazines quickly proved to be powerful social and economic weapons for the new generation of engineers, innovators and businessmen in promoting and legitimizing new concepts, new values and new trends in society. The digital nerd became an avant-garde artist, a potential billionaire and a creative hero. The print news media responded by introducing specialists in the digital area, developing special sections and supplements for editorial comment, news and advertising.

An interesting feature of business information and news expansion in the Nordic region is the proliferation of weekly news-sheets. Originally, these newssheets consisted of print and fax-distributed newspapers, like *Managements Politiske Ugebrev* in Denmark for instance, founded by Erik Rasmussen in 1981 and later succeeded by *Ugebrevet Mandag Morgen* (1989), and *Økonomisk Ugebrev* (1994) and *Ugebrevet A4* (2002). The latter was established by the Danish Confederation of Trade Unions (LO) after the closure of the social democrat daily *Aktuelt*. Its idea and format have been imported and copied in the other Nordic countries. With the arrival of the Internet, more of these print-based newssheets have turned themselves into web-based publications with conditional access.

Although the practice of business journalism and the contents of business news have both been expanding, this has also been a period during which the print media platforms for business news have had to look into their future role in the national and global media orders. These platforms face growing competition, as a result of the recent technological changes and also because the spread of audiovisual media platforms increases the general saturation of the print media market. The latest figures from 2005 thus show a slight decline for several of the Nordic business niche newspapers and magazines, which can be interpreted as a consequence of the increasing popularity of the Internet, rather than as part of a general weakening in audience attention or interest in business news. For instance, according to a report in *Aftenposten* on the 4th of April 2005, *Dagens Industri* has managed to discourage further decline due to 'net cannibalization' by reducing the number of articles freely available in their web edition. Besides which, the print platforms for business news are often more stable and more protected from competition since their position in the media orders is already privileged compared to that of most other platforms: the specialized business news platform and the main general-interest newspapers are both privileged when it comes to advertising revenues, and the business community (and thus also the market for potential readers) is growing rather than declining. Consequently, although the figures for general newspaper reading are falling in all the Nordic countries at present, the print media platforms for business news remain surprisingly stable.

In Sweden, *Dagens Industri* reported a big increase in sales from 73,243 copies sold in 1990 to 126,500 in 2000, followed by a slight drop to 117,500 in 2005. These sales are impressive, not least since they occurred at a time when circulation for the Swedish daily press as a whole was declining from around 3,400,000 copies daily in 1990 to below 3,000,000 in 2000 (Grafström 2005). Sales of *Finanstidningen* also rose from 4,500 copies in 1990 to more than 27,000 in 2000 (Grafström 2006). However, in 1998 when *Finanstidningen* was acquired by the Swedish-based international, Modern Times Group, its new owners began to compete more directly with *Dagens Industri*. The strategy failed, and in 2002 *Finanstidningen* was merged with the media and public-relations weekly *Vision* under the name of *Finans Vision*. This did not help much and the newspaper was liquidated in January 2003. *Veckans Affärer* also faced uneven sales, but its situation has never become dramatic. After a peak in 1990 with 48,000 copies sold, the figure has dropped to 34,000 in 2005.

In Denmark, *Børsen* 'turned pink' in 1993 and further consolidated its position as Denmark's leading specialist business paper. The general-interest newspapers were also concentrating more on their business coverage. In 2002 the monthly magazine *Børsens Nyhedsmagasin* was purchased by Berlingske Officin — which since 2000 had been owned by the Norwegian media group Orkla (sold to Mecon Media in 2006) — and was renamed *Berlingske Nyhedsmagasin*. The following year Berlingske Officin bought out *Erhvervsbladet* from the Bernhard family. *Berlingske Tidende* however, continued to have economic problems even after its reconstruction. On the other hand, Jyllands-Posten, originally a regional publication, managed to redefine itself as a national newspaper. Again, one of the strategies for achieving this goal was to develop the paper's national business news coverage. Thus the business news field continues today to be a highly competitive field.

In Finland, the owners of *Helsingin Sanomat*, Sanoma OY started *Taloussanomat* (Economic News) in 1997 as the country's second largest daily business newspaper. The paper is reported to have sold 34,782 copies on weekdays and as many as 64,894 on Saturdays in 2003. Thus *Kauppalehti*, with its circulation of 80,894 copies in 2003 and 81,006 in 2005, still occupies the top position in the specialized business newspaper market, drawing on the symbolic capital of being Finland's old original business daily. And in 2004, in order to combat the competition from *Taloussanomat*, *Kauppalehti* also developed their Saturday edition to become *Presso,* an independent platform. *Presso* has a wider and younger readership than *Kauppalehti* and offers a lighter and a more entertaining content. *Presso*'s circulation was around 50,000 copies in 2005. *Kauppalehti* has also been able to diversify its products successfully to television and the Internet by launching *Kauppalehti Online* in 1996 and by fronting prime time financial programs on the private television channel MTV3, which since 1991 has been owned by the same group, Alma Media Group. Since 1987 *Kauppalehti* has also been publishing *Kauppalehti Optio,* a business magazine issued twice a month as a supplement of *Kauppalehti.* On the general-interest front, *Uusi Suomi* was taken over in 1991 by the Alma Media Group, the second largest owner group in the Finnish media industry. This group also owns *Aamulehti*, the predominant daily in the Tampere region, and *Iltalehti,* the national tabloid rival of the Sanoma group's *Ilta-Sanomat.* In addition, they own the major private television channel *MTV3*, and several other media platforms. Bonnier owns 23% of the Alma Media Group.

In Norway, *Dagens Næringsliv* maintained its steady increase of sales during the second half of the 1990s and became Norway's fourth largest daily. Since 2000 sales have varied between 70,000 and 75,000 and have secured the economic base for the largest team of business journalists in Norway. But it was the more specialized *Finansavisen* that was rated the most profitable newspaper in Norway in 1997, with its 30% profit margin and sales rising to 12,000.[20] The paper continued to rise throughout the period and have a present level of 21,800. Other publications in the business field have continued to prosper, for instance *Kapital* (40,000), *Dine Penger* (83,505) and free print outlets as *Finansfokus* (36,800) and *HK-nytt* (59,400). The innovative media-owner Trygve Hegnar also extended his publishing empire during the same period with the launch of *Kapital Data, PC-Magasinet* and *Interiørmagasinet.* Adding book publishing to his other activities, Hegnar established Hegnar Media as a media company. He now also hosts a television show called *Kapital-TV.* The Internet service *Hegnar Online* was established as far back as 1996, but it never became an effective platform. Hegnar continues to be a significant investor and publicist. In 2003 he also bought a 24% share in the respected Norwegian publishing house *Gyldendal.*

An interesting feature of this recent phase of expansion is the way in which business news has become an important spearhead for the media owners' more general strategies for expanding into new markets and new technologies (see also Finneman 2006, Slaatta 2003). In Sweden, Bonnier remains the dominant player when it comes to business information and news production, and Bonnier has used its special insights from business information publishing to expand within and across the Nordic borders. Having first become firmly positioned in Denmark with the ownership of *Børsen,* Bonnier — through Dagens Industri Holding AB — has expanded further into the Eastern and Central European countries. In 2005 it is successfully running business dailies

---

[20] Geelmeuyden 2002: 379.

in Bulgaria, Croatia, Estonia, Latvia, Lithuania, Poland, Russia and Slovenia (see also Risberg & Ainamo in the present volume). Through Bonnier Affärsinformation Holding AB, the company has also recently been positioning itself as strongly in the Internet services market, providing directories, various forms of business information outlets, direct marketing and Internet consultancies in a wide range of European countries (Harrie 2003, 2006). However, in its own home market in Sweden Bonnier has encountered growing competition from abroad. The Norwegian company Schibsted has entered both the general-interest and the boulevard newspaper market with the purchase first of *Svenska Dagbladet* and subsequently of *Aftonbladet*. One of their strategies for the renewal of the two newspapers has consisted of re-designing their business news sections. Their latest investment has been the news website *E24* which offers business news and is the result of co-operation between *Svenska Dagbladet* and *Aftonbladet*. In Finland, Sanoma has to some extent followed Bonnier and created business news agencies and print media in Estonia and Russia. But Sanoma's main international strategy has been connected with its investments in the European magazine industry, while other industrial movers in the Nordic region are connecting business news platforms on the Internet to cable television channels and mobile phone service providers.

A related development on the business news front has involved a certain re-orientation of news values into other forms of journalism, entertainment and news production, with a general shift in interest towards money, fortune making, speculation and risk-taking. To some extent macro-oriented reports on the ups and downs of national economies and the big nationally owned corporations have always appeared as leading news in national news programs on the national public service broadcasting channels. However, business news and economic information increased significantly in the 1990s to become a major ingredient in the standard news programs. It has become a development strategy among the private news purveyors with public service obligations programs to take on and/or expand business news. *TV2* in Norway provides an example of this. In 1999 their journalists were instructed to choose an economic news story every day to be one of their top stories, and to give business news a slot later in the program as well. For two years *TV2* designated a section in its main news program to economic news, and ran a ticker showing stock exchange index information at the bottom of the screen, like the major international channels did. However, these rather radical strategies for a business news re-orientation were abandoned, since when television's economic orientation has tended to abandon hard-core business news production and economic trading information in favor of a more personalized and popularized coverage of investors and owners. The late 1990s also saw an increase in infotainment programs with a personal focus on betting, quick private fortune-making (how to be a millionaire) and investment strategies (how to invest your money).

Although there are few signs as yet that the digital media are leaving the printed media behind as obsolete and unfashionable news platforms, the industrial movers do seem to be attuning their business strategies towards a more digital and mobile media order. With the recent improvements in Internet-based financial and information services, it may be that the printed platforms for business journalism have reached their peak. It seems more than likely that newspaper sales in all the Nordic countries will fall in the years to come, and that the competition which has so far existed between newspapers becomes much fiercer in the Internet market. The transition has already led to growing market concern regarding the availability of news and information and the limited opportunities for media companies to charge for such services. There is an increasing reluctance — particularly among the young audiences — to pay for news, which is being regarded more and more as a public good and is taken for granted as such.

The effect of all these changes on the practice of journalism in the Nordic region has been profound. The changes in the technological environment and the changes in ownership structures and media company strategies on the one hand and the expansion of business news production and distribution on the other have together had complex implications for the relations between the fields of journalism and economy. There is no unilateral impact causing a comprehensive loss of autonomy for journalism. Rather, still taking a relational perspective on symbolic power, there is reason to believe that the subfield of business journalism has taken over — or is about to take over — the professional hegemony that political journalism has previously enjoyed, thus becoming the most prestigious and best-paid specialized field in the news industry.

New sources of information have become important to the business news specialists who now turn less to companies themselves and more to the world of shareholder interests and investors, taking the stock exchange index as an indicator of performance. It is no longer necessary to talk to the board-members or to top management to find out what is happening; stock values tell the journalists all they want to know.

Thus, as a result of their new practice, journalists are continually engaged in the symbolical reification of the stock exchange as the central source for information about the economy.

A new generation of information workers with strong roots in the new media has arrived, although the dominance of its members is not yet complete. But they are getting there. Web journalists in traditional news media are used to work with little time available, small resources and meager office space, and the new industrial owners of media organizations are eager make decisions about cost allocation, time-saving, employee cuts, etc. The competition is thus between work methods and platforms. Which of them will win to become the spearhead of the media brand? So far, the print and audiovisual media are powerful identity platforms, but things are changing rapidly. Just now there is no doubt that content is changing, due to growing experience and new editorial strategies, adjusting to the greater speed in the discourses and the information circuits to which their positions are connected. It seems increasingly likely that speed, rather than accuracy or exclusiveness, is becoming the essential sine qua non for all news production.

Conclusion

We have now observed over a period of almost fifty years the emergence and course of old and new platforms for business journalism in the four Nordic countries. We have traced the expansion of the business press in four phases. The personal — and soon the public — careers of the early innovators of the new magazines and newspapers were shaped by the new opportunity structures of the 1960s and 1970s in the field of journalism and in the economic field. New ideological and economic demands in the media market that could now, it seemed, be met. A new international wave of neo-liberal economic theory was flowing their way, and successful international business publications such as *Business Week, Fortune* and *Economist* provided them with models for new market opportunities in the individual national media orders. Apart from the cultural and ideological inducements, there was also possibility of making money from the production of news. Thirty years later these new business news platforms had become a spectacular success — economically, industrially and culturally.

More recently, the expansion of business news has perhaps been most marked for its association with wider cultural and other non-economic changes in the Nordic countries. Its effects on the economy and on the business firms should be regarded not only in terms of increasing sales and the number of news stories, but also of the way other parts of society — in particular the cultural industries such as sports, the arts, visual culture and entertainment — have become increasingly influenced by the dominant form of knowledge in the economic field.

It has thus been a spectacular story, and the expansion of business journalism in the Nordic news media orders has been considerable and lasting. Its success in the print media markets has occurred just when the global marked for newspapers generally has been declining. For some time it has been taken generally for granted that newspapers would suffer increasing competition from television, film and radio. But, with the exception of Denmark, newspaper circulation in the Nordic countries was on the increase throughout the 1980s, and in Norway and Finland even into the early 1990s.[21] As the present study has shown, part of this success is also due to the expansion of the business press.

	Finland	Sweden	Norway	Denmark
1950	419	497	462	368
1979	557	549	519	337
1990	558	526	611	343
1998	453	438	598	307
2004	522	489	651	301

Table 2.1: Total Circulation of Newspapers per 1000 Inhabitants in the Nordic Countries 1950-1998
Source: Salokangas 1999, Suomen Lehdistö - Finlands Press 6-7/1998, 7; http://www.sanomalehdet.fi/maailmantilasto.html, World Press Trends 2005

Media consumption as a whole reveals a different trend, and the audiovisual media are clearly accounting for a growing proportion of the time devoted to the media by Nordic audiences. Thus, overall, the first half of the period studied here is characterized by increasing circulation of newspapers. The second half, however, is a period of de-

---

[21] The decline in the number of titles is steep in Denmark, where local monopolies in the newspaper market developed early. As regards circulation, this development came somewhat later and was less steep. Measured in terms of total circulation, the decline in regional and local titles has been offset by increasing circulation for the national press and the central Copenhagen newspapers (*Politiken and Berlingske Tidende*). Interestingly, the regional newspaper *Jyllands-Posten* has also managed to achieve a spectacular transformation from regional to national newspaper with increased circulation. According to Søllinge, the Danish tabloids were already in decline in the early 1980s (Søllinge 1999). Høst notes that a different development has taken place in Norway, where both tabloids and local newspapers have increased their circulation (Høst 1999).

cline, with the possible exception of Norway, where circulation figures have remained remarkably stable. However, the decline does not really affect the main platforms for business news. The case of Sweden can illustrate this point. In the 40-year period the two general-interest newspapers *Svenska Dagbladet* and *Dagens Nyheter* have increased their joint sales from 450,000 copies in 1970 to 540,000 in 2000. During the same period the four newcomers - *Dagens Industri, Finanstidningen, Affärsvärlden* and *Veckans Affärer* - have increased their sales from almost 40,000 in 1970 to 220,000 in 2000.

The economic motivation of the innovators, the owners and the publishers was obviously strong. The early market was associated with the arrival of new educational institutions, new forms of knowledge, new generations of business managers and new technologies for developing print media design. Later, the growing demand for financial news on the part of financiers, banks and brokers has spawned many minor specialist services, which in turn provide openings for yet more news-sellers, news-analysts and news commentators and so on. There is a functional circle of reinforcement within the media order, whereby information generates a greater supply of information services providing more information, as well as more media generating an even greater demand for new information supplies, new specializations, and so on.

In addition to this functional logic for expansion in the media order, there is an important social aspect to the expansion of business journalism, whereby specialized business information platforms (web pages, print media, formats and programs) tend to turn towards including political, cultural and social information, creating and reinforcing the social identification and stratification of business communities with news about theories of management, business commentaries, business personalities, life-style information, and news about variously conspicuous consumption goods. As this social expansion continues, the advertising market also expands, adding another important economic reason for regarding business news production as a business in itself. Thus, like Reuters before them, international news companies have moved on from specialized business news to news in general. And so the show will go on...

Bibliography

Ainamo, A., J. Tienari & E. Vaara (2002) The Emergence, Legitimization and Naturalization of Business Journalism in Finland. Paper presented at the Sixth European Business History Congress, Helsinki, Finland, August 22-24.

Ainamo A., J. Tienari & E. Vaara (2006) Between West and East: A Social History of Business Journalism in Cold War Finland. *Human Relations* Vol. 59 (5): 611-636.

Bjørklund, T. & Hagtvet, B. (Eds.) (1981) *Høyrebølgen - epokesjifte i norsk politikk?* Oslo: Aschehough.

Boréus, K. (1994) *Högervåg: Nyliberalismen och kampen om språket i svensk debatt 1969-1989.* Stockholm: Tidens Förlag.

Boréus, K. (1997) The Shift to the Right: Neo-liberalism in Argumentation and Language in the Swedish Public Debate since 1969. *European Journal of Political Research* Vol. 31(3): 257-286.

Bourdieu, P. (1984) *Distinction. A Social Critique of the Judgement of Taste.* Cambridge: Polity Press.

Bourdieu, P. (1996) *Sur la television.* Paris: Raisons d'agir.

Bringert, L. & B. Torekull (1995) *Äventyret Dagens Industri: Historien om en tidnings födelse.* Stockholm: Wahlström & Widstrand.

Byrkjeflot, H. (2001) The Nordic Model of Democracy and Management. In Byrkjeflot, H., S. Myklebust, T. Myrvang & F. Sejersted. *The Democratic Challenge to Capitalism. Management and Democracy in the Nordic Countries.* Bergen: Fagbokforlaget.

Duval, J. (2004) *Critique de la raison journalistique. Les transformations de la presse èconomique en France.* Paris: Seuil.

Engblom, L.-Å. (2002) Tidninger dör men pressen lever. In Gustafsson, K. E. & P. Rydén (Eds.) *Den svenska pressens historia IV.* Stockholm: Ekerlids Förlag.

Engwall, L. & V. Samagni (1998) *Management education in historical perspective.* Manchester: Manchester University Press.

Engwall, L. (1992) *Mercury meets Minerva: Business studies in higher education - The Swedish case.* Oxford: Pergamon Press.

Finneman, N. O. (2006) The Internet and the Public Space. In Carlsson, U. (Ed.) *Radio, TV & Internet in the Nordic Countries.* Gothenburg: Nordicom.

Fonsmark, H. (1996) *Børsens Danmarkshistorie 1896-1996.* Copenhagen: Børsens Forlag.

Fagerfjäll, R. (1991) *Affärsvärlden 1901-1991.* Stockholm: Affärsvärldens Förlag.

Geelmeuyden, N. C. (2002) *Hegnar.* Oslo: Schibsted.

Grafström, M. (2006) *The Development of Swedish Business Journalism. Historical Roots of an Organisational Field.* Doctoral Thesis No. 121. Department of Business Studies, Uppsala University.

Grafström, M. (2005) The Expansion and Change of Business News Content in Sweden, 1960-2000. Working Paper, Center for Business and Politics, Copenhagen Business School.

Gustafsson, K. E. (2002) I datoernes värld (efter 1975). In Gustafsson, K. E. & P. Rydén (Eds.) *Den svenska pressens historia IV*. Stockholm: Ekerlids förlag.

Hadenius, S. (2002) *Dagens Nyheters historia. Tidningen och makten 1864 - 2000*. Stockholm: Bokforlaget DN.

Hallin, D.C. & P. Mancini (2004) *Comparing Media Systems*. Cambridge: Cambridge University Press.

Harrie, E. (2003) *The Nordic Media Market. Media Companies and Business Activities*. Gothenburg: Nordicom.

Hegnar, T. (1973) *Hvordan unnslippe skatten*. Oslo.

Herkman, J. (2005) *Kaupallisen television ja iltapäivälehtien avioliitto: median markkinoituminen ja televisioituminen*. Tampere, Finland: Vastapaino.

Hernes, G. (1978) *Blandingsadministrasjon og Forhandlingsøkonomi*. Oslo: Universitetsforlaget.

Høst, S. (1999) *Avisåret 1998: stabilt totalopplag, svake aviser tilbake*, Fredrikstad: The Norwegian Institute of Journalism.

Høyer, S. (1995) *Pressen mellom teknologi og samfunn*. Oslo: Universitetsforlaget.

Jonsson, S. (2000): Göteborgs Handels- och Sjöfartstidnings om- och nedläggning. In Gustafsson, K. E. & P. Rydén (Eds.): *Konkurrens och förnyelse*. Sweden: Nordicom.

Jyrkiäinen, J. (1994) Sanomalehdistön keskittyminen –joukkoviestinnän ja erityisesti sanomalehdistön keskittymisilmiö, sen kulku ja seuraukset jälkiteollisessa yhteiskunnassa 1980- luvun lopulla. Acta Universitatis Tamperensis ser A vol. 409, Doctoral dissertation, University of Tampere.

Kjær, P. & Langer, R. (2005) Infused with news value: Management, managerial knowledge and the institutionalization of business news. *Scandinavian Journal of Management* Vol. 21 (2): 209-233.

Lamont, M. (1992) *Money, Morals and Manners. The Culture of the French and the American Upper-Middle Class*. Chicago: University of Chicago Press.

Harrie, E. (Ed.) (2003) *The Nordic media market*. Nordic Media Trends, no. 7 Nordicom. Sweden: Gothenburg University.

Harrie, E. (2006) *Media Trends 2006: Radio, TV & Internet*. Nordic Media Trends, no. 8. Nordicom. Sweden: Gothenburg University.

Palmer, M., O. Boyd-Barrett & T. Rantanen (1998) Global Financial News. In Boyd-Barrett, O. & T. Rantanen (Eds.) *The Globalization of News*. London: Sage.

Parsons, W. D. (1989) *The Power of the Financial Press. Journalism and Economic Opinion in Britain and America*. Aldershot: Edward Elgar Press.

Paterson, C. (1998) Global Battlefields. In Boyd-Barrett, O. & T. Rantanen (Eds.) *The Globalization of News*. London: Sage.

Salokangas, R. (1999) From Political to National, Regional and Local. The Newspaper Structure in Finland. *Nordicom Review* Vol 20 (1): 77-105.

Schultz, I. (2006) *Bag nyhederne*. Fredriksberg: Forlaget Samfundslitteratur.

Slaatta, T. (2003) *Den norske medieorden*. Oslo: Gyldendal Akademisk.

Stråth, B. (Ed.) (1992) *Language and the Construction of Class Identities*. Gothenburg University: Department of History.

Sundqvist, S.-I., (1989) Datorernas intåg. In B. Nordell (Ed.) *Stormarnas hus: En krönika om DN 1964-1989*. Stockholm: DN Förlaget.
Søllinge, J. (1999) Danish Newspapers: Structure and Developments. *Nordicom Review* Vol. 20 (1): 31-76.

CHAPTER 3

The Professionalization of
Business Journalism in Finland

ANTTI AINAMO, JANNE TIENARI
& EERO VAARA

Introduction

Over the last few decades, we have wittnessed the growth and proliferation of business journalism across the globe (Herman & Chomsky
1988, Yamaguchi & Harris 2004, cf. Nordfors et al. 2006). Business
journalism has emerged as a key carrier of discourses relating to
business and management (Sahlin-Andersson & Engwall 2002, Kjær
& Langer 2005, the chapters in this volume), and has become an established part of national media orders (Slaatta 2003). While the
roles of business journalism in global discourses and national media
orders are beginning to be generally understood, the particular *processes* of professionalization have up to now received less research attention than have the role of business journalism or business news.

In this chapter, we examine the process whereby business journalism in Finland professionalized. For the most part, we take most of
the established literature on professionalization (e.g. Abbott 1988) as
a point of departure. We also look for fresh inspiration in the research
of the French sociologist Pierre Bourdieu and those who have followed his method (e.g. Bourdieu 1998, Benson & Neveu, 2005). We
find from all this how many of the institutional processes and outcomes in Finland appear to resemble those in Denmark, Norway and
Sweden, those in the UK and the U.S., as well as those in France
(Slaatta 2003, Kjær & Langer 2005, Grafström 2006, Parsons 1989,
Duval 2004). But we also find that the Finnish case contains specific
traits of its own that are due, for example, to Finland's peculiar post-
World War II position between the West and the Soviet Bloc. Bearing this in mind we focus on what we regard as the characteristic features and essential turning-points in the development of business

journalism in Finland. We set out to answer a general question: what kinds of processes have characterized the professionalization of business journalism? We specify ways in which business journalists in Finland over the last 50 years or so have created and institutionalized a key position for themselves as representing a specific profession in the context of their own particular local society and economy.

While the present chapter draws on our recent paper on Finnish business journalism in the context of the political and ideological struggles of the Cold War (Ainamo, Tienari & Vaara 2006), the focus here - the actual process of professionalization – is a different one. In order to confirm the potential generalizability of our findings, we characterize the Finnish experience and compare it with that of the other Nordic countries. Next, we provide a review of the existing literature, and follow this with a brief historical account of our empirical data, based on our access to the numerous interviews conducted by Antti Mikkonen, an experienced Finnish business journalist between 1996 and 1998. Finally, we offer some conclusions based on our analysis to suggest why - and how - the case of Finland appears to generate insights that may be of general interest for anyone studying business journalism, professionalization, or both.

Journalism as a Field and a Profession

The traditional approach to the study of professionalization in any field has been to examine the emergence and institutionalization of a new profession in relation to the national system of regulation, the norms created and nurtured in professional associations, and the system of education preparing graduates for the profession concerned (Abbott 1988). Breaking to some extent from this approach, our analysis of the professionalization of the journalistic field in the present chapter is inspired by Pierre Bourdieu's research. Bourdieu turned his attention to the mass media and journalism in the 1990s (1993, 1998, 2000). Bourdieu came up with a conceptual frame of reference that has since been a source of inspiration for some researchers who have focused on the historical development of business journalism in a particular context (Slaatta 2003, Benson & Neveu 2005). Our approach is a complex one in that we diverge also to some extent from Bourdieu's approach. Our approach both complements and departs from the traditional approaches to professionalization and from the work of Bourdieu and of those most faithful to his method. In this chapter we do not pretend to make a rigid application of any established conceptual and methodological tools in relation to the field of journalism. This said, our approach is most inspired by Bourdieu's work in, for example, bearing in mind his repudiation of the uncritical use of the term 'profession' (Bourdieu 1988: xii).

Two selective readings of the work of Bourdieu and his colleagues brings this work quite near to the core literature on the system of professions by Abbott (1988) and his colleagues. The first of these is to say that any talk of 'profession' is a discourse mainly serving to enhance the self-identity of those involved (Bourdieu 1988; Aldridge & Evetts 2003). In both research by Bourdieu and by Abbott, talk and discourse are portrayed as strategies for accumulating capital specific to a particular domain that then becomes institutionalized as a particular 'professional field' for those involved and those not involved. Another selective reading is that Bourdieu's work on the media and journalism must have been inspired by his earlier work in fields such as cultural production and academic production (Bourdieu 1990, 1993). Within this reading, spanning the outermost boundaries outwards and bringing barriers to entry ever closer to the most inward core are relevant parts of almost any collective project.

Thus, our Bourdieu-inspired analysis builds on the premise that journalism and business journalism are remiscent of other professions and of other cultural fields. In our view, a new genre of culture or professional discourse will generally develop by way of individual practitioners or small groups who are able to set new examples that attract followers in the field (cf. Bourdieu 1993). We take it that, like other professions and other cultural fields, journalism and business journalism have originated from systems of apprenticeship and professional associations (e.g. Aldridge & Evetts 2003, cf. Abbott 1988, for other professions). The origins and dispositions of the earlier generations serve as the 'ideal' (Bourdieu 2000) for those coming after. The 'ideal', as this concept is used by Bourdieu, refers to the set of integrated institutionalized beliefs that functions as a semi-barrier to entry for anyone wishing to enter the profession. This 'ideal' acquires practical significance by way of such social mechanisms as education and training. It affects those who enter journalistic discourse and, thus, the field to which this discourse is related. It affects those who accept the status quo, as well as those who attempt to establish a new genre within the discourse. All journalists operating in the journalistic field 'must' share specific norms, values and practices. These are specific to the field and may evolve over time. As a result of various processes of socialization, the *habitus* or dispositions of any journalist prepare and guide him or her cognitively toward sensing, perceiving, thinking, and acting (Bourdieu 1993, 1998, 2000).

Central to Bourdieu's method in all its applications is that it does not focus only on the institutional field as a semi-autonomous field with its own 'rules of the game' and particular 'economy' of exchange and rewards. Essential to these exchanges are also various forms of capital – cultural, social, economic – that are accumulated over time and available for the actors concerned. A frame of reference of this kind provides a link between the journalistic field and the economic and political fields in that their inter-field relations are central to an understanding of the role that journalists have played, and now play, in society. Important in the journalistic field are, for example, the cultural capital that established media and professionals possess, the social capital that is connected with the relationships between the journalists and their informants, and the economic capital whose role is becoming stronger as the media become increasingly profit-oriented.

The boundaries between business journalism and other forms of journalism are obviously not fixed. Nordfors et al. (2006), for example, argue 'innovation journalism' is a new genre that includes key parts of, and builds on, business journalism. Business journalism has nonetheless also developed a number of specific practices and norms of its own (Read 1992). In particular, business journalists have relations vis-à-vis other actors inside and outside the boundaries of their field that differ from those of journalists in general. Business journalism now includes particular outlets that specialize in the dissemination of economic, business and management news on a daily or weekly basis. The increasing medialization and commercialization of society has been one force behind the growth in the significance of the role that business journalists play in society, to such an extent that these journalists are now a crucial part of a society's "media order" (Slaatta 2003).

Despite the obvious advantages of using Bourdieu's method, the fact is that almost all his work is geared to French conditions. While some of the observations reported undoubtedly apply to many other contexts as well, we cannot assume that they all do so (Benson & Neveu 2005). None of Bourdieu's studies take note of the kind of specific and subtle differences that may make business journalism different from other forms of journalism or make one context different from another. Thus, the historical development of business journalism in specific contexts needs looking into. Bearing Bourdieu's general approach and this particular reservation in mind, we focus here on the development of business journalism as a semi-autonomous field within a broader specialized field, embedded in a particular local context, and thus more than likely linked to more than one regulatory, technological, economic and political field.

Our analysis also takes into account that since the 1970s the development of business journalism as a specific journalistic field has been touched by globalization (Hermann & Chomsky 1988). The effects of globalization on the media were revolutionary, particularly in the 1970s (Read 1992, Ojala & Uskali 2005). The financialization of the global economy meant that companies had to invest in specialized relations with investors and the media, and had to try to manage these relations in as 'effective' ways as possible (Tainio et al. 2003). This meant more than a dramatic challenge to change local status quo from one local optimum to another. It heralded a succession of new global practices for business journalism requiring genuine innovation not only in journalism but in other fields of society and the economy as well (Kjær & Langer 2005, cf. Uskali, 2004).

In the following pages we will look in particular at two potential sources of diversity in the way that business journalism has become professionalized at different times and in different milieus. First, unlike some of the classical professions such as medicine or law (Abbott 1988), business journalism is not a highly regulated field in Western countries. However, there are certain laws and regulations that do affect the journalists's possibilities to engage in critical inquiry. These pertain to the protection of sources of news and to a prevention of too great a focus on the personal life of political or economic decision-makers. In application, such laws and regulations in journalism are largely indirect and tacit rather than direct. Self-governance rather than official regulation has characterized the field of journalism, although the distinction between the two has not always been very clear. Ainamo et al. (2006) describe how business journalists in Finland have sometimes considered state interests to an extent that clearly borders on self-censorship. The complex relations between journalistic conventions and the system of journalistic self-governance have thus, at least in the past, offered a platform for collusion or hybridization across fields in Finland.

Second, forms of such hybridization can differ significantly across countries in terms of relations among business journalism, business organizations, and various fields of society. On the one hand, the fact that the journalism is self-governed rather than being legally regulated has meant that journalistic development has not been much slowed down by the kind of built-in conservativeness that tends to characterize most Western legal institutions. In the Nordic countries, moreover, the nation-state has generally played an important role in setting up and financing new arrangements for education in journalism. On the other hand, all across the Western world, national ideology and broadsheet journalism have been related phenomena (Dacin 1997). Because of this ideological relation, self-governance and state-sponsored education have remained affected by politics. In the field of journalism, generally, and in the case of its various subfields, the process of professionalization has in many instances remained a volatile project, characterized by 'politics' in the original sense of the word as 'affairs of the state'. We will concentrate below on the historical development of business journalism as a profession in Finland, looking particularly at certain characteristic features and critical moments from this 'political' interpretation of Bourdieu's method.

Empirical Material

Our empirical material is based largely on interviews with business journalists and corporate managers and is complemented by an analysis of selected examples from Finnish media outlets. Antti Mikkonen, a well-known Finnish business journalist working for *Talouselämä*, conducted 153 interviews with journalists and important decision-makers in Finnish society and the economy in 1996 and 1997. His intention was to carry out the interviews to document the development of Finnish business journalism from the Second World War to the mid-1990s. He also wrote a popular book on this topic (Mikkonen 1998). We obtained full access to Mikkonen's interviews and other material he had collected.

Antti Mikkonen's interviewees include most of the key figures in Finnish business journalism, such as retired journalists and others still active in the mid-1990s, as well as important corporate decision-makers in Finnish business organizations. Business news, after all, is a co-constructed outcome of interactions between journalists and their sources (Kjær & Langer 2005). Most of Mikkonen's interviewees are male. The interviews focus on topics such as the development of journalistic practices, the emergence and development of specific 'genres' or recognized traditions within business journalism, the professionalization of the business press and its changing role in the

Finnish media, and the relationship between business journalists and the political and management elite. The interviews usually take up on specific topics such as 'scoops' or breaking news that journalists have made over the years. All the interviews were fully or partially transcribed by Mikkonen himself. The quotations in the following sections are our translations from the Finnish.

We have also studied selected media texts in leading Finnish outlets. Our analyses of the media texts and of the interview material all focus on interpreting and understanding the events and actors in two leading broadsheet newspapers, *Helsingin Sanomat* (HS) and *Uusi Suomi* (US), and in one leading business daily, *Kauppalehti* (KL), and one leading business weekly, *Talouselämä* (TE). Apart from *Uusi Suomi*, still today, these outlets continue to be occupy a central position in the Finnish-language business press. See Table 3.1 (cf. Ainamo et al. 2006).

Outlet	History and Characteristics
Uusi Suomi (US) 1847	From 1809 until 1917, Finland was a Grand Duchy in the Russian Empire. In 1847, the first major daily newspaper in the Finnish language was established. *Suometar* ('Maiden of Finland') was the product of a cohort of Finns who were overtly nationalistic. Russian censorship authorities forced the publishers to change the newspaper's name. In 1869, it became *Uusi Suometar* ('New Maiden of Finland') and in 1919, *Uusi Suomi* ('New Finland'), which remained closely linked with the Conservative Party in Finland. In 1958, *Uusi Suomi* acquired *Kauppalehti*, the business daily (see below). In the 1960s, the financial performance of *Uusi Suomi* began to deteriorate rapidly although *Kauppalehti's* profits helped to cover Uusi Suomi's losses. In the 1980s, *Aamulehti* acquired *Uusi Suomi*. In 1991, *Aamulehti* abandoned *Uusi Suomi*, the operations of which were then closed.
Helsingin Sanomat (HS) 1889	In 1889, *Päivälehti* was established by yet another cohort of nationalists. The founders consisted of Finnish-speaking entrepreneurs and politicians. The Russian authorities closed the paper down in 1903, but it was re-established as *Helsingin Sanomat* ('Helsinki News') in 1904. In the 1930s, *Helsingin Sanomat* began to cut itself off from its origins in the Finnish nationalist movement and to reinvent itself as an independent and neutral outlet. It repositioned itself as liberally rightwing or neutral. Today, *Helsingin Sanomat* has the largest daily subscription rate of printed media outlets in the Nordic countries. SanomaWSOY, a media corporation that grew up around *Helsingin Sanomat*, remains controlled by the descendants of Eero Erkko, the founder of *Päivälehti*. Among other papers, it publishes the largest Finnish tabloid, *Ilta-Sanomat*. From the 1970s onwards, SanomaWSOY has been internationalizing itself.
Kauppalehti (KL) 1898	In 1898, the Finnish Businessmen's Association established *Kauppalehti* ('The Commerce Journal'), a newspaper specializing in issues of economy and business. Ever since, *Kauppalehti* has remained in an important position in the Finnish business press. Since 1919, it has been appeared five (or at times six) times a week.
Talouselämä (TE) 1937	In 1937, a group of Finnish businessmen dissatisfied with *Helsingin Sanomat's* coverage of economic news established *Talouselämä* ('Economic Life'). Printed in magazine format, *Talouselämä* emerged as the largest business weekly in Finland. Challengers to *Talouselämä's* dominance as the main weekly business magazine in Finland have appeared particularly since the 1980s. *Talouselämä* has managed to maintain its dominant position as a business weekly.

Table 3.1: Major Outlets of Business Journalism in Finland
Source: Ainamo, Tienari & Vaara (2006)

The Professionalization of Business Journalism in Post-War Finland

We will now describe four periods in Finnish business journalism since World War II. These periods are: (1) the dissemination of information, from the 1940s onwards, (2) taking sides in how business and politics mix, from the 1960s onwards, (3) the 'casino period' and its 'backlash', from the 1980s, and (4) protecting and promoting the rules of the game of the global economic order of neo-liberal capitalism, from the 1990s onwards. Every period is described in terms of emerging practices among journalists as regards the economy and business, and of the development of particular genres within journalism. But each period also reveals the challenge of breaking new ground in the development of journalistic practices for reporting business phenomena in Finland. In some cases we find a blindness regarding the shape of things to come, and in other cases clairvoyant but fallacious projection of short-term trends. By and large, the periods reveal the field of business journalism as a series of shifting positions in relation to the economic and political fields in the post-war Finnish economy and in Finnish society as a whole.

From the 1940s Onwards: The Dissemination of Information

In 1948, Finnish journalists with an inclination for business journalism founded *Taloustoimittajain kerho*, The Business Journalists' Club. The mission of the club, as one of the founders put it, was 'to free members from simply being a conduit for trade statistics or financial quotes, as was the pre-war practice in Finland.' The club aspired to act as a 'pressure group...to develop the professional competence of business journalists, particularly with respect to the national economy.' What began as an informal club was transformed into a registered professional association in 1952[1]. 'The professional journalists and the economy experts who were there to advise the journalists were side by side in the club,' a pioneering business journalist recalls. 'In the 1950s, business firms were able to pay more than newspapers so, overall, there was a shortage of business journalists in Finland.'

In the first decades after World War II, a cadre of men closely united by their wartime experience formed the dominant political and managerial elite in Finland (Virtanen 2001). They differed widely in their education and political orientation, but many of them shared a

---

[1] An apparent contrast, worth noting is that business journalists in Sweden established an association for themselves as late as 1979 (Grafström 2006).

fundamental interest in the '*national cause*', or the national project of modernizing and developing Finnish society and the Finnish economy. Their premise was one of collective agency, whereby they allowed the nation-state a powerful role in terms of developing infrastructure, in terms of maintaining the essential elements of regulation, and in terms of acting as the central node in centralized wage negotiations between representatives of central associations of employers and the labour unions.

When key members in this 'co-operative' kind of Finnish elite organized meetings and various social functions, they invited prominent journalists to join them. It was expected that the state-led or private firms hosting these events would arrange for plenty food and alcohol to be served. The stakes were often stacked in favor of the latter so that a lunch meeting, for example, was often effectively 'quite wet'. It became the custom among business journalists to attend such events, to come away with a full stomach and sometimes rather drunk, and then to head for the office to type out the news story, usually based on a corporate handout or press release. According to a veteran journalist, the most important thing was 'if you were really drunk, to be able to stick the sheets of paper together, three sheets in the right order, so you wouldn't end up with 1, 3, and 2.' Access to free food and drink was seductive for modestly paid journalists in a society still plagued by rationing and a shortage of luxury goods. After getting the information, journalists were expected to promote knowledge of the economy among members of the public and, in particular, to bring up the special interests of the firms concerned in their texts. Individual business journalists could become quite knowledgeable about business events and issues, but were not usually able to show off such knowledge in written form. The captains of Finnish industry expected them to communicate what was regarded as factual information about new contracts, deals, investments and economic growth in general. In the post-war reconstruction period, the 'Finnish cause' called for an inherently positive outlook on the events and issues covered.

In the 1950s and 1960s, apart from these 'official' corporate press releases, it was meetings and functions that provided business journalists with their personal networks and background information. Also, by placing their advertisements in media outlets – withdrawing or replacing them at will – firms could in practice affect the way in which they were treated by more than one of the media outlets that reported on their activities. This was especially the case for the outlets specialized in business matters. Business journalism was not a recognized and certainly not a very respected part of the Finnish media order. The number of journalists who specialized on covering business issues was small, albeit gradually increasing.

Finnish industrialists and executives regarded most financial information as 'business secrets', a nondisclosure practice allowed by Finnish accounting legislation. A tradition of self-censorship prevailed. Business journalists and their sources both believed that 'leaks' would damage a company's business and companies, in turn, were regarded as the foundation on which the Finnish nation of the post-war era would be reconstructed. Within this context of carefully controled public exposure, business journalists would publish what they were asked to, and they would not rush to publish something if not asked. As a well-known business journalist maintained, 'the principle was that someone organized a press conference or a function in the evening, and they didn't even have to ask ... [before] journalists suggested that, "hey, we won't write anything about this for tomorrow's papers now".' Business journalists conformed to the expectations and needs of influential industrialists and business executives, as well as to their own desires of leisure. As late as 1968, it was estimated that two-thirds of all company press releases were published more or less word-for-word in *Helsingin Sanomat* (HS) and *Uusi Suomi* (US), the two major Finnish broadsheets that were also one of the main platforms for developments in business journalism (Mikkonen 1998: 42).

It was once said that the business weekly *Talouselämä* (TE), for example, attracted 'fourteen pages of ads in order to cater for fourteen pages of journalistic material.' All in all, it is thus evident that in the 1950s and 1960s, the original goal of The Business Journalists' Club 'to free members from simply being a conduit for trade statistics or financial quotes' was only realized in part. On one hand, the practice of disseminating information was alive and well. On the other hand, the societal context (state regulation and secretive firms) meant that journalists complied in a form of self-censorship, and thus restrictring the professional development of business journalism in Finland. 'Back in the 1960s, there was hardly any way we would ever make [corporate executives] angry, we didn't personalize the stories.' In effect, the outcome of this kind of compliance – apart perhaps from a low level of expert knowledge about business and the economy – was similar to that in Sweden (Grafström 2006: 91). A Finnish industrialist put it bluntly: 'The professional skill of business journalists was improving from the mid-60s onwards, but from an interviewee's point of view it was really poor back then...especially in relation to the micro level, the firms.' Nonetheless, despite the various pressures and requirements, skillful business journalists were beginning to be in demand. Moreover, in the late 1960s, a few individual journalists began actively to break away from the convention that business journalists did not report what they knew as news.

From the 1960s Onwards: Taking Sides in How Business and Politics Mix

From the late 1960s onwards, Finnish society became increasingly politically charged. The radical left gained ground especially after the 1966 parliamentary elections. Dr. Urho Kaleva Kekkonen, President of the Republic (1956-1981), came from the centre-right-wing Agrarian Party, but had excellent personal contacts with the Soviet *nomenklatura*. He soon had excellent personal contacts also with the radical left in Finnish politics. Throughout this revolution of the political map, the President governed with fiat also the political-managerial elite. The political-managerial elite was less of an integrated actor than earlier, and by now began to include an array of political thought spanning liberal market economy ideals, social-democratic ideals of market reform, and agrarian ideals of cooperatives that returned any economic surplus to the members of the cooperative.

By hindsight, it is notable in this intense politically charged atmosphere, *Helsingin Sanomat* (HS), the newspaper with the largest circulation in Finland, managed to maintain a relatively neutral image. Although principally liberally right-wing and hence pro market-economy, this newspaper also strove to be neutral and tolerant and, in exchange, was tolerated and, at times, even appreciated by many moderate leftists. HS was to become the crucial platform for the development of Finnish business journalism. In 1965, Aatos Erkko had succeeded his father, a former Foreign Minister, as the managing director of HS. Erkko's personal interest in business journalism marked a new start for the broadsheet business pages. Erkko declared an explicit policy of journalistic independence vis-à-vis advertising sales. 'We started to look critically at the way companies operated,' an experienced business journalist recalls. 'For example, I remember an incident connected with a state-owned firm, where we really managed to infuriate the CEO...that must have been in the late 60s...he then arranged for a boycott on ads...but, you know, it only lasted for a couple of weeks.' This mentality was in stark contrast with the situation only a few years earlier, when business journalists made sure that they did not make any business executive angry.

In 1972, following the example of Sweden's *Dagens Nyheter*, HS expanded its business section on its Tuesday edition to allow for longer stories on significant business events. It also acquired exclusive Finnish rights to Dow Jones's electronic economic and business news services, and began to make frequent use them of them. While it was thus quite transnational in its coverage of business news, HS was also careful not to upset representatives of the Finnish or Soviet states in its coverage of other news (Klemola 1981).

Ever since the 1940s, trade with the Soviet Union had been important to Finland, as a result of the peace treaty, and the war reparations and trade that it entailed. Trade was bilateral. Finland imported oil from the Soviet Union, and this trade spiraled upwards with increases in the world price of oil in 1973. Finland's trade relations with the Soviet Union generated a new form of self-censorship, whereby the Finnish business media refrained from criticizing the Soviet Union and its policies. Finnish journalists would – at best – 'write between the lines' (Uskali 2005, cf. Klemola 1981).

It was not easy for individual journalists to remain neutral in the highly political atmosphere that had now invaded the busines media, after its earlier seclusion from mainstream politics. Thus, many executives in Finnish firms became even more reluctant to talk to the press. Another reason why the tradition of secrecy persisted was that it was now considered risky to talk about profit and profit-making. One journalist put it as follows: 'If [a firm] was doing well, you didn't talk about it.' Instead, executives would declare their participation in carrying out' a social mission, providing jobs.'

HS, with its greater circulation compared to US, was enjoying advantages of scale in distribution and advertising. *Uusi Suomi* (US) had a distinct correlation between a company's advertising and the amount of space allotted to news about this company's operations. Because of shrinking circulation and growing per-copy distribution cost, US ran into into serious financial difficulties in the early 1970s. It was kept afloat by *Kauppalehti*, which enjoyed significant first-mover advantages as the first business daily in Finland and a rising circulation. [2]

---

[2] Interestingly, the same connection between advertising and news spaces for companies that can be found in US for these years can be found in *Kauppalehti* (KL).

In 1974, a group of right-wing businessmen established a national think-tank called *Elinkeinoelämän valtuuskunta* (EVA). In contrast to what the founders perceived as the Soviet model, the EVA mission was to promote a 'market economy' model. According to an EVA memo, HS offered 'too much space for all kinds of political opinions' (quoted in Sanomalehtimies-Journalisten 1978-07-03). To provide more room for positive views of the interests of private industry and Finnish corporations, EVA began to subsidize US. There is an interesting resemblance here to developments in Sweden where, in the 1970s, the Swedish Employers' Confederation and Timbro (a right-wing think-tank) set up their own news agency called 'The Press Service of the Industry' because there were 'anti-corporate and anti-social tendencies in the formation of public opinion' (Grafström 2006: 81).

As EVA had hoped, a significant number of business journalists saw themselves as proponents of the Western/EVA market economy model. 'Back then, business desks in newspapers were the centre for faith in the market economy, unlike the other desks.' The business journalists at US and KL, in particular, tried – for ideological reasons –not to write as much as the others about Soviet trade (Tolvanen 1982), but this made things rather difficult for them. Finnish firms doing business with the Soviet Union 'blacklisted' KL as regards advertising, as they wanted to remain on favourable terms with the politicians who negotiated bilateral agreements with their Soviet counterparts and who often, in practice, dictated the terms of trade for individual companies. 'With a heavy heart, this profile [with limited trace of Soviet trade] was gradually worked on,' a leading journalist in KL put it. This meant in the first instance that KL ran a series of articles about Finland's trade with the Soviet bloc.

The growing bilateral trade between Finland and the Soviet Union generated significant business opportunities for Finnish industry and trade. The Finnish media in general -the leftist political press in particular –and even many business journalists took a pro-Soviet view of the increasing economic co-operation with the Soviet Union (Tolvanen 1982). In an ironical twist of history, the Soviet trade all of a sudden meant that it was in the interest of Finnish 'market-economy' industrialists that the Finnish media refrain from explicit criticism of the Soviet Union. This collusion was made complete when, for the journalists, significant Soviet deals were obviously big news. A prominent business journalist described the situation as 'great business for the media…with big Finno-Soviet deals to be covered, very important to the Finnish economy…gigantic trade agreements and deals.'

The Finnish accounting legislation was being revised, and the adjusted version came into effect in 1974. Many business journalists began to work on new kinds of financial analysis regarding companies, as well as commenting more thoroughly and sometimes more critically on their strategies. TE –the leading business weekly – began to differentiate its profile by offering analyses of the financial results of Finnish companies, together with commentaries that were more like feature articles than mere news briefs. Sweden's *Veckans Affärer* was one of the models used here, although the outcome was a unique product.

From 1978 onwards, HS began to combine financial analyses with colorful commentaries on the company' business and corporate management 'to get ordinary people interested' in business issues. The 1974 accounting legislation made it possible for companies to continue to conceal a good deal of their profit in their financial statements to minimize their tax, on the one hand, and to provide financial analysts with the necessary information to analyze this information and to show a company's 'real' results on the other. This led to a new type of business journalism, whereby the journalist was a critical analyst. According to one seasoned business journalist: 'In the late 1960s, these guys changed business journalism into something totally different, into normal journalism, it was no longer just a question of reproducing company handouts in the newspaper.'

Together with the development of the new type of journalistic practice at TE and HS, the reorientation of KL in 1977 was a turning point in Finnish business journalism. The intent of the new young editor-in-chief was 'to achieve something that others hadn't done before.' His paper introduced a stream of business news independent from others in Finland. The idea, it was later explained, was 'to actively take part and to take stands…to profile ourselves as different from Helsingin Sanomat…My reporters don't have to know how to write,' the editor-in-chief explained, 'it's enough for me if they come with "breaking" news every day. I'll handle the writing. News is the primary product of a daily paper.' This was a 'photo-journalistic' style. There were more pictures. The text he wrote was impressionistic, meant to be read at a glance rather than carefully studied. Here, *Kauppalehti* was to be a model for *Dagens Industri* in Sweden (see chapter by Risberg and Ainamo, in the present volume) even if, undoubtedly, the imitation was to run both ways.

Meanwhile, apart from the pioneering work at TE, HS and KL, it cannot be denied that the practice of dissemination of information on business issues had now acquired a strong political flavor reflecting the general atmosphere of the Finnish societal context at that time, characterized by continued regulation by the State, increasing Soviet trade, and persistently secretive firms. This atmosphere could not but affect the professional practice of business journalism in the country. Despite the specific features of Finnish political and economic spheres, the situation was rather similar to that of Sweden in the 1970s. The Swedish case is described by Grafström (2006: 81, cf. Boréus 1994, Stråth 1998: 201-242) as follows: 'voices from the Swedish corporate sector were raised and lobbying activities emerged in an attempt to influence and shape public opinion to become more friendly toward and interested in corporations and corporate activities and events.' Another similarity between Finland and Sweden was the significant role of key inviduals – or institutional entrepreneurs, as Grafström (2006) calls them – in developing the practice of business journalism. However, the practices and the way in which they were developed appear to have happened with a time lag in Finland, when compared to their timing in Sweden. As a prominent business journalist put it: 'everything happened in Sweden four or five years before it happened in Finland.'

While now a clear second in terms of circulation and logistics, US still had close links to industry. Its journalists had superior access to top managers. As an experienced Finnish business journalist put it 'it was now a fight between HS and US,' a decisive fight for precedence. The other major outlets for printed business news were also acquiring distinct profiles of their own. TE invested in carefully crafted feature articles. KL focused on small and medium-sized business.

From the 1980s Onwards: The 'Casino Period' and its Backlash

By the early 1980s, the political right had regained ground from the political radical left in Finland, and the state regulation of business became a contested issue in much the same way as in other Western nations. Change was subsequently so rapid that a new era in the Finnish economy and Finnish society can be said to have opened. The deregulation of the Finnish financial system began in 1983 (Halttunen & Suvanto 1988) and power blocs in business and industry that had been established in the previous era began to crumble (Kuusterä

1990). 'Significant events started to unroll: deregulation, mergers, takeovers and other major business events,' as one prominent business journalist put it. Also, Finnish companies started to invest seriously in internationalization, for example, by making foreign acquisitions. Then, in the mid-1980s, foreign investors began in turn to show interest in Finnish companies. Finnish banks provided financing for the booming economy, and their customers took full advantage of deregulation. This was a time when it seemed that no investment could ever go wrong –a mood that has since become popularly known in Finland as the 'casino economy'. In retrospect, the late 1980s was an era of unprecedented hype, unsurpassed in the country's history except perhaps for the late 19th century when the the country was first industrialized.

The atmosphere was increasingly friendly towards business and deal-making. The business journalistic models of *Kauppalehti* (KL), *Talouselämä* (TE) and *Helsingin Sanomat* (HS) began to attract followers in the form of new outlets. A new generation of journalists entered the field. Finnish industrialists and executives no longer guarded business secrets as they had in the past. 'A choir of deep throats emerged in 1985-87; big shots using publicity for their own purposes. Back in the old days you could trust a big shot, but not anymore…they've learned to use the media for their own purposes.' Journalists now, for the first time, personalized business news. As a reward, some business journalists got 'scoops' to report about these dramatic events. Several young and eager bankers and business executives emerged in the media as heroes whose actions were seldom questioned. One seasoned business journalist recalls that 'in the 1980s, analysts and stockbrokers first appeared on the scene, and with modest experience, too.' The 'big boys realized that the only way to survive was to go along with this.' Executives began to try using the media to build up their personal reputations as well as for the benefit of their companies.

The boom turned into a bust. Finland plunged into a deep and dramatic recession in 1990-1991. The downturn was due to the collapse of the Soviet Union, which was still Finland's most important individual trading partner. Liquidity bankruptcies became very common in the Finnish economy after the collapse of Soviet demand and Soviet trade. The Finnish banking system ran into severe problems with so many of its clients going insolvent. With lay-offs in the industry, the banking, and other sectors alike, unemployment soared from five percent to around twenty. This proved to be a major watershed for Finnish business, for the country's economy and society as a whole. The recession also affected the development of business journalism. Retrospective self-criticism was one manifestation of this. In 1994, one prominent business journalist wrote:

> *We are the children of a prolonged period of regulation. For some sixty years, Finland was a regulated economy characterized by deal-making, talk in the sauna,[3] and centralized planning. Only the recession made the rotten structures visible. [...]* **[B]usiness journalism has only existed in Finland for 10-15 years. It takes a long time for independent and critical business journalism to mature.** *The Economist has been around for some 150 years, The Financial Times for a 115. Business journalism is [still] plagued by political journalism. In a small country, talk of power battles is often justified, but [still] too often business journalists are offered conspiracy theories and too often they accept these theories at face value.* Journalisti 1994-02-28 [our emphasis].

Once the recession set in, there was a 'backlash' among Finnish business journalists who regretted their 'lap dog journalism', that is, their simple-minded and uncritical enthusiasm and lack of criticism of the casino economy of the late 1980s (Mikkonen 1998). As one experienced journalist put it: 'Looking back at those years between 1987 and 1989 in particular, [we were behaving like] third rate detectives. We were only good at writing the news of the day. That's sad...but what was happening was just so damned dramatic!' Another experienced colleague of his added: 'That's the original sin of business journalists. ...You write glossy stories about lots of apparently successful businessmen, and you don't really ask the essential question: is this logical, can anyone really produce the kind of results that these guys appeared to have produced?'

Another prominent business journalist, describing the casino-economy period retrospectively, maintained that journalists had been carried away by a mixture of hype and cynicism: hype was accompanied by an incapacity for analysis, which was then compensated for by the constructing and recounting of simple stories, with their own heroes and villains, easy for readers to understand (Journalisti 1993-02-04). Self-censorship was transformed into a naïve enthusiasm for

---

[3] This refers to the practices of the post-WWII political and managerial elites – the tightly knit networks – who often met to bathe in the sauna, drink and 'talk business and politics.'

new heroes and heoric actions. Together, the bold deregulation of the Finnish economy that began in the early 1980s and the period of the casino-economy that it engendered set the stage for the transformation of the 1980s and demonstrated the long and winding road towards the professionalization of business journalists.

At the height of the casino economy in 1987-1988, the professional journalists writing columns in the journal of Finnish business journalists were already debating the question of their ownership of stocks or shares. Ethics of ownership triggered titles for the columns such as 'Journalists acting as stock exchange geniuses have reinforced the stock craze' (Journalisti 1987-11-09), and 'The double somersault of the newspaperman's ethic: the business journalist as insider' (Journalisti 1988-06-06). It was only from 1989 that Finland took its first steps towards 'comprehensive legislation' in the Western sense to provide transparent rules for trading in securities and insider trading.

After the collapse of the Soviet Union in 1991 and the dramatic consequences it had in Finland, business journalists found themselves in a new role. They began to hunt stories down proactively in the spirit of American investigative journalism, rather than waiting passively for news to unfold. The scoop about the merger between a toppling Finnish bank and its main rival in 1995 that brought forward an official statement from the banks several days before the originally intended date is still today regarded as a major event in the history of Finnish business journalism. As one journalist put it, '[this] illustrates the strength of real-time media.' The practice of investigative journalism that had previously appeared only sporadically (Mikkonen 1998), quickly became institutionalized as an integral part of Finnish business journalism. One seasoned business journalist and editor-in-chief reflected upon the new working ethic: 'It's the mentally lazy business journalists that annoy me most. Many of them don't even bother to check the archives of their own paper to prepare for an interview or for writing a story. The excuse is that there's no time. For the most part, I think that's just crap.'

During the 1980s and early 1990s, business journalism was thus expanding as a viable force in Finnish society. The number of outlets grew, the content of business news became more diversified, and business issues were generally being given more space in the various branches of the media. Again, this expansion, together with the shifting news content and the general process of institutionalization resembles developments in Sweden (Grafström 2006), Denmark (Kjær

& Langer 2005), and elsewhere (Drori 2006). In Finland, however, business journalists' knowledge about the workings of the economy or about finance in general was still rather haphazard in the 1980s. Thus, journalists' holdings in the companies covered by their stories was an issue discussed only sporadically in public. 'Your role as journalist should be crystal clear. You have to be very careful not to get involved as an actor when you know the people or the issues that you're covering. But this isn't always the case in practice,' one business journalist remarks. 'At the end of the day, autonomy is up to every individual journalist,' adds another.

From the 1990s Onwards: Protecting and Promoting the Neo-Liberal Global Order

The deregulation of the Finnish economy climaxed in 1993, when the last restrictions were abolished on foreign investors buying stocks traded on the Helsinki Stock Exchange. With the opportunities for attracting foreign investors, Finnish executives began to regard investor relations as an important part of their job, and the media became an important professional partner in the endeavor. And, yet, some proponents of neo-liberalism still believed that a persistent 'lack of analysis and a [constant] fear of the establishment striking back' still characterized Finnish business journalism more than anything else. These proponents were concerned with what they perceived as the legitimate concerns of owners and investors. The result was a predominating discourse in the Finnish business press wary of any criticism of the market economy or its neo-liberal ideals (Vaara & Tienari 2002). In broadsheet newspapers, this kind of an economic and financial rationale and the economic or business perspective spread rapidly from the business sections into other sections of newspapers and the media (Mikkonen 1998, Heikkilä 2001, cf. Kjær & Langer 2005)[4]. Whereas the late 1980s had revealed Finland's 'deviation from the ideal of the market economy,' the developments of the 1990s ensured that discourses in business journalism were clearly 'within the parameters of the market economy' (Mikkonen 1998).

---

[4] This contemporary dominance of the neo-liberal market content in the Finnish media is discussed in greater detail in Chapter 7 of the present book. In this respect, developments in Finland since the 1990s reminded of simultaneous processes of transition from a Soviet-run command economy into a market economy in post-socialist Central and Eastern European states (see Risberg and Ainamo, in the present volume, Drori 2006, Ainamo & Cardwell 1998) even if Finland was never formally a socialist country.

In the autumn of 1994, a referendum was held on Finland's membership of the European Union. A heated public debate on the pros and cons of EU membership preceded the referendum. *Helsingin Sanomat* (HS) actively supported Finland's bid for membership and contributed to the domestic debate by hosting its own 'Europe Seminar'. Generally speaking, too, 'the Finnish press was harnessed in favour of EU membership,' as a journalist in a regional newspaper recalls. The 'free' market business perspective –together with national security – was the main argument of those in favour of joining the EU.

Supporters of EU membership won by a narrow margin, and Finland joined the European Union on 1 January, 1995. Some have remarked sardonically that the recession really only ended when Finland won the World Championship for ice hockey in 1995 for the first (and, so far, for the only time) ever. The atmosphere and mood in society became positive. The business cycle took a turn for the better. As Finland fully recovered from the recession, an unprecedented volume of financial investment came from abroad (Tainio et al. 2003). The global breakthrough of Nokia mobile phones played an important part in both the financial investment and the economic recovery (Pulkkinen 1997, Ainamo 1997, Tainio 2003). In this dramatic recession-recovery cycle, the importance of the economy and business moved centre stage in the Finnish media landscape (Herkman 2005).

An increasing number of young and enthusiastic journalists were entering the field. Referring to the debate about the 1995 bank merger, an up-and-coming business journalist maintained that

> *...we have nothing to be ashamed of. Everyone has some kind of an interest. If you fail to find issues in which someone has an interest, you can't really report anything. It's all a question of balancing interests. Maybe we could have thought a bit more about some of the stories, but in the end there's not much that we need be ashamed of.*

The professional practices of business journalists continued to to take shape. 'Business journalists live by chatting with financial analysts. We didn't really have an analyst profession in Finland until the 1990s,' a prominent businessman has claimed. Today, a network of other corporate sources is a self-evident asset for business journalists. The network is exploited by way of personal contacts, unlike the company briefings (and the 'wet' meetings and functions) of the 1950s and 1960s. An ex-journalist remarked with apparent regret: 'Well, these sharp young business journalists...from a more mature perspective, it's a bit painful...the traces of their sources are so evident.'

Antti Mikkonen conducted most of his interviews in the autumn of 1997. Even at that time, another major influence on business journalism was already evident. 'Basically', one Finnish business man declared, 'business journalists in printed media are no longer able to "break" news, it's the electronic media that does that. Printed media does the analysis.' At the same time, a business journalist working for one of the tabloids maintained that 'business news simply don't sell well. Business, politics and all that are worst possible headlines.' Thus, the popularization of business news seems to be a more complicated matter than one might think at first sight. It is all part and parcel of other fundamental developments in the media field.

During the 1990s, the media field in Finland was subject to consolidation and the concentration of ownership (Jyrkiäinen 1994, Herkman 2005, Ojala & Uskali 2005). Dramatic developments in digitalization, communications technology and deregulation all coincided to encourage this process: '...the IT-boom coincided with the triumphal march of the market economy' (Herkman 2005: 69, cf. Tainio 2003). Within the media world, cross-pollination of content between tabloids, television, the Internet, and so on was both a significant corporate goal (Ainamo & Pantzar 2000) and a prominent outcome of media consolidation and concentration (Herkman 2005: 69). Business journalists were for the first time caught up in the convergence of digitalization and communication in the environment for their own media activities, and in the convergence of the media output for which they were responsible (Ojala & Uskali 2005, Nordfors et al. 2006). Large media companies grew in size and began to dominate the scene. In view of this, the journalists' failure to criticize the market economy and its accompanying neo-liberal ideals appears unsurprising and 'natural'. Business journalists were a profession that had coevolved with the news about the market economy they have covered.

Essentially, the professional practices of business journalism continued to be moulded by the contemporary societal and political atmosphere in which they found themselves, and which now included an insistence on the prime importance of financial results. Private media corporations had come to resemble other corporations in

Finland. They sought profit. The emerging trends of the 1990s were 'medialization' or 'entertainalization' (Ainamo & Pantzar 2000) whereby the currently prevailing professional practices in 'genres' or branches of journalism were to lose, at least in part, their credibility as news carriers in the 21st century. During the new century, Herkman (2005) warned against over-estimating the capacity of business journalists or students of business journalism to maintain an independent professional ethic and a non-public system of self-governance in business journalism and its study. Those who mention the threats that might arise from the concentration of media ownership are often accused of over-reacting. On the basis of such an interpretation, while the historical record may be less than conclusive, there is nonetheless historical evidence that business journalism has developed some professional conventions and routines that are distinct to it. It may also be interpreted that locally peculiar conventions and routines serve to balance the power relations and hierarchies of those adhering to the global profit-seeking order of neo-liberalism and those adhering to the local bases of political power and positions in society and the economy.

Conclusion

The events reported in this chapter tell a story of the increasing professionalization and influence of Finnish business journalism in the local media and the economy, as well as society as a whole. But it has also been a story of trial-and-error, of what in some instances by hindsight seem obvious collective fallacies. Retrospectively, we could say that business journalism in Finland appears to have been caught up in the international expansion of the Western business and management discourse, which emerged as a dominant discourse in Finland, too. Finnish business journalists developed several rudimentary variants of international business journalism in their own own country, at a time when representatives of many other fields were still maintaining close relations with the Soviet Union. Within this context, business journalism emerged as a collective container for Western market economy discourse that could not be spelled out in text, printed, published and distributed.

From the 1940s and up to 1991, close political and trade relations with the Soviet Union imposed certain constraints on business journalism, in that a lack of economic transparency was sometimes combined with self-censorship 'in the national interest'. While no genre or branch of journalism in Finland was ever explicitly censored, the pressure to conform was considerable. Consequently, the autonomy of business journalism in Finland was rather different from that in the other Nordic countries. The professionalization of business journalism in Finland was affected by certain unique features and transformations in the economic and political fields. The long presidency of Urho Kekkonen (1956-1981) was a singular feature, while the 1973 oil crisis and the decline of the Soviet Union were examples of global discontinuities. Both these phenomena were associated with the emergence of a specific (new) cadre of business journalists and of particular conventions which in the next generation were largely accepted as established practices and conventions.

This way of interpreting the historical evidence does not belittle the deliberate efforts of business journalists to develop their practice according to their new professional specialization. The very success of their collective strategy supports our conclusion that the strategy was not only about coping with contemporary challenges but also about the progressive development of new professional practices. Nonetheless, we find that the emerging professionals described above lent their identities and their legitimacy to specific political practices, such that the materialization of their discourse was contingent on changes in their field in its relations with other fields. Finnish business journalists did not lean towards the West as their model from choice or by serendipity. Nor did they acquiesce to the 'national cause' by censoring themselves. Rather, the project for professionalizing Finnish business journalism was, to a large extent, an evolutionary outcome of political struggles and the path dependencies to which they gave cause, whereby 'politics' is used here in the original meaning of the word as being related to the affairs of the (nation-) state.

We can conclude, in the spirit of Bourdieu, that an ever new generation of business journalism had its own peculiar relations with Finland's corporate and political elite, and that it created and nurtured its own particular kind of social or other field-specific capital. The absolute and the relative roles of this capital changed considerably over the years. The propensity of individual journalists to change or to develop new practices seems to have sprung out of their positions vis-à-vis the economic or political fields with which they were linked.

While our description and interpretation of the Finnish case undoubtedly has certain singular features, we believe that it can also serve as a more general indication of the importance of developments and long-term trends that are not immediately apparent. The evidence reported in this chapter suggests that the professionalization of business journalism was never a question of simple progress towards a universal code. Rather, it was a complex phenomenon both in itself and its relation to other contingent factors. Our findings complement those of similar developments in Norway, Denmark, and Sweden (Slaatta 2003, Kjær & Langer 2005, Grafström 2006), and the growing influence of the business press in contemporary society. This chapter represents one first part on which to build further historical and comparative analysis of the process of professionalization in the case of business journalism. Our findings also indicate novel directions for research: why does professionalization deserve a historical description of its own and a discussion about how it occurs in a society? As regards future research, it would be particularly interesting to examine in detail the role of politics in systems of education and in professional associations.

Bibliography

Abbott, A. (1988) *The System of Professions*. Chicago: University of Chicago Press.

Ainamo, A. (1997) Evolution of the Finnish System of Innovation: The Contribution of Nokia. In: Fynes, B. & S. Ennis (Eds.) *Competing from the Periphery: Core Issues in International Business*. Ireland: The Dryden Press.

Ainamo, A. & W. Cardwell (1998) After Privatisation: Economic Development, Social Transformation and Corporate Governance in the Baltic States. *Journal of Eastern European Management Studies*. Vol. 3 (2): 134-163. Special Issue on Mergers and Acquisitions.

Ainamo, A. & M. Pantzar (2000) Design for the Information Society: What Can We Learn from the Nokia Experience. *Design Journal* Vol. 3 (2): 15-26.

Ainamo, A., J. Tienari & E. Vaara (2006) Between West and East: A Social History of Business Journalism and Management in Cold War Finland. *Human Relations* Vol. 59 (5): 611-636.

Aldridge, M. & J. Evetts (2003) Rethinking the concept of professionalism: the case of journalism. *British Journal of Sociology* Vol. 54 (4): 547-564.

Benson, R. & E. Neveu (2005) *Bourdieu and the journalistic field*. Cambridge: Polity Press.

Boréus, K. (1994) *Högervåg: Nyliberalism och kampen om språket I svensk debatt 1969-1989*. Stockholm: Tidens Förlag.

Boudon, R. (1986) *L'idéologie ou l'origine des idées recues*. Paris: Fayard.

Bourdieu, P. (1988) *Homo academicus*. Stanford: Stanford University Press.

Bourdieu, P. (1993) *The Field of Cultural Production. Essays on Art and Literature*. Cambridge: Polity Press.
Bourdieu, P. (1998) *On television*. New York: The New Press.
Bourdieu, P. (2000) *Pascalian Mediations*. Cambridge: Polity Press.
Dacin, T. (1997) Isomorphism in Context: The Power and Prescription of Institutional Norms. *Academy of Management Journal* Vol. 40 (1): 46-81.
Doyle, G. (2006) Financial News Journalism: A Post-Enron Analysis of Approaches towards Economics and Financial News Production in the UK. *Journalism: Theory, Practice & Criticism* Vol. 7 (4): 433-452.
Drori, G. (2006) Governed by Governance. The New Prism for Organizational Change. *Globalization and Organizations: World Society and Organizational Change*. New York: Oxford University Press.
Duval, J. (2004) Critique de la raison journalistique. Les transformations de la presse économique en France, Paris: Seuil.
Grafström, M. (2006) *The Development of Swedish Business Journalism. Historical Roots of an Organizational Field*. Uppsala University: Doctoral Dissertation No. 121.
Halttunen, H. & A. Suvanto (1988) Rahoitusinnovaatiot ja Suomen rahamarkkinat. In Honkapohja, S. & A. Suvanto (Eds.) *Raha, inflaatio ja talouspolitiikka*. Helsinki: Valtion painatuskeskus.
Heikkilä, H. (2001) *Heikko ja vahva journalismi*. Tampere, Finland: Tampereen yliopisto.
Herkman, J. (2005) *Kaupallisen television ja iltapäivälehtien avoliitto: median markkinoituminen ja televisioituminen*. Tampere, Finland: Vastapaino.
Herman, E. & N. Chomsky (1988) *Manufacturing consent*. New York: Pantheon Books.
Jyrkiäinen, J. (1994) *Sanomalehdistön keskittyminen – joukkoviestinnän ja erityisesti sanomalehdistön keskittymisilmiö, sen kulku ja seuraukset jälkiteollisessa yhteiskunnassa 1980- luvun lopulla*. Acta Universitatis Tamperensis ser A vol. 409, Doctoral dissertation, University of Tampere.
Kjær, P. & R. Langer (2005) Infused with news value: Management, managerial knowledge and the institutionalization of business news. *Scandinavian Journal of Management* Vol. 21 (2): 209-233.
Klemola, P. (1981) *Helsingin Sanomat – sananvapauden monopoli*. Helsinki: Otava.
Kuusterä, A. (1990) Taloudellisesta vallasta Suomessa: Historiaa – käsitteitä – empiriaa. *TTT Katsaus* 4/1990: 31-40.
Mikkonen, M. (1998) *Rahavallan rakkikoirat: Tositarinoita talousjournalismista*. Porvoo: WSOY.
Nordfors, D., M. Ventresca, A. Hargadon, T. Uskali, A. Ainamo, S. Jonsson, S. Grodal, A. Weinstein, M. Kennedy, P. Svensson & F. Reid (2006): Innovation Journalism: Towards research on the interplay of journalism and innovation ecosystems. *Innovation Journalism* Vol. 3 (2): 1-18.

Ojala, J. & T. Uskali (Eds.) (2005) *Mediajättien aika: Uusia heikkoja signaaleja etsimässä.* Helsinki: Infor.

Parsons, W. (1989) *The power of the financial press: Journalism and economic opinion in Britain and America.* Aldershot: Edward Elgar.

Pulkkinen, M. (1997) *The Breakthrough of Nokia Mobile Phones.* Helsinki School of Economics and Business Administration, Acta Universitatis Oeconomicae Helsingiensis A-122.

Read, D. (1992) *The power of the news: The history of the Reuters.* Oxford: Oxford University Press.

Sahlin-Anderson, K. & L. Engwall (2002) *Carriers of Management Knowledge.* Palo Alto: Stanford University Press.

Slaatta, T. (2003) *Den norske medieorden: Posisjoner och privilegier.* Oslo: Gyldendal Norsk Forlag.

Stråth, B. (1998) *Mellan två fonder: LO och den svenska modellen.* Stockholm: Atlas.

Tainio, R. M. Huolman, M. Pulkkinen, J. Ali-Yrkkö & P. Ylä-Anttila (2003) Global Investors Meet Local Managers: Shareholder Value in the Finnish Context. In M-L. Djelic & S. Quack (Eds.) *Globalization and Institutions: Redefining the Rules of the Economic Game.* Cheltenham: Edward Elgar.

Tolvanen, O. (1992) Suomen tärkeimpien sanomalehtien suhtautuminen taloudelliseen yhteistyöhön Neuvostoliiton kanssa vuosina 1961-1971. Master's thesis, Political history, University of Helsinki.

Uskali, T. (2005) Talousjournalismin historia, rajat ja tulevaisuus. In Ojala, J. & T. Uskali (Eds.) *Mediajättien aika: Uusia heikkoja signaaleja etsimässä.* Helsinki: Infor.

Virtanen, M. (2001) *Fennomaanien perilliset: Poliittiset traditiot ja sukupolvien dynamiikka.* Helsinki: SKS.

Yamaguchi, T. & C. K. Harris (2004) The economic hegemonization of Bt cotton discourse in India. *Discourse & Society* Vol. 15 (4): 467-491.

CHAPTER 4

Expansion of the Nordic Business Press
Äripäev in Estonia as a Carrier of Western Discourses

ANNETTE RISBERG & ANTTI AINAMO

The media can act as carriers of a variety of societal discourses. Over the last twenty years or so Western business media have become increasingly important in bringing discourses relating to business and management into new domains (e.g. Yamaguchi & Harris 2004, Meyer 2002). Media are still disseminating business and management discourses within national borders but they also carry such discourses across national borders, across regions and across cultures (cf. Sahlin-Andersson & Engwall 2002). In this chapter we will tell the story of the Estonian business newspaper *Äripäev*, which is owned by the Swedish publishing house Bonnier and was launched by Bonnier's own business newspaper *Dagens Industri*. We will see how *Äripäev* acted as a carrier of market ideology and business discourse into Estonia, a country which at the time still was part of the command-based Soviet empire.

Since the late 1980s Western-based media companies, and other types of organizations too, have been introducing a business and management discourse from Western Europe and North America into the countries of Central and Eastern Europe. One reason for this may be, as Kostera suggests, that 'it is widely believed that the east should "learn" from the west' (1995: 337). In our specific case, *Äripäev* was based on the idea of a newspaper concept focused on reporting in particular on market actors, entrepreneurship, the stock exchange and other symbols of a market economy. This was, however, something of a challenge in that when *Äripäev* was established Estonia was still part of the Soviet Union, a socialist command economy, and there was hardly any market economy to write about, nor was there a market waiting for this type of news. So part of *Äripäev's* mission, as presented by its owner's managers, was to help to 'educate' the Estonians in the ideas and ways of a market economy and thus also helping to construct the ideologies and mentalities that were to provide the base for such an economy in their country. One way of fulfilling this educational mission was to present the Estonian readers with ideas about liberal market ideology and business discourses. A similar approach was adopted in other former socialist countries as well with a helping hand from Western 'idea producers' such as consultants, academics and, as in our case, Western-owned media outlets.

Journalists play an important part as the translators of business ideas while at the same time the media provide outlets for others who also produce these and similar ideas (Thrift 2001). In this chapter, we build on the notion of idea production and transfer of ideas from the journalists themselves to the media outlets in which they work. The case of *Äripäev*, as we try to show in this chapter, is revealing in that as a business newspaper it was first conceived and then quickly institutionalized as the holder of a key position in Estonia as a translator and distributor of capitalist and Western based management ideologies, norms and emerging rules of the game.

The media is often portrayed as the Fourth Estate, that is to say it not only reflects the society but also has an impact on it (e.g. Read 1992). In Estonia the media became an important part of the changes and transformations taking place. One aspect of the entry of Western media and the development of Western types of media in Estonia was the media's participation in what we call 'constructing the market' or the 'construction of the concept of a market'. Although the Soviet Socialist Republic of Estonia was something of a laboratory in the Soviet Union when it came to ideas about the market economy (Ainamo & Cardwell 1998), the 'market' (as meaning a free or liberal market economy ideology and the equivalent practice) hardly existed in Estonia as a key concept so long as the country was still part of the Soviet Union.

The traditional approach to the role of media in societies such as the Nordic countries (e.g. Heikkilä 2001) has been to investigate the state and the government, often in a critical way, to increase transparency, justice and fairness in society (cf. e.g. Ainamo, Tienari & Vaara 2006, Ainamo, Tienari & Vaara, this volume). We look at how *Äripäev* started as a Western alternative partly critically investigating the economy and society both before and after the transition into a democratic society and a market economy started.

Bonnier did not choose Estonia or, later, the other Baltic countries, out of serendipity. Estonia has long had historical links with the Nordic countries, especially Denmark, Finland and Sweden. Since the liberation from the Soviet Union, Swedish and Finnish firms have been the largest foreign direct investors in Estonia[1]. In some ways it almost seems as though Nordic companies were internalizing the Baltic states into the Nordic Region from an early stage (Ainamo & Cardwell 1998). For this reason we have chosen to describe the case of a Swedish daily business newspaper entering the Estonian newspaper market to illustrate the spread of the Nordic business press into an extended Nordic region, as well as noting early indications of an international expansion of a Nordic business and management discourse.

The present chapter will thus look at the way media expansion into new markets can act as a carrier of societal discourses. In particular we describe the expansion of a Western business and management discourse from the Nordic countries into Estonia, where a discourse of this kind was more or less non-existent. We start by describing the internationalization activities of Nordic newspaper companies in their neighbouring countries including the Baltic states and Eastern and Central Europe. Thereafter taking the case of *Dagens Industri*'s expansion into Estonia we show how media can act as the carrier of business discourses. The case will show that *Dagens Industri* aimed to introduce a free market ideology and a management discourse to Estonia, and that it intended, from the start, to take part in constructing Estonia as a market economy.

We believe that *Äripäev – Dagens Industri*'s Estonian sister newspaper, as its managers call it – is a particularly illuminating example of the business press as a carrier of business and management discourse. We suggest that it was not the news content or the newspaper itself that were internationalized by Bonnier, but the concept of the business newspaper (cf. Risberg & Melin 2005). The concept as depicted by *Dagens Industri*'s management is described later in the chapter. This specific concept can be seen as a carrier of ideas from the West and, together with the news, it can be a carrier of specific discourses.

---

[1] www.investinestonia.com. 2005-12-05.

The Internationalization of the Newspaper Industries in the Nordic Countries

Up to the late 1980s the daily press was rather a domestic affair in the Nordic countries, (Sundin 2003b). One reason for this may have been that the daily press was seen as a largely nationalistic endeavour (Ainamo, Tienari & Vaara 2006, Dacin 1997). Towards the end of the 1980s the ownership as well as the scope of Nordic newspapers gradually became more international. A few Nordic publishing houses expanded their businesses into other countries in the Nordic region during this period (Harrie 2003), including countries in the Baltic states, partly due to changes in the regulations of foreign media ownership in these countries. In the case of the former socialist countries it could be said that an open attitude to foreign ownership was also an ideological question.

The newspaper market in the Nordic countries has seen big changes in terms of the restructuring of ownership by way of mergers and acquisitions. As a result, the number of newspapers in the Nordic countries began to decline during the late 20th century. Another change was that some ownership became foreign – something that was quite new for the newspaper industry but not for the publishing industry as such (cf. Sundin 2003b).

In the present section we will take a further look at the foreign ownership and internationalization patterns of Nordic newspapers, focusing on the extended Nordic region (in which we include other countries round the Baltic Sea as well as parts of Eastern and Central Europe). Iceland is not included in our description since its newspapers have no foreign owners, nor have they expanded abroad (at the time when the data for this chapter was being collected). Below we briefly describe the market situation and internationalization pattern in each of the Nordic countries during the late 1990s and early 2000s.

The Danish newspaper market has been dominated by three newspapers – *Berlingske Tidende*, *Politiken* and *Jyllands-Posten* – all previously Danish-owned (Harrie 2003). A structural change occurred at the beginning of 2003, when the two organizations owning *Politiken* and *Jyllands-Posten* merged (the tabloid *Ekstra Bladet* was also included in the merger). All three newspapers still exist. In late 2000 the Norwegian company Orkla Media acquired *Berlingske Officin*, the publishing house of the daily *Berlingske Tidende*, the tabloid *B.T* and *Weekendavisen*. Orkla Media is not the first foreign owner on the Danish newspaper market, however. For example, Swedish Bonnier acquired shares in the business newspaper *Børsen* in 1970 in what seems to have been a rare exception in terms of foreign newspaper ownership in the Nordic countries at that time.

After a series of mergers, the Finnish media market has been dominated by two key actors: SanomaWSOY and Almamedia. Sanoma is the largest newspaper owner and Almamedia is the second largest in the industry. SanomaWSOY publishes a number of newspapers, among them the two largest *Helsingin Sanomat* and *Ilta-Sanomat,* as well as the business newspaper *Taloussanomat.* Until 2003 SanomaW-SOY owned 30% of the Norwegian A-pressen which was then sold to the Norwegian co-owners (Harrie 2003). In 2005, Sanoma bought, among other printed media, the two leading newspapers in English, *Moscow Times, the St. Petersburg Times,* and the leading business newspaper in Russian in Russia, *Vedomosti,* (Ainamo 2003, 2005). Almamedia publishes a range of newspapers of which the largest are *Aamulehti,* the tabloid *Ilalehti* and Finland's largest business newspaper *Kauppalehti,* with no signs of expansion internationally. The Swedish publishing house, Bonnier, owns 33% of Almamedia.

The Norwegian newspaper market has been dominated by three media companies: Schibsted, Orkla Media and A-pressen. Two Swedish publishers of regional newspapers, Nya Wermlands-Tidning and Herenco AB, have small share holdings in the regional papers *Bergens Tidende* and *Stavanger Aftenblad* (Harrie 2003). Schibsted's largest newspapers are the tabloid *Verdens Gang* (the largest newspaper in Norway) and *Aftenposten,* and it publishes a number of regional newspapers as well. Outside Norway it owns the two Swedish newspapers *Aftonbladet* and *Svenska Dagbladet* and, through its Estonian company Eesti Media, it also owns *Postimees,* a national daily newspaper, *SLÖhtuleht* and a number of local newspapers (Harrie 2003; www.schibsted.no 2006-02-02). Schibsted also publishes a free newspaper called 20minutes in several cities in Spain, Switzerland and France (Sundin 2003a, www.20minutes.fr 2005-12-14). A-pressen is a group consisting of labour newspapers publishing a large number of regional – often second – newspapers (Harrie 2003; www.apressen.no 2006-02-02). Internationally A-pressen has minority holdings in some Russian newspapers, *Nizhegordskij Robochij* (45.5%), *Prizyv* (47.5%), and owns 25.05% of the ZAO Publishing House Komsomolskaya Pravda[2] which publishes, among other newspapers, *Komsomolskaya Pravda*[3]. Orkla Media, like A-pressen, publishes local and regional newspapers. Internationally, Orkla Media is the owner of the Danish

[2] E-mail from Reidar Karlsen, A-pressen 2006-02-03.
[3] E-mail from Reidar Karlsen, A-pressen 2006-02-03.

Berlingske Officin as well as newspapers in Sweden, Poland, Lithuania and Ukraine (www.orkla-media.no 2006-02-02[4]). In Poland it owns shares in thirteen newspapers, of which the largest is *Rzeczpospolita* (51%). In Lithuania it owns the largest regional newspaper *Kauno diena* (100%), and in Ukraine the regional newspaper *Vysokyj Zamok I Lviv* (50%) (www.orkla-media.no 2006-02-02). In Sweden Orkla Media owns the small regional newspaper *Norrländska Socialdemokraten* (49%) (Harrie 2003). In the fall of 2005 it tried to acquire the Swedish newspaper company Centertidningar, but failed.

The Swedish newspaper market started to consolidate in the early 1990s, and today a small number of actors dominate the industry (Sundin 2005). Since the early 1990s when it started to acquire regional newspapers (Sundin 2005), Bonnier has been the largest owner of newspapers in Sweden, with eight newspapers located in different regions, among those the largest daily *Dagens Nyheter* and the tabloid *Expressen*. The second largest actor is the Norway based company Schibsted. The third largest actor is the Stenbeck group with its free daily tabloid, *Metro*. In Gothenburg *Göteborgs-Posten*, a large daily, is owned by the Hjörne family. There are mainly three newspaper companies that are engaged in foreign ownership. The Bonnier group owns newspaper companies in Denmark (*Børsen*), Finland (shares in *Almamedia*), the Baltic states and Eastern and Central Europe. Through its business newspaper *Dagens Industri* it owns business dailies in Lithuania, Poland, Estonia, Latvia, Russia, Austria, and Slovenia. Bonnier also has shares in *Diena*, a daily newspaper in Latvia and *Super Express*, a daily in Poland (Sundin 2003a). Earlier it had shares in one Estonian daily and one tabloid, *Eesti Päevaleht* and *SLÖthuleth*, owned today by Schibsted. The Stenbeck sphere was very successful in expanding its free newspaper *Metro*, which was established in 2005 in 18 countries and 81 cities. Finally, the Hamrin/Herenco group, that publishes regional and local papers in Sweden, has a small share in the Norwegian *Stavanger Aftenblad*.

The Nordic newspapers' foreign ownership in the Nordic region[5] is summarized in Table 4.1. The table, and the description above, indicates that cross-border ownership in the Nordic context is not very common and that the newspaper industry is still fairly domestic. There are a few actors, mainly Norwegian and Swedish newspaper-owners that have expanded their market abroad. Few newspaper-owners have

---

[4] In September 2006 Orkla sold Berlingske Officin to the Mecom Group plc.
[5] This information is based on Sundin (2003) and on company material such as home pages in 2005 and 2006 and annual reports in 2004.

expanded outside the Nordic countries, but in those cases where it has happened, they seem to expand east, to the former Eastern Bloc. Estonia and Russia are the two dominating host countries.

In Table 4.1 an interesting dimension can be discerned in the processes of development and ownership of the Nordic business press in its expansion southwards and eastwards. By 2006 the Norwegian newspaper companies A-Pressen, Orkla, and Schibsted had expanded into Denmark, Sweden, Estonia and Russia, Finnish SanomaWSOY into Russia and Swedish Bonnier and Stenbeck/Metro into Denmark, Finland, Estonia, Latvia, Lithuania, Poland, and Russia. An example of expansion south and east by Nordic newspapers is thus Bonnier's *Dagens Industri*. *Dagens Industri* has followed the southward and eastward expansion pattern by starting business newspapers in the Baltic states, Russia and Poland (Risberg & Melin 2005). After the dissolution of the Eastern Bloc all these societies have evolved towards more Western European models.

Country of Origin, Owner	Host Country	Shares %	Newspaper	Type of Newspaper
Norway				
A-pressen	Russia	45.5	Nizhegordskij Robochij	Local daily
		47.5	Prizyv	Local daily
		25.05	Komsomolskaya Pravda	National daily
Orkla	Denmark (Det Berlingske Offi-cin)(until 2006)	100	*Berlingske Tidende* B.T	National daily Tabloid
Schibsted	Sweden	49.999	Aftonbladet	National tabloid
		99	Svenska Dagbladet	National daily
	Estonia	92,5	Postimees	National daily
	(Eesti Meedia)		*SL Öhtuleht*	National tabloid
			A number of local news-papers	
Finland				
SanomaWSOY	Russia	N.i.	The Moscow Times	Daily
	(Independent Media)		St Petersburg Times	Daily
			Vedomosti	Business news-paper
Sweden				
Bonnier	Finland	33	Aamulehti	Regional daily
	(Alma Media)		Kainuun Sanomat	Regional daily
			Kauppalehti	Business daily
			Lapin Kansa	Regional daily
			Pohjolan Sanomat	Regional daily
			Satakunnan Kansa	Regional daily
			Iltalehti	National daily
			Various newspapers	15 locals
	Denmark	100	Dagbladet Børsen	Business daily
	Russia	100	Delevoj Petersburg	Business daily
	Latvia	100	Dienas Bizness	Business daily
	Poland	100	Puls Bizneu	Business daily
		68	Super Express	National daily
	Lithuania	73	Verslo Zinios	Business daily
		20	Diena	National daily
	Estonia	100	Äripäev	Business daily
Hamrin/Herenco	Norway	9,8	Stavanger Aftenblad	Regional daily
Stenbeck/Metro	Finland	100	Metro Helsinki	Free newspaper
	Denmark	70	MetroXpress Copenha-gen, Århus	Free newspaper
	Poland	100	Metropol	Free Newspaper

Table 4.1: Nordic Newspaper Ownership in the Nordic and Baltic Countries, Russia and Poland
Sources: Sundin (2003a), www.metropol.pl 2005-12-08,
www.medieregisteret.no 2006-02-02, www.apressen.no 2006-02-07,
www.sanomawsoy.fi 2006-02-07, www.bonnier.se 2006-03-02,
Metropol International S.A Annual Report 2004.

The Case of *Dagens Industri's* Eastward Expansion

A pronounced example of the expansion southward and eastward and into emerging markets is Bonnier's *Dagens Industri*. The fact that *Dagens Industri* was the first among the Nordic newspaper companies to expand into the Baltic states, Russia and Poland (Risberg & Melin 2005) is one reason why we chose to focus on the *Äripäev* case in this chapter. Another reason is that a specialized business newspaper can be regarded as a more obvious carrier of a business and management discourse than, for example, the business section of a broadsheet newspaper. A third reason for focusing on *Dagens Industri* is that its Äripäev project represents a specific and possibly extreme and revelatory type of international expansion, compared to the activities of most other Nordic newspaper companies: instead of acquiring foreign newspapers, *Dagens Industri's* unique strategy was to start a new newspaper. This mode of entry gave *Dagens Industri* control over the concept and over the production of content. Once the owners and managers of *Dagens Industri* had control over the concept and the principles of running a newspaper, they were also able to control the transfer of discourses migrating from the west to Estonia.

Method

Our analysis of the *Dagens Industri* and *Äripäev* case builds on a 12-year process of systematic data collection, analysis and interpretation. The first of the present authors made a study on the international expansion of *Dagens Industri* and its declared intentions to assume a role in the societal changes of the former Soviet state. Seven managers at *Dagens Industri* and Bonnier were interviewed in the fall of 1999 and the spring of 2000. In March 2000 a field study was carried out at *Äripäev*, Tallinn. Eleven people representing administrative and editorial management and staff were interviewed. The first editor-in-chief of *Äripäev*, who no longer works for the newspaper, was also interviewed. During the week spent at *Äripäev* the researcher was given a desk in the same room as the net-based newspaper and spent the whole working day there, making observations in between interviews. She also attended an editorial meeting as an observer. Additional material, including internal company material, published material and newspaper articles on the subject, has been collected up to 2006.

We also use data collected on-site in the Baltic states by the second author, between 1994 and 1997, as background information for the current case. The data was geared mainly to inherent tensions between investors and management in Estonia, Latvia and Lithuania as well as tensions between 'national pride' and the very idea of 'global investors'.

The recombination and analysis of these two streams of data collection produced something in the nature of a 'thick description' that opened up broader horizons of discourse and discourse interpretation (cf. Geertz 1973) in relation to *Äripäev*. We describe the case of *Dagens Industri* with its launching of the business newspaper *Äripäev* in Estonia and the pivotal role that this played in the social construction and institutionalization of the market economy concept in Estonia.

Accordingly our idea is to describe not only the launching of a business newspaper in Estonia by *Dagens Industri* but also the function and significance of this particular newspaper in the Estonian economy and in Estonian society. Our analysis does not seek to prove the extent to which *Äripäev* has – or even whether it has – influenced this construction. Instead, we start from the explicit claim put forward by *Äripäev* and *Dagens Industri's* representatives in the interviews, and from the company material we have seen, about the way they believe(d) the company had impacted changes in Estonian society and the Estonian market. Representatives of *Dagens Industri* and *Äripäev* claimed that these newspapers were carriers of a certain ideology in Estonian society, a claim that our other sources of data did not contradict. Enquiry into the validity of such a claim should be interesting to any discussion of the media's role more generally as a carrier of discourses in society.

Dagens Industri: a Business Newspaper and a Concept[6]

Dagens Industri is a Swedish business newspaper that was launched in 1974 by Bertil Torekull (editor-in-chief 1976-1980). The newspaper was based on the idea of a business newspaper not just for businessmen but for all decision makers within and connected with industry. During its early years *Dagens Industri* struggled to achieve acceptable circulation figures (Risberg & Melin 2005). By 1979 the newspaper reported a profit for the first time, and has continued to do so ever since (this was an undisputed fact at least up to 2006). Business newspapers in other Nordic countries reported a similar development (see Chapter 2 in the present volume).

Dagens Industri, is often described, by people in the industry as well as in academia, as a successful newspaper both in terms of circu-

---

[6] The description of the concept is based on interviews held with *Dagens Industri* employees in 1999 and 2000, if no other reference is given.

lation and profit (cf. Hadenius & Weibull 1999, Gustafsson 1996). Its success can be explained in terms of three advantages, ownership, timing and target-group selection (Bringert & Torekull 1995), as well as in terms of the newspaper concept. *Dagens Industri*'s concept turned out to be of special importance in the internationalization of the newspaper as it was the concept rather than the news that was brought to the new markets. Therefore we will spend some time on describing this concept.

From the start as a business newspaper, the *Dagens Industri* concept has remained more or less the same but for a few changes over the years. The *Dagens Industri* concept can be said to rest on three pillars. 1) The newspaper should be easy to understand. 2) It should take little time to read. 3) It should be a tool for managers. This three-pronged concept implies that all readers targeted by *Dagens Industri* are decision-makers, and not just on top management level but, at all levels in private and public organizations. *Dagens Industri* describes it as a non-élite target group. To reach this target group the journalists in *Dagens Industri* seek to present and explain complex economic facts in a way that is easy for all its readers to comprehend. The newspaper's layout consists of short, easy, and simple headlines, with plenty of diagrams and visuals making the news articles quick and easy to read. By reading *Dagens Industri* the reader should be able to improve his or her productivity, as well as career and career development. The newspaper focuses mainly on company activities rather than on macro-economic news. This element in the concept supports the role of *Dagens Industri* and its Estonian sister paper *Äripäev* as carriers of a management discourse. We return on this point later when we tell the story of *Äripäev*. First, however, we will briefly describe the internationalization of *Dagens Industri's* concept.

The Internationalization of *Dagens Industri* Concept[7]

The internationalization of *Dagens Industri* began in 1989, with the launching of the business newspaper *Äripäev* in Estonia. In subsequent steps towards internationalization the concept described above was exported to the Baltic states, and later to other parts of central and Eastern Europe. The management of Bonnier and *Dagens Industri* decided to export a concept that should appear to be 'universal' rather than national in origin. It was intended that every subsequent 'sister newspa-

[7] The information in these sections is based on interviews with the Bonnier and *Dagens Industri* managements and on company information from company pamphlets and the company's website.

per' of *Dagens Industri* would appear as an original artefact appertaining to the particular target country and able to produce a news content in any 'Western type context', beginning with Estonia.

When newspaper companies enter new markets they do so typically by acquiring existing newspapers. Above we noted examples of many Nordic media companies that grew by acquiring newspapers abroad. This has not been *Dagens Industri's* chosen strategy, however. Instead management decided to launch a series of new business newspapers based on its own concept. One reason for choosing this strategy was that the Bonnier and *Dagens Industri* management wanted to monitor the start-up processes of the sister papers closely in order to keep closer control over the implementation of the newspaper concept and over the knowledge of their journalists and managers (see Risberg & Melin 2005). Acquiring existing newspapers would not allow for such control, as Bonnier would be buying into an existing and possibly quite powerful heritage. Building a newspaper from scratch involves fewer compromises with the intended concept. Thus, the internationalization of *Dagens Industri* rather resembled a system of franchising where control of interior and exterior design and atmosphere is vitally important (cf. Ritzer 1993).

The internationalization of the concept has been quite extensive, and by 2006 *Dagens Industri* had, what its management calls 'sister newspapers' in seven countries: Estonia, Lithuania, Latvia, Russia, Austria, Poland and Slovenia. There were also two earlier sister newspapers in Hungary and Scotland, but these were closed down fairly soon after start-up, for different reasons.

The following section is based on interviews with managers and employees at *Dagens Industri* and *Äripäev*. We will describe from their point of view, the aims and efforts that went into building up the Estonian business newspaper *Äripäev*. We will also describe how *Dagens Industri* with its concept and type of ownership, and *Äripäev* with its physical newspaper and its news services may have influenced the process of constructing a free market economy in Estonian.

Dagens Industri as a Carrier of Western Discourses

In the middle of the 'singing revolution'[8], *Dagens Industri* launched a business newspaper in Estonia. It all grew from the vision of the *Dagens Industri's* editor-in-chief, Hasse Olsson, for expanding the concept of the paper eastwards. As a newspaper *Dagens Industri* differed from the Soviet model. While Soviet newspapers – at about six pages – were thin, given over long articles, always in black and white, and without photographs, and the price was low, *Dagens Industri* in its turn was thicker, ran short concise articles and used colour, photos and other images and the paper was also quite expensive.

Dagens Industri aims to be best-seller in any market it enters[9], and it succeeded in this when it established *Äripäev*. In many of its expansion ventures it has achieved this goal by being one of the first foreign actors on the scene. At that time the Baltic states differed from Western markets in many respects. Not only was there no competition from existing (actually non-existing) business newspapers, but the readers were also unfamiliar with the product as well as with the news genre itself. Although Estonia was a testing-ground for pan-Soviet experiments in liberalizing trade, the country was still part of the Soviet Union when the business newspaper *Äripäev* was established in 1989. Private enterprise had only just been made legal and most people were unfamiliar with the very idea of market economy (cf. Ainamo & Cardwell 1998). *Dagens Industri* saw this as a challenge as well as an opportunity. It was a challenge to the *Dagens Industri* management in that they were deciding to sell a newspaper concept with which the potential readers were completely unfamiliar. In the Baltic states, *Dagens Industri* was not only entering a virgin market for their product; they were also getting a chance to take part in constructing these markets by acting as a carrier of Western-based ideas, ideologies and discourses. They met the challenge in a variety of ways, as will be described below.

Launching *Äripäev*

The story of *Äripäev* began when Hasse Olsson from *Dagens Industri* visited Estonia to sound out the possibility of starting a business newspaper there. As a result of what he learned the management of *Dagens Industri* and Bonnier decide to produce a trial edition. Hallar Lind, an

---

[8] The movement that led to Estonia's liberation from the Soviet Union is known as 'the singing revolution' after the great nationalist song festivals that were arranged in the course of the revolution.
[9] "Tvåan är hans olyckstal", Dagens Nyheter 2000-09-30. Bo E. Åkermark.

Estonian journalist who later became the first editor-in-chief of *Äripäev,* was invited to Stockholm for the occasion. During his visit Lind became acquainted with the *Dagens Industri* concept: he learnt about editorial and technical matters, about how to sell advertisements and other things connected with publishing a Western type of newspaper. On their part, the managers from Bonnier and *Dagens Industri* learnt about market conditions in Estonia. Before Lind left Stockholm it had been decided that the newspaper was to be launched within a month, in October 1989. For technical reasons of production, the first issue was printed in Stockholm.

If a non-Soviet citizen wanted to start a business in Estonia, a local partner had to be found. This problem was solved by way of a partnership with Mainor, a Tallinn-based company and the first editorial office was located on its premises. Four people were recruited to join Lind in producing the trial edition. During this first month this team, besides writing the articles also designed the layout, tried to find a solution to the distribution and planned for possible future editions if the launching was successful. As the layout of the newspaper is an important part of the *Dagens Industri* concept the local staff got help from Stockholm.

Äripäev was launched on a Monday, 9 October, 1989. On 8 October Lind was interviewed on a popular Estonian TV show. He told the viewers something new and exciting would be happening the next day. He described the newspaper itself and described how people could subscribe to it.[10] The first issue was a success and sold 30,000 copies. It was decided that *Dagens Industri* would go on with the project, and by December that year the circulation had risen to 40,000. At the beginning of December *Äripäev* signed an agreement with newsstand distributors to sell the business newspaper. By January 1990 it had over 40,000 subscribers and its circulation reached 55,000. Despite a population much smaller than that of Sweden, *Äripäev's* circulation matched that of the Swedish *Dagens Industri*. For the rest of 1989 the paper came out monthly, from January to April 1990 it appeared twice a month, and from May 1990 it appeared as a weekly newspaper. In 1992 *Äripäev* began to come out three times a week, and in 1996 it became a daily (five times a week). The large circulation and the popularity of the business newspaper suggest that it may have had a significant impact on its readers at that time. It was through *Äripäev* that

---

[10] The Soviet subscription system was quite different from the one prevailing in the west. Subscriptions were registered at the post office once a year, around the New Year.

many readers first became aware of Western newspaper style, Western journalism and Western business and management discourses.

Äripäev's Perceived Role in the Changes in Estonian Society

Some might claim that the news-media merely reflect the society on which they are reporting. Others might argue that the news-media cannot avoid influencing society by what they report and how they do so. Yet others would claim that the role of the media is to influence those in power (politicians or business leaders). In this section we will describe how people working at *Äripäev* and *Dagens Industri* perceive their newspapers' influence on the economic and political changes in Estonia after 1989. According to our informants, this influence has taken place in different ways, which will be discussed in the following sections.

Dagens Industri's Objectives in Launching Äripäev

If managers in any field are asked why they enter a new market the answer usually includes objectives such as reaching new markets, economies of scale in production, reaching new customers, or other business-oriented goals. Although one of the objectives that Bonnier and *Dagens Industri* had in mind was obviously to reach a new market and to make more money, their managers mentioned other seemingly less business-oriented objectives as the main goal of the expansions concerned. Hasse Olsson, the initiator and driving-force behind the expansions to the east, emphasized a more educational mission as underlying the decision.

> *I see the start-ups of the newspapers in the Baltic not so much as a matter of making money as one of transferring knowledge. We wanted to create copies of Dagens Industri. It was also about personal engagement on my part. I would call it a mission and I see the establishing of the newspapers in the Baltic as striking a blow for* **the freedom of the press**. *The mission consists of a belief in the freedom of the press. In the Baltic countries, where Dagens Industri has established newspapers, it has mostly been about* **teaching the readers about the market economy**, *that is, we have a pedagogical purpose.* Hasse Olsson, interview September 1999 [our emphasis].

His expressed objective was thus to introduce certain ideas, beliefs and knowledge from the west into Estonia. It is possible to discern three elements of educating in this statement of Olsson. 1) One concerns producing a copy of *Dagens Industri*. This implies an intention to transfer the concept to the local staff. In order to do this it was necessary to teach the local staff how to produce a Western type of newspaper and to introduce them to Western journalism, and probably also to teach them something about Western management. It was perhaps a question of *journalistic and press knowledge*. 2) Another element concerned the transfer of an ideology about *the freedom of the press*, which could probably be achieved simply by publishing *Äripäev* and making a newspaper different from the old Soviet newspapers. This was not anything that came up in other interviews so we will not address this issue in the present chapter. 3) A third element was a desire to *teach the Estonians about market economy*, a last mission that was performed in two steps. In order to be able to educate their readers the journalists themselves had to learn about market economy, Western ways of doing business and Western management. After this they would be able to pass on this knowledge to their readers through the articles they would write. In effecting this transfer of knowledge the *Dagens Industri* organization and management acted as carriers of journalistic knowledge, of opinions about the freedom of the press and of the ideology about free market economy.

In the following pages we will describe the way in which *Dagens Industri* trained its local staff in the Western type of journalism, how the journalists learnt about market economy and about Western type of business and management, as well as the way in which *Äripäev* in turn acted as a carrier of these discourses vis-à-vis the readers.

Training the Local Journalists

It was important to *Dagens Industri* to be able to form and influence the local staff. In preparation for the first issue of *Äripäev* the local journalists were taught about the concept itself, about how to achieve the desired layout, and how to write short concise articles. This local journalist training was important to further recruitment. Olsson tells how the *Dagens Industri* management preferred to hire young people, and that they often sought people with no journalistic training, who – they felt – were unaffected by the soviet style of journalism (Olsson interview September 1999). These people often held a university degree in some other fields such as engineering, economics, arts or teaching. This strategy, and a system of in-house training, meant that *Dagens*

Industri and *Äripäev* could have an influence on the journalists' way of working and on their view of business and the economy. In the early days people were sent to Stockholm to learn from the journalists at *Dagens Industri,* and staff was sent from Stockholm to train people locally in Tallinn at *Äripäev.*

To be able to educate the Estonians in the market economy the local journalists had to learn about this themselves. They sent for books from Sweden, they read foreign business magazines and they got help from professors at Tallinn University of Technology (Lind interview March 2000). This tradition of training the staff at the place of work has been continued at *Äripäev* (at least until the time of the interviews in 2000). In 2000 *Äripäev* spent around 1.5 percent of its turnover on training and education of its staff. Several of the middle managers have worked for an MBA in their own time. *Äripäev* is proud of its skilled workers, and its local management has declared that 'it is necessary to spend so much on training, because *Äripäev's* only assets are its people'.

The idea of transferring the *Dagens Industri* concept to *Äripäev* and its staff seems to have been successful. The *Dagens Industri* concept is reflected in *Äripäev*'s business idea (see Box 4.1.) and most of the newspaper's journalists and staff in general seem to have adopted the concept. The notion of *Äripäev* as a tool for entrepreneurs was mentioned in most of the interviews and the idea of being useful to the readers appears to have permeated the organization. All the products developed by the company[11] have been intended as tools for decision-makers. They all aim to provide the necessary information and knowledge for the individual decision-makers in their jobs. These tally with the pedagogical purpose envisaged by Olsson and Bonnier when launching *Äripäev*, which has thus trained and educated entrepreneurs and managers in all that is necessary for running a business, and has defined what this actually means. The idea of being a tool – rather than just providing news – and of training and educating the readers, suggests an ambition on the part of *Dagens Industri* and *Äripäev* to assume an active role in influencing society and business life.

Äripäev continues to act as a carrier of discourses of the free market economy and Western business and management ideas. The Bonnier publishing house and the Bonnier family that owns it are well known

---

[11] Besides the business newspaper *Äripäev*, the company *Äripäev* publishes a weekly business newspaper in Russian and a business magazine. It also produces handbooks on various management topics and organizes management seminars. See *Äripäev*'s homepage www.aripaev.ee for more information.

in Sweden for their liberal ideology. As a business newspaper *Dagens Industri* has a clear market-driven business ideology. The market economy ideology is present at *Äripäev* today, just as it is described in *Äripäev's* official documents: 'The objective is to promote a free market economy, protect the interests of small businesses and assist in the development of a more prosperous, open and ethical society' (see Box 4.2.). *Äripäev's* aim as a newspaper is thus not only to reflect what is happening in the business community but also to influence the developments concerned in a certain direction. We now turn to the question of the possible impact of *Äripäev* on the contemporary situation of society and especially on the changes occurring in Estonia during the 1990s.

Impact on the Readers and Contemporary Society

According to the people working for the newspaper *Äripäev* has had, and still has, an impact on the Estonian society. One group that may have been influenced by the news discourse in *Äripäev* consists of its readers. By reading *Äripäev* people learnt about Western ways of doing business, about Western management and the market economy. In the newspaper's early years the idea of influencing the readers was obvious from the very style of the articles. Lind explains:

> *In 1989 the Swedes intended that from the first issues we should be another Dagens Industri. That was impossible at the time. People – the readers – were not ready to understand things. At that time, for example, we did not have a stock market as we do now. What was normal knowledge in the west was unknown here. It was therefore necessary to explain, and for the first few years it [the newspaper] was like a schoolbook. If you look at the newspapers from that time you will find terribly long full page stories, and two page stories about very simple things presented in a way that was easy to understand. It could perhaps explain what a joint venture is. So we used to write two pages to make a story, because there were no books about such things in Estonian at that time.*
> Hallar Lind, interview, March 2000.

In the early years the journalists thus wrote long articles on different aspects of the market economy and Western business. There were also special newspaper supplements about business, economics and the market economy. Once a month the newspaper included something called research pages describing the basics of market economy. Lind continues:

> *So, for the first two years it was our* **mission to educate the Estonian people about business and the market economy**. *It took a couple of years before companies were established that could provide special training for people, companies where people could get training and attend short courses to learn about business in different industries. By then there was no need to publish "educational" articles or to try to be like a schoolbook.*
> Hallar Lind, interview, March 2000 [our emphasis].

Äripäev aimed to influence its readers by writing about the market economy and did so explicitly during the first few years. By teaching the journalists about the market economy and training them to write about it, *Äripäev* acted as a carrier of Western-based business management discourses. The purpose of this educational input was to prepare the readers for the product to come, that is, the business newspaper *Äripäev*, but it was also to educate Estonians in general.

Bonnier and *Dagens Industri*, on their part, claim that *Äripäev* was involved in the changing and shaping of Estonian society after the liberation. In conversation, some of the *Äripäev* staff agree with this up to a point. The very size of *Äripäev's* circulation in the yearly years, namely 55,000, suggests that it may well have had an impact on the way Estonian society developed. *Äripäev* was popular and was read by a great many people, including politicians, who were taking part in shaping the new state. It was mentioned in one of the interviews that *Äripäev's* critical articles and critical editorials have made an impact on politicians. Since its launch *Äripäev* has been promoting a free market economy, and Estonia is today one of the most deregulated markets in Europe. What part *Äripäev* may have played in these deregulations we cannot tell, but representatives of the newspaper itself claim that they have been able to influence the politicians' decisions. A similar claim is made in *Äripäev's* business idea: 'Thanks to sharp criticism in editorials in Äripäev, officials and politicians have changed several regulations or laws that were harmful to entrepreneurs' (see Box 4.1).

The impact on society could be exercised in other ways too. One of the *Äripäev* managers talked about the down-side of the management training discussed above. He claimed that other media companies benefit from the money that *Äripäev* spends on its own position by recruiting the newspaper's skilled staff. 'We are producing knowledge-able and well-educated people. Sometimes other companies' headhunting is a problem for us', as one of the managers put it. The *Dagens Industri* kind of journalism, as practised at *Äripäev*, thus appears to have made an impact on the practices of other Estonian newspapers that recruit from *Äripäev*. Similar points came up in the interview with Lind. He described how *Äripäev* has become a breeding-ground for new managers in Estonia (cf. Kokk 2006). According to him, *Äripäev* trains managers in Western management practices and these managers are then often recruited by other Estonian companies. Among them, Lind says, the press secretaries of two ministers used to work for *Äripäev* and were trained by them. Lind is not alone in this view of *Äripäev*. The commercial director at *Äripäev* itself mentioned that several of their managers had moved to prestigious positions at other Estonian newspapers in the late 1990s.

Another factor mentioned to explain the impact that *Äripäev* had made was, what its employees call the 'professionalism' of the paper. *Äripäev* is an independent newspaper, according to its employees, that does not run to do its owners' bidding. The journalists are free to write on any subject they want to and are often critical about various people or groups in the society. As one of the editors put it, 'No other newspaper focuses on economic issues and our sources are very reliable. We have ample resources and have often acted as trainers or teachers of Estonian entrepreneurs.' Thus, to judge from statements like these, *Äripäev* has influenced business life and society in Estonia, and still does so.

On several counts, then, the *Dagens Industri* concept and various Western journalist and management discourses have successfully been transferred to *Äripäev*. Two aspects of the concept are prominent in the present newspaper organization, as it was presented on its homepage (see Box 4.1 and Box 4.2). First, decision-makers and entrepreneurs emerge clearly as the target group. Second, the nature of the newspaper as a management tool is also emphasized: '*Äripäev* offers heads of companies and entrepreneurs information they require for their work' [sic] (Box 4.1). Part of its concept is that the newspaper should not take long to read and its articles should not be too complicated. This point is not mentioned in the business idea but it is included in a description of the newspaper intended for its advertisers with a reference to the 'brief and clearly written stories' (Box 4.2) offered by the paper. The ideological thrust promoting free market economy and private companies is also reflected in the business idea: '*Äripäev* does all in its power to protect the interests of its main reader – the head of a small company. Thanks to sharp criticism in editorials in *Äripäev*, officials and politicians have changed several regulations or laws that were harmful to entrepreneurs' [sic] (Box 4.1). Later in the same statement *Äripäev* also asserts its ability to take part in the restructuring of Estonian society. Thanks to its journalism, it is written, laws and regulations have been changed in such a way as to favour private enterprise.

Äripäev 's Business Idea

Äripäev offers heads of companies and entrepreneurs information they require for their work, and also serves as a channel for advertising between entrepreneurs.

In its other products *Äripäeva* Kirjastus has also focused on the production and sale of business and economic information. Private individuals who consume business information are also included in our target group.

A successful business advertising channel can be a media product only when its readership includes a sufficient number of decision-makers - people who are authorised to make decisions not only about the use of their personal money, but also about a company's money.

The dominant position of *Äripäev* among decision-makers is confirmed by the Decision-makers' Media Survey carried out by BMF Gallup Media in autumn 2002, in which it transpires that 65% of Estonian decision-makers read *Äripäev* .

Äripäev supplies its readers with both interesting and fresh news and also thorough and comparable information about the prices and quality of goods and services.

Äripäev does all in its power to protect the interests of its main reader - the head of a small company. Thanks to sharp criticism in editorials in *Äripäev*, officials and politicians have changed several regulations or laws that were harmful to entrepreneurs.

As a result of the work of *Äripäev* journalists, readers have obtained information that has helped many to save their company money or has opened up new, excellent opportunities to earn money.

Box 4.1: Äripäev's Business Idea
Source: www.aripaev.ee 2005-12-15

While *Äripäev* is a politically independent newspaper, it has quite a clear political agenda. In its business idea (see Box 4.1) it talks about protecting the interests of those running small companies, an aim that has guided its operations since 1989. On its homepage *Äripäev* describes that its 'newspapers are independent and edited in a liberal spirit'. Its mission closely resembles the objective as given by Olsson in the above quotation, namely to teach the Estonians about the market economy. In 2005 and early 2006, for example, *Äripäev* emerged prominently in its self-proclaimed role as watchdog of the market economy in Estonia, when it drew attention to the way in which a recently listed local Estonian corporation had produced what looked like insufficiently transparent accounts and inadequate systems of corporate governance (see e.g. *Äripäev*, February 16, 2006).

Dagens Industri arrived in Estonia as a carrier of market, business and management discourses. *Äripäev* has continued along this path and today is promoting a free market economy in order to protect the interest of their readers. *Äripäev* is also continuing the liberal Bonnier tradition (see for example www.bonnier.se), when it declares its support for 'a liberal organisation of life, minimal state interference in the economy and citizens' private life' [sic] (See Box 4.1).

Äripäev, which is printed on weekdays, is Estonia's leading economics newspaper. The paper's readers are heads of companies and entrepreneurs. *Äripäev* offers them information they require in their work and also serves as an advertising channel between entrepreneurs. *Äripäev* does not compete with the daily papers in the area of general news, but does provide better Estonian business news.

Format and brief and clearly written stories make it possible to read the paper quickly before the workday begins. *Äripäev* supports a liberal organisation of life, minimal state interference in the economy and citizens' private life.

The objective is to promote a free market economy, protect the interests of small businesses and assist in the development of a more prosperous, open and ethical society.

Box 4.2: A Description of Äripäev for Potential Advertisers
Source: www.aripaev.ee 2005-12-15

Äripäev has thus adopted the *Dagens Industri* concept as well as the ideology of its owner. This concept and *Äripäev*'s business idea together still seek to influence their readers and the society in which they live. Starting from this concept and its liberal ideology *Äripäev* – as a newspaper – acts towards its readers as a carrier of certain discourses. Assuming that its main target group consists of managers and entrepreneurs and that these groups adopt the *Äripäev* discourse, then the ideology would in turn influence the companies that these people lead. If, again, we see *Äripäev* as providing its readers with a tool, then the ideas and ideologies projected in the news discourse will be implemented in the companies by the decision makers. If *Äripäev*'s readers are many or powerful, they may in turn make an impact on the way in which the Estonian market economy is constructed. Although we may not be able to say anything explicit about the impact of *Äripäev* on Estonian society on a basis of our case analysis, it is worth noting that Estonia is one of the former Eastern Bloc countries that, has changed the most over the last 15 years, from being an example of a communist political regime to its present state as an extreme market economy.

Discussion

Estonia is but one example of a former Eastern Bloc country that has experienced tremendous changes over the last fifteen years. Since its liberation in 1991 Estonia has abandoned the socialist ideology and the concept of the command economy and has moved towards capitalism and the free market economy. This transition was driven by the Estonian government. 'Whatever ideas there were by that time about the future of the new state [Estonia], they can be summarised in a few words: First, an abandonment of the previous economic and political systems, and a wish to keep Russia at a distance. These two elements represent the *negative* side of the revolutionary discourse. On the *positive* side, there were nothing else than vague ideas of "Western" capitalism and liberal democracy, and an idealised picture of the pre-WWII society. Out of this virgin soil were the sprouts of the new social order to spring up' (Lagerspetz 2000:12, emphasis as in the original).

These ideas of Western capitalism did not reach Estonia singly. Czarniawska and Joerges (1996) observed that organizational changes are often introduced by many organizations at the same time. They call this phenomenon the 'travel of ideas'. Looking back we can see that many Eastern European countries introduced market liberalism and deregulated their economies and societies according to the neo-liberal model at about the same time. These ideas travelled or were carried from the west to the east. *Dagens Industri* is only one example of many Western actors bringing Western market and business discourses to the east. Other examples include management consultants (Kostera 1995), Western companies (e.g. Hood, Kilis & Vahlne 1997), or university scholars from Western universities involved in teaching collaboration and joint ventures of all kinds (cf. Sahlin-Andersson & Engwall 2002). In emphasizing the role of *Dagens Industri* as a representative of the Nordic business press and, more generally, of Western management and business discourse, one could compare this case with descriptions of the way Western civilization had previously carried Western ideas and ideologies to all parts of the world by ways of colonialism and trade (Spybey 1996: 173). We suggest that forms of 'colonialism' are still to be seen in action today, as more and more countries are adopting market liberalism. While the role played by international organizations cannot be denied, it has also been acknowledged that their role explains a limited part only of the processes of transformation (Ainamo & Cardwell 1998). We believe that such systemic change as the transformation of a country's economic paradigm is an open-ended and discursive process of transformation rather than a rationally planned transition from one economic system to another

If ideas are to travel as part of such a discursive process of change, they must be socially constructed and objectified (Czarniawska & Joerges 1996) before they are reproduced by entrepreneurs and institutionalized as components in the economic rules of the game (Spybey 1996, Djelic & Quack 2003). Czarniawska and Joerges (1996: 30) further refer to ideological control, 'that is control which takes place by influencing ideologies held by organizational actors, shaping their ideas about what reality is like, how it should be and how to achieve the desired state'. We believe this is relevant to our present context. Our case shows how the editors, journalists and managers of *Dagens Industri* and *Äripäev* sought to influence the ideologies of the journalists and their readers by shaping their idea of reality. They did so by introducing their ideas about journalism and market liberalism into the *Äripäev* news discourse. Here the ideology was made explicit in ideas about the way businesses should be run, how there should be a free liberal market, and how the ideal state should be achieved, by the way of deregulations and by promoting entrepreneurs and private companies in the Western sense. By communicating their ideas repeatedly, through their work and in news discourses about ways of approaching and operationalising the concepts of business and management, the ideas were forcefully brought to the readers' attention. The *Dagens Industri* ideas were carried over into the *Äripäev* news discourse, whence they were carried over by the readers into Estonian society as a whole.

By introducing ideas about the market economy into the *Äripäev* news discourse and by repeatedly writing about such things *Äripäev* had assumed an agenda-setting role. Carroll and McCombs (2003) describe the way in which the media affect the public agenda on a variety of issues and, not just public issues or politicians. In our case we could claim that *Äripäev* has been involved in changing the public discourse in Estonia by introducing a new discourse which, in turn, has paved the way for institutional changes in the economy and society as a whole.

Äripäev also had an agenda-setting effect due to its large circulation during the early years. Many people in Estonia read it and many of them were influential people, such as politicians and business leaders. What the media includes in its agenda in turn affects the public agenda

(Carroll & McCombs 2003). If many people read *Äripäev* the newspapers discourse is likely to affect the public agenda as well as the public discourse. Carroll and McCombs (2003) point out that the set of priorities appearing on the agenda of the new media will become in time the agenda of the reading public. We can thus conclude that as *Äripäev* was disseminating a particular discourse, carrying certain beliefs and ideologies over a long period, then this discourse can be expected to influence the newspaper's readers. Over time, and if they continue to read *Äripäev*, the readers are very likely to incorporate this discourse into their own beliefs and start taking it for granted.

It thus appears that the news media set the public agenda, or at least takes part in doing so. The public agenda may have been set 1) by *Äripäev*, 2) by other Estonian media influenced by *Äripäev*, 3) by *Äripäev* managers and journalists who were recruited to other Estonian media, and 4) by readers who enacted or operationalised the Western business and management discourse in the Nordic model adopted in Estonia.

Thus, having identified general and specific patterns of ownership and control over the generic and particular concepts, we suggest that business newspapers are carriers of societal discourses. As such they participate in the setting of societal agendas and discourses in the contexts concerned. First and foremost, business newspapers carry business and management discourses and the ideologies and mentalities with which these are connected. While this idea is hardly new (see e.g. Herman & Chomsky 1988, Engwall & Kipping 2002, Meyer 2002, Sahlin-Andersson & Engwall 2002), we put forward another, albeit, related argument. We suggest that Western business media which succeed in becoming institutionalized carriers of discourses connected with business and management often expand into new domains (cf. Kjær & Langer 2005). The new domains will involve moving across national borders and cultures, unless the expansion meets resistance in the shape of other discourses that are systemically incompatible and/or stronger than the expansive force.

In this chapter we have described how the Estonian newspaper *Äripäev* acted as a carrier of market ideology and business discourse. We suggest that other business-newspaper companies and other business newspapers too, are likely to exhibit a similar pattern so long as our currently neo-liberal world society continues to allow business newspapers to have an important part in shaping and controlling the market mechanism, the spread of which as yet appears hardly controllable by any other kind of voice.

Bibliography

Ainamo, A. & W. Cardwell (1998) After Privatisation: Economic Development, Social Transformation and Corporate Governance in the Baltic States. *Journal of Eastern European Management Studies* Vol. 3 (2): 134-163. Special Issue on Mergers and Acquisitions.

Ainamo, A. (2003) A Small Step for Insiders, Great Leap for Outsiders - The Case of the 'Tiger Leap' of SanomaWSOY. In Mannio, P., E. Vaara & P. Ylä-Anttila (Eds.) *Our Path Abroad: Exploring Post-war Internationalization of Finnish Corporations*. Helsinki: Taloustieto.

Ainamo, A. (2005) An evolutionary or strategic outcome: The birth, development and reorientation of SanomaWSOY (in Finnish). In Ojala, J. & T. Uskali (Eds.) *The Time of the Media Giants*. Helsinki: Infor.

Ainamo, A., J. Tienari & E. Vaara (2006) Between West and East: A Social History of Business Journalism in Cold War Finland. *Human Relations* Vol. 59 (5): 611-636.

Äripäev (2006) Minister Savisaar ärimees Hanschmidti PR-vankri ees. *Äripäev*, February 16, 2006.

Bringert, L. & B. Torekull (1995) *Äventyret Dagens Industri*. Borås, Sweden: Wahlström & Widstrand.

Carrol, C. E. & M. McCombs (2003) Agenda-setting effects of business news on the public's images and opinions about major corporations. *Corporation Reputation Review* Vol. 6 (1): 36-46.

Czarniawska, B. & B. Joerges (1996) Travels of Ideas. In Czarniawska, B. & G, Sevón (Eds.) *Translating Organizational Change*. Berlin, New York: Walter de Gruyter.

Dacin, T. (1997) Isomorphism in Context: The Power and Prescription of Institutional Norms. *Academy of Management Journal* Vol. 40 (1): 46-81.

Dagens Nyheter (2000) *Tvåan är hans olyckstal*. Bo E. Åkermark, September 30, 2000.

Djelic, M.-L. & S. Quack (2003) (Eds.) *Globalization and Institutions: Redefining the Rules of the Economic Game*. Cheltenham: Edgar Elgar.

Engwall, L. & M. Kipping (2002) *Management Consulting: Emergence and Dynamics of a Knowledge Industry*. Oxford: Oxford University Press.

Geertz, C. (1973) *The Interpretation of Cultures*. New York: Basic Books.

Gustafsson, K. E. (1996) *Dagspressen i Norden. Struktur och ekonomi*. Lund, Sverige: Studentlitteratur.

Haldenius, S. & L. Weibull (1999) *Massmedier. Press, Radio & TV i förvandling*. Falkenberg, Sverige: Albert Bonniers Förlag.

Harrie, E. (2003) The newspaper market. In E. Harrie (Ed.) *The Nordic Media Market. Media Companies and Business Activities*. Gothenburg: Nordicom.

Heikkilä, H. (2001) *Heikko ja vahva journalismi*. Tampere: Tampereen yliopisto.

Herman, E. S. & N. Chomsky (1988) *Manufacturing Consent*. Pantheon Books.

Hood, N., R. Kilis & J.-E. Vahlne (1997) (Eds.) *Transition in the Baltic States*. London: MacMillian Press Ltd.

Kjær, P. & Langer, R. (2005) Infused with news value: Management, managerial knowledge and the institutionalization of business news. *Scandinavian Journal of Management* Vol. 21 (2): 209-233.

Kokk, A. (2006) Owner and CEO of Eesti Päevaleht. *Personal correspondence*, August 22, 24, and 26, 2006.

Kostera, M. (1995) The Modern Crusade. The Missionaries of Management Come to Eastern Europe. *Management Learning* Vol. 26 (3): 91-118.

Lagerspetz, M. (2000) *The construction and hegemonization of post-socialist order in Estonia.* Working papers no. 54 Department of East European Studies. Uppsala University.

Metropol International S.A Annual Report 2004.

Meyer, J. (2002) Globalization and the Expansion of Standardization of Management. In Sahlin-Andersson, K. & L. Engwall (Eds.) *The expansion of management knowledge: carriers, flows and sources.* Stanford, California: Stanford University Press.

Read, D. (1992) The *power of the news: The history of the Reuters.* Oxford: Oxford University Press.

Risberg, A. & L. Melin (2005) *Dagens Industri* Goes Abroad - the Internationalization of a Successful Newspaper Concept. In Picard, R. G. (Ed.) *Media Product Portfolios: Issues in Management of Multiple Products and Services.* Mahwah, New Jersey: Lawrence Erlbaum.

Ritzer, G. (1993) *The McDonaldization of Society.* Thousand Oak, CA: Pine Forge Press.

Sahlin-Andersson, K. & L. Engwall (2002) Carriers, Flows, and Sources of Management Knowledge. In Sahlin-Andersson, K. & L. Engwall (Eds.) *The expansion of management knowledge: carriers, flows and sources.* Stanford, California: Stanford University Press.

Spybey, T. (1996) Global Transformation. In Czarniawska, B. & G. Sevón (Eds.) *Translating Organizational Change.* Berlin, New York: Walter de Gruyter. Pp.

Sundin, S. (2003a) *Den svenska mediemarknaden 2003.* MedieNotiser Nr. 2, Nordicom-Sverige: Gothenburg University.

Sundin, S. (2003b) Trends in media ownership in the Nordic countries. In E. Harrie (Ed.) *The Nordic Media Market. Media Companies and Business Activities.* Gothenburg: Nordicom.

Sundin, S. (2005) *Den svenska mediemarknaden 2005.* MedieNotiser Nr. 3, Nordicom-Sverige: Gothenburg University.

Thrift, N. (2001) 'It's the romance, not the finance, that makes the business worth pursuing': disclosing a new market culture. *Economy and Society* Vol 30 (4): 412-432.

Yamaguchi, T. & C. K. Harris (2004) The economic hegemonization of Bt cotton discourse in India. *Discourse & Society* Vol. 15 (4): 467-491.

WWW-sources:

www.20minutes.fr 2005-12-14
www.20minutes.fr 2005-12-14
www.apressen.no 2006-02-02, 2006-02-07
www.aripaev.ee 2005-12-15
www.bonnier.se 2006-03-02
www.medieregisteret.no 2006-02-02
www.metropol.pl 2005-12-08
www.orkla-media.no 2006-02-02
www.sanomawsoy.fi 2006-02-07
www.schibsted.no 2006-02-02
www.investinestonia.com. 2005-12-05

PART II

BUSINESS NEWS, PUBLIC KNOWLEDGE AND MEANING

CHAPTER 5

Transforming Business News Content
A Comparative Analysis

PETER KJÆR, NIINA ERKAMA & MARIA GRAFSTRÖM

Introduction

Over the last four decades business news has become an important sub-field of journalism in the Nordic countries. The emergence of this field is the outcome of a process of innovation in the course of which new journalistic ideals, formats and practices have been introduced. The process of innovation began primarily in the niche segment of the business press, but has spread into the business press as a whole and even to other media platforms altogether.

The previous chapters described this process of innovation and diffusion with particular emphasis on key actors and their strategies in national media contexts. We now turn from the actors to the actual product with which they are engaging and which they are struggling over, namely newspaper content concerned with business issues, and we ask how the innovation process has manifested itself in this context? How, in terms of content, has a particular sub-field been carved out for business news in the four Nordic countries, and what can we say about the overall development of this sub-field in regard to changes in content?

The most obvious aspect of this development concerns the expanding *volume* of business and economy news. Up to now studies of business news have indicated a dramatic expansion in both the total and the relative volume of business and economy news, suggesting that business news has become a distinct and prioritized area of interest that appeals to new audiences and constitutes a new and expanding source of advertising revenue (Volden 1996, Barnes 1998, Henriques 2000a, Mazza & Strandgaard Pedersen 2004, Kjær & Langer 2005). In general we would expect the institutional innovations in the field to lead to an overall expansion in the volume of content. At the same time, the timing and the clear patterns of expansion could yield interesting insights into the dynamics of different national contexts, while also allowing us to speculate about the role of other contextual factors, such as changes in economic policy regimes in the countries concerned (See also Slaatta 2003: 114ff). A study of the expansion process would also enable us to consider the development of business and economy content relative to other fields of specialization, something that has been an issue in the debate about the expansion of business journalism in which there has been frequent concern about the way business news has come to marginalize other perspectives and areas of interest (E.g. Lindhoff 1998, Davis 2000, Goozner 2000, Henriques 2000b, Vaara & Tienari 2002).

The creation of a sub-field is also connected with *professionalization and popularization*. The professional projects and strategies undertaken by innovators in the business press, as described in the previous chapters, suggest that much more was at stake than simply a shifting balance between general types of content. According to the new ideals of business journalism, business and economy news was to be produced and presented in new ways which, while adhering to the professional norms of journalism, would also extend the readership of business news. Some observers have described the recent development of business journalism as signifying a 'golden age', implying that the most prominent representatives of business journalism today are reaching new levels of professionalism and that what used to be a highly specialized area of interest is now appealing to a much wider audience (E.g. Roush 2004: 1ff, Welles 2001).[1] We will be looking here not at journalistic quality so much as the way in which the content of business and economy texts in general has come to reflect a concern with journalistic professionalism and popular appeal. In other words, is the actual content of the texts indicating changes in the way business news is being produced and presented to its audiences?

Finally, the renewal of the business press is also nourished by an ambition to change the very way in which the economy, or business activity, is to be *represented* in the news. Many of the innovators have had definite ideas about what counts as business news, i.e. what themes were to be handled in the brave new world of business journal-

---

[1] Many students of the business press however also emphasize the variation in professional standards in the field, and how business journalists face particular challenges in the relationship to the sources of news (Henriques 2000a, Davis 2000, Ekonomiska Samfundets Tidskrift 2003).

ism, and who would be the actors populating it (see also Slaatta with Kjær, Grafström & Erkama in the present volume). At the same time many outside observers have been concerned about trends towards 'corporatization', or the uncritical diffusion of an 'enterprise culture', or 'managerialism' in popular discourse (Keat & Abercrombie 1990, Lindhoff 1998, Gavin 1998, Mazza & Alvarez 2000). The question therefore is whether the innovation process is reflected in changes in the way 'the economy' is being represented journalistically.

Although this chapter is intended to be primarily descriptive, it is also informed by an institutional perspective, whereby news production is regarded as inseparable from its institutional context, i.e. the rules, routines or world views that have become institutionalized within the field (Powell & DiMaggio 1991, Scott 1995, Cook 1998). In an institutional perspective we would thus expect changes in the content of business news to be connected with changes in the institutional contexts in which news is being produced and distributed. The following analysis explores two such contexts, namely national media orders and media platforms.

Media orders we define as the historically evolving structure of positions and relations among media organizations and technologies such as it has been institutionalized in a particular society (Slaatta 2003, Bourdieu 1993, Benson 1998, Benson & Neveu 2005). We would expect the timing and the degree of change to differ between national media orders, given that these orders are continually evolving in distinct interactions with other social fields, such as the economy or the political system. *Media platforms* are the technological and organizational sites for the production and circulation of news and information within particular media orders. The historical analysis in Chapter 2 of the present volume suggests that the development of business news is clearly linked to changes in the niche platforms dedicated to business news, and we should therefore expect distinct patterns of expansion, professionalization and popularization in niche and general-interest platforms in the four countries concerned.

We will now first introduce our methodological base, after which we offer a quantitative content analysis of changes in eight newspapers in the Nordic countries between 1960 and 2000. The analysis describes patterns in the overall expansion, changes in the formats used, i.e. type of texts and illustrations, and changes in the way the news is structured, i.e. in the way economy and business are represented thematically and in terms of the actors concerned. We conclude with a discussion of the role of the institutional context in the expansion and transformation of business news content.

Methodology

The analysis is concerned with historical changes in newspaper content in the Nordic countries. Given this broad focus, our definition of 'business news' has to be flexible – ranging from a general orientation towards the coverage of economic and business issues in newspaper outlets, then on to the various specialized platforms and genres developed in general-interest and niche newspapers focusing on business coverage, and finally to the particular thematic selections made by different journalists when covering business. We thus first defined our data set as including all edited content in a given number of newspapers. We then developed and examined specific definitions of business news within this data set.

We make a basic distinction between economic and non-economic content. In its broadest sense 'economic content' refers to articles, tables, illustrations, etc., which are identified as belonging to the 'economic' sphere by the newspaper concerned or which have 'economy' as a primary or secondary theme.

The analysis will map three aspects of change in the news: volume, format and representation. *Volume* refers the overall magnitude of material relating to business and economy relative to other general subject matters. *Format* is connected with the way in which business and economy news are presented in terms of particular text types or types of visualization. *Representation* is connected with the way in which business and economy news handles its subject matter, how the worldview of business and economy news is structured thematically.

Our time frame comprises the period between 1960 and 2000. 1960 has been selected as a starting-point, because it represents the period before the dramatic changes in the business press that occurred in all the Nordic countries after the mid-1960s. For practical reasons the year 2000 constitutes 'the present' in our analysis.

Our data is drawn from eight Nordic newspapers. From each newspaper the content during a single week was coded at ten-year intervals: 1960, 1970, 1980, 1990 and 2000. The ten-year intervals were selected to provide sufficient detail for a longitudinal study, while still limiting the total number of items to be coded. The intervals make it possible to detect broader patterns of change but not the smaller shifts that may be caused by changes in the business cycle in media markets, one-off changes in editorial policy etc.

The analysis covers Denmark, Finland, Norway and Sweden. In each country two newspapers have been selected for analysis, namely one leading business daily and one national general-interest newspaper with a particular focus on business. In Denmark *Berlingske Tidende* is one of three large national general-interest dailies, but it has a long history as an important national newspaper with a business orientation. It thus seemed highly relevant to the purposes of our analysis. *Børsen* was selected as our Danish niche newspaper in view of its long history and more or less unrivalled position as a national business newspaper. *Helsingin Sanomat* is the dominant general-interest newspaper in Finland, while *Kauppalehti* stands out as the leading Finnish business daily. In Norway we selected *Aftenposten*, a leading national daily with a strong business focus, and *Norges Handels- og Sjøfartstidning/ Dagens Næringsliv* as the leading niche newspaper.[2] *Svenska Dagbladet* was selected as the general-interest newspaper for Sweden. It is the second largest general-interest newspaper with nationwide circulation but, unlike its somewhat larger competitor *Dagens Nyheter*, it has had a fairly persistent interest in business coverage. The business daily *Dagens Industri* was established as recently as 1976 but soon became the leading business daily not only in Sweden but in the Nordic countries as a whole.[3] Taken together the four niche and four general-interest newspapers represent a significant part of the market for business news in the Nordic newspaper market.

When possible a full week each year was coded in order to capture the varied news content on different weekdays. Rather than coding a particular week, which could be 'polluted' by extraordinary events (e.g. elections and disasters), we constructed a 'composite week' consisting of Mondays, Tuesdays, Wednesdays, etc., from different weeks each year.[4]

A total of 296 newspaper issues and 43,106 items were coded in the four countries. The total material also included commercial advertisements and official announcements, but since the analysis is geared to edited material, advertisements and announcements have been filtered

---

[2] *Norges Handels- og Sjøfartstidning* changed its name to *Dagens Næringsliv* in 1987.
[3] Given the time frame of our study, we considered supplementing *Dagens Industri* with the older business daily *Göteborgs Handels- och Sjöfartstidning*, which was closed down in 1973. However, since there were no clear links between the two – in either editorial or ownership terms, we decided against including GHS.
[4] In most cases we have coded the number of weekly editions actually published, typically ranging between 5 and 7 editions, since some business dailies do not have weekend editions. However, in the case of *Dagens Industri*, which in 1980 was only published two days a week, we coded four additional newspapers for that year.

out,[5] leaving us with some 34,000 articles, one-third of which are 'economic' articles. Figure 5.1 shows the total volume of edited content in the coded newspapers:

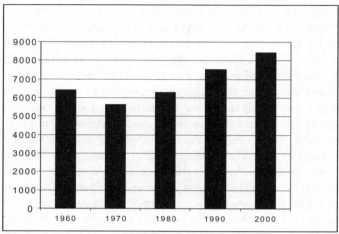

Figure 5.1: Total Volume of Edited Content

The newspapers were coded with the help of a joint code sheet comprising 20 main variables (see Appendix for code sheet). All articles were coded, but only larger items defined as 'economic' articles were coded in depth.[6] This allowed for a general description of the relative expansion of economic news vis-à-vis other types of content, while also enabling a closer study of economic and business news as such.[7]

---

[5] Non-edited content, such as official announcements and advertisements, was included in the original code sheet to allow us to consider possible changes in the relationship between commercial information and journalism. In the coding process, coders often had to group advertisements and announcements, since many newspapers place these under common headings. The total number thus gives an inaccurate picture of the volume of non-edited content.

[6] The in-depth coding of themes and agents/source etc. included 'economic' news articles and commentary, but excluded what was defined as 'non-economic articles' as well as 'small notes', 'formalia', 'economic information' etc. Non-economic articles were coded for 'economic indicators', however (Points 4 and 5 in the code sheet, see Appendix).

[7] Given that coding was to be carried out in five different national settings, detailed coder instructions were developed, and the code sheet was tested several times. Due to problems of inter-coder reliability about 5% of the issues were recoded after the initial coding had taken place. A few more experimental categories, such as 'discourse' and 'sources' were subsequently scrapped due to reliability problems, but we have included them in the code sheet in the Appendix. See Grafström (2005) and Kjær (2005) for details of the coding process.

The Expansion of Economic News Content

In the following we define 'economic content' as material dealing with issues pertaining to work, production and economic transactions in the private and public sectors. Economy may be the dominant concern in this context, for instance when an article describes changes in interest rates or the investment potential in a given industry, or it may be an important albeit not a dominant theme that overlaps with other concerns such as politics, sport or culture – for example reporting a government initiative to support research in industry or to improve efficiency of the public sector. In both cases, we consider the content to be 'economic' because both indicate a direct or indirect concern with economic affairs.[8]

Figure 5.2 shows that since 1960, and more markedly since 1980, there appears to have been a marked increase in the number of economic articles and other economic items, which have doubled, in the newspapers studied:

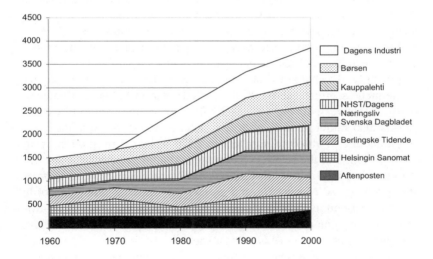

Figure 5.2: Number of Economic Articles, all Newspapers

---

[8] In cases where economic aspects are mentioned but not obviously as either a primary or a secondary concern, we have defined items as 'non-economic'. It should be noted that we have also coded items as economic when they appear under an obviously 'economic' page or section heading such as 'trade and industry'; 'economy and trade'; 'finance' etc.

The expansion process seems to fall into three fairly distinct phases.[9] Between 1960 and 1980 there was a steady increase in the total number of economic articles. This was followed by a period of more dramatic growth between 1980 and 1990. Finally, between 1990 and 2000 the growth rate seems to have settled at a steadier level. Even in relative terms, i.e. economic content as a share of all edited content, the same overall pattern of expansion can be observed, indicating that although there is an overall expansion in the volume of newspaper content (see Figure 5.1) the share of economic content was increasing steadily up to the 1990s.

The overall growth pattern supports the observation (see Slattaa with Kjær, Grafström & Erkama in the present volume) that the 1960s and 1970s can be regarded as a period of innovation, during which business news became an object of editorial concern and journalistic professionalization, while the 'real' expansion occurred during the 1980s and 1990s when the full market potential of business news was exploited. After 1990 the rate of growth has been more modest, partly due to the decline in the newspaper advertisement market and the expansion of competing platforms from the late 1990s onwards.[10]

There are important differences in the pattern of expansion as between the niche and the general-interest newspapers. First, and not surprisingly, the share of economic articles is persistently much higher in the niche segment (above 80% in 2000) than in the general-interest segment (between 20 and 40% in 2000). Second, the pattern of expansion is also rather similar, with the niche newspapers experiencing a slight decline in absolute numbers in 1970 followed by growth up to 1990. In terms of the relative volume of economic content, the growth is even more uniform, with *Kauppalehti, Norges Handels- og Sjøfartstidende/Dagens Næringsliv* and *Børsen* all moving from a profile whereby economic content answered for approximately half of all articles and then gradually moving on to command an 80 or 90% share. The late-comer *Dagens Industri* is a special case in that it experienced a minor drop in the number of articles per issue, and because it actually reduced the relative space allotted to economic matter in 1990 and

[9] Please note that we only have data for *Dagens Industri* from 1980 to 2000.
[10] The 'space' occupied by economic content has increased even more dramatically. In Finland the total size of economic content doubled from 1960 to 2000, but in Norway the total size increased fourfold, in Denmark the increase was five-fold, and in Sweden the increase was even more dramatic. The increase in size suggests that the format of business news has changed towards larger content pieces and the creation of specialized business supplements. See Grafström (2005), Kjær (2005), Herskedal (2004), Ainamo et al. (2004).

2000. It should be noted, however, that it started from a very high level.

The pattern of expansion in the general-interest newspapers is less uniform. While all newspapers have expanded their economic coverage in both absolute and relative terms since 1960, only *Svenska Dagbladet* has shown a steady increase in economic coverage over the years. *Berlingske Tidende* remained quite stable until 1980 and then increased dramatically in 1990 only to cut down its economic coverage somewhat in 2000. *Helsingin Sanomat* experienced an early increase, after which its coverage decreased in 1980 in both relative and absolute terms, not reaching its 1970-level again until 1990. Finally, *Aftenposten's* economic coverage remained remarkably stable from 1960 until 1990, and then increased between 1990 and 2000.

Changing Formats

Newspaper formats have changed dramatically since the 1950s. Just a quick glance at the pages of both general-interest and niche newspapers reveals a profound transformation in the way news is presented to the reader. To a contemporary eye a typical newspaper page in 1960 looks rather confusing with its combination of a few large articles and many small articles on a wide range of subjects. A newspaper in 2000 consisted instead of dedicated pages, sections and supplements (typically linked to particular advertising segments), with each page clearly divided between major feature stories and minor news briefs, often placed in particular columns. Similarly, the text of a 1960 newspaper was very dense, there were few illustrations and not many visual guidelines to help the reader to prioritize or interpret the various news stories. In 2000, the textual density had lessened. Differentiated headlines, photographs and other illustrations now provided visual assistance to the reader.

Changes like this in the way journalists and editors present things to the reader tell us something about how news is produced and consumed in a given context. The design and format of text and visual matter may thus indicate the degree to which journalistic ideals have penetrated the practices of business news production, for instance by prioritizing journalistic content over other types of content or by prioritizing particular ways of addressing business-news audiences. In concrete terms, we will now describe changes in format in two dimensions. First, we deal with changes in the textual format (text type), some of which – specifically feature news articles – will be taken as an indication of a trend towards journalistic professionalization while others – economic information – can be interpreted as a sign of popularization and of market orientation. Secondly, we deal with changes in the visual format (e.g. illustrations and photos), which will be seen as indicating a trend towards the popularization of business and economy news.

Feature news articles and news briefs are the prevalent types of text for economic content in all the coded outlets.[11] Together the two constitute about 75% of the coded content over the years. The interrelationship between feature news and news briefs is complex and has changed over the years.[12] Formerly there was often an equal amount of feature news articles and news briefs. However, the expansion in economic content tended to lead to an expansion in feature news, at the expense of news briefs. This can be interpreted as a sign of increasing journalistic ambition, since feature news articles written by staff reporters were being prioritized over the more routine use of material lifted from news wire services, etc. However, since 1980, the number of news briefs has increased again, in both general and economic content, suggesting that in the period of rapid expansion news briefs constituted a cheap (and popular) way of expanding economic content without increasing the number of journalists.

In terms of text types, economic content differs from general content primarily in the particular attention given to the presentation of various forms of standardized economic information.

Economic information, in the shape of currency lists, stock market quotations, price indexes, etc. constitutes a classical type of text in economic news.[13] With the changes in business journalism from the mid-1960s onwards, this type of text was expected to make way for a more journalistically oriented content, i.e. feature news. However, as Figure 5.3 suggests, the amount of economic information has increased dramatically since 1980, parallel with the overall increase in economic content.[14]

---

[11] We distinguish between ten general types of text: feature news, news briefs (brief notes, news telegrams), economic information (tables, lists, and indexes), reviews, formalia, internal commentary, external commentary, entertainment, pictures and 'other'. See code sheet in the Appendix for details.

[12] See e.g. Grafström (2005) on changes in text types in Swedish newspapers since 1960.

[13] See Parsons (1989). In our coding procedure we distinguished between tables, indexes, etc., used to illustrate news articles etc., and economic information presented in the shape of separate textual entities, e.g. on designated pages. Only this last has been coded as 'Economic information'.

[14] Simply counting the number of items dedicated to economic information (e.g. stock market quotations in tables) yields rather a conservative estimate of the importance of this kind of information, since tables and lists may occupy whole pages or even sections – while each table is only counted once.

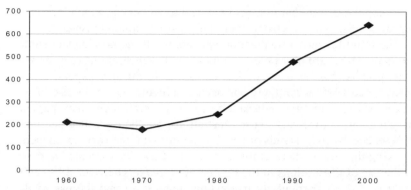

Figure 5.3: Economic Information, All Newspapers

The development of economic information indicates both a trend towards journalistic professionalization, and a parallel trend towards a stronger market orientation. The development of *Børsen* in Denmark is a good case in point. During the editorial reorientation in 1970 the new editors-in-chief first wanted to do away with stock lists, etc., in the name of journalistic modernization. However, the editors soon realized that a large section of the readership was unwilling to trade stock market information for critical journalism (Fonsmark 1996: 189). In the case of *Dagens Industri* in Sweden, the owners did not at first allow the newspaper to publish stock market lists, for fear of competing with other outlets in their own possession, but this policy had to be reversed a few years later (Grafström 2006: 110, Bringert & Torekull 1995: 106f, Slaatta with Kjær, Grafström & Erkama, in the present volume).

Niche newspapers and general-interest newspapers seem to follow different patterns of change when it comes to types of text. Most general-interest newspapers seem to give priority to news articles over news briefs from an early stage, while the emphasis on feature news develops somewhat later in the niche segment. While all newspapers, with one exception (*Aftenposten*), have given priority to economic information ever since 1980, the niche newspapers carry much more economic information than their general-interest counterparts.

Having described changes in the choice of textual formats, we now turn to the use of visuals. The 'visualization' of economic content can be examined in quantitative terms by looking at the use of various types of illustration, including photographs. The results indicate that while economic content has evolved as a specialized type of content involving distinct types of text, business and economy news has also

141

been popularized in that it seeks to appeal to audiences which lack any highly specialized knowledge about business or economic issues.

The trend towards visualization appears in all the newspapers studied here. The share of articles accompanied by illustrations (e.g. drawings, graphs) has been increasing uniformly in all newspapers, especially since 1990, when there has been a dramatic rise in the use of illustrations (see Figures 5.4a and 5.4b). In general, niche newspapers have a greater propensity to use illustrations, but there are also national differences. Norway stands out as the country with the two newspapers showing the largest share of illustrations in 2000. The extreme increase in the use of illustrations in the Finnish *Kauppalehti* between 1980 and 1990 is perhaps particularly interesting, suggesting that the use of illustrations can also be subject to conscious editorial and strategic decisions.

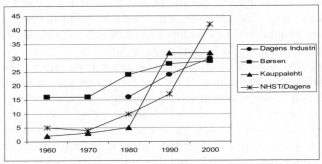

Figure 5.4a: The Use of Illustrations in Niche Newspapers (Percent of Economic Content)

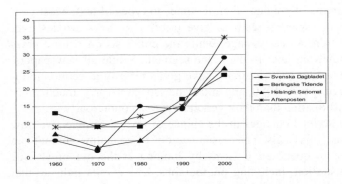

Figure 5.4b: The Use of Illustrations in General-Interest Newspapers (Percent of Economic Content)

142

A closer inspection of the different types of illustration reveals that the overall increase is first and foremost a matter of using more numerical illustrations. Illustrations thus becomes condensed ways of presenting quantitative data, but the increase in numerical illustrations probably also reflects the diffusion of standardized quantitative indicators of economic performance in relation to both macro-economic and corporate or financial performance.

The use of photographs is another element of the visual presentation of a newspaper's content (see Figure 5.5). Generally speaking, we would associate increasing use of photographs with a trend towards popularization, particularly if it coincides with increasing use of illustrations. However, the use of photographs is also affected by the greater technological possibilities available to newspapers as layout- and printing technologies are improved.

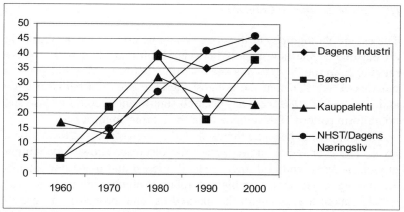

Figure 5.5a: The Use of Photographs in Niche Newspapers (Percent of Economic Content)

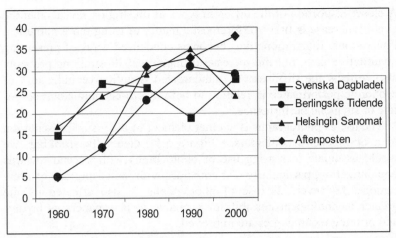

Figure 5.5b: The Use of Photographs in General-Interest Newspapers (Percent of Economic Content)

The use of photographs to illustrate economic articles has increased in all but one of the newspapers between 1960 and 2000 with a share ranging from roughly 5% to a share shifting between 23% and 46%. In most cases we find that the greatest increase occurred between 1960 and 1980. After 1980 there has been no significant overall increase and no uniform pattern of development in the Nordic countries.

There appear to be some trends shared by newspapers at the national level. The Norwegian newspapers, for instance, show very similar growth patterns, and both their general-interest and niche newspapers are among those with the highest relative number of photographs, which - taken together with the marked national propensity to use illustrations - indicates that economic news in Norway is noticeably 'visual'.

There is a marked difference in the use of photographs between niche and general-interest platforms. With the possible exception of the Finland's *Kauppalehti*, the niche newspapers use photographs to a much greater extent than the general-interest newspapers. This suggests that while all Nordic newspapers have seized the technological opportunities in photography and have 'modernized' their presentation of news, the niche newspapers - inspired by the mode of presentation in the tabloids - have adopted a more 'popular' type of format than the general-interest newspapers.[15]

All in all, it seems that the choice of visual formats applied to the economic content of newspapers in the Nordic countries has been undergoing a process of popularization. Historically, the use of photographs appears to have preceded the widespread use of illustrations. While both trends are common to all newspapers, the trend towards visualization is strongest in the niche newspapers. Thus the niche newspapers seem to be combining a pronounced editorial specialization with a strong and fairly persistent tendency towards popularization.

Changes in the Representation of Economic Activity

We now turn to the question of how 'the economic' is represented in the business and economy news. Although we have tentatively defined economic content as referring in some way to work, production or economic transactions in the public or private sectors, there are very different ways of representing the economic world even within these perimeters.

To examine changes in the representations of 'the economic' we have looked at two variables, namely themes and agents.

Regarding the former, we consider changes in the subject matter: *what* are economic articles about? We limit ourselves to articles in which economy is the dominant theme, which gives us a sample of around 5800 articles (the rest do not have a main economic theme or they were not subjected to detailed thematic coding, as was the case regarding lists or tables concerned with 'economic information'). We take up four broad thematic categories: Business & industry; Labor & labor market; Government policy and 'Other' (e.g. morals, ethics, law, etc.):[16]

---

[15] It should be noted that we only counted the frequency, and not the size, of photographs. Thus, in the case of *Helsingin Sanomat*, the decline in relative frequency seems to be compensated for by the use of larger photos.

[16] The four themes considered here are aggregates of eleven predefined themes, plus a few more added during the coding process.

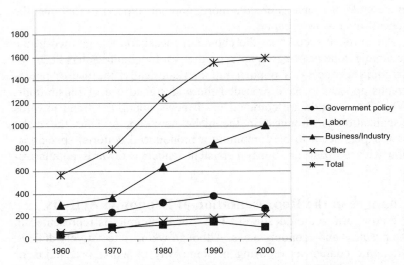

Figure 5.6: Dominant Themes in Economic Content, All Newspapers

Since 1960 the number of articles concerned predominantly with business has tripled. From representing about 50% of the total, business articles now comprise almost two-thirds of all economic articles. In contrast, the number of articles concerned with government policy shows only a moderate rise, and the relative share of such articles has dropped from 31% to 17%. The number of articles on labor market issues was showing a moderate increase up to 1990, but by 2000 its overall share was back to the 7-8% that it represented in 1960.

If we disaggregate these changes, a very varied picture emerges. Apart from overall growth for business themes at the expense of government policy, there are few common patterns at the Nordic level. Surprisingly, it is also hard to detect any national patterns. While the national media do sometimes reveal similar patterns for a while, for instance both Finnish outlets seemed to be focusing fairly strongly on labor market issues in 1990,[17] there is little or no long-term covariation between the media at the national level.

Marked differences can be detected between the niche and general-interest outlets. On the whole niche outlets have been more business-oriented throughout, with business-oriented articles rarely dropping below a 50% share. With the exception of *Aftenposten* in 1960 and 1970,

---

[17] The emphasis on labor market issues in Finland in 1990 is probably closely connected with the severe economic depression that hit Finland in conjunction with the decline in trade relations with the Soviet Union.

general-interest newspapers have been less business-oriented, as well as showing a greater propensity for government policy and labor market issues. On the other hand, it seems that the niche outlets focus on a wider range of business issues than their general-interest counterparts. Thus *Børsen* in Denmark is sometimes described as a 'general-interest business newspaper', whereas *Berlingske Tidende* focuses on a narrower range of firms, industries and problems.

As regards the process of thematic change, we find that most niche media appear to follow a fairly regular pattern. In Figure 5.7 we show changes in the share represented by the 'business' theme in the niche newspapers:

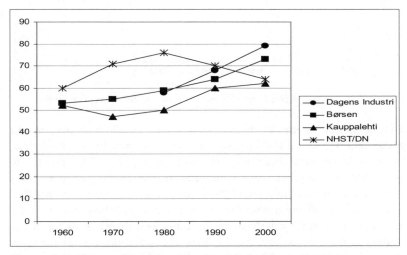

Figure 5.7: Share of Business Themes, Niche Newspapers

Figure 5.7 shows how *Børsen, Kauppalehti* (after 1970) and *Dagens Industri* (starting in 1980) showed an increasing emphasis on business, while de-emphasizing governmental policy. Up to 1980 *Norges Handels og Sjøfartstidende* put increasing emphasis on business themes, after which this theme shows a relative decline from its rather high maximum level.

The general-interest newspapers on their part reveal a common initial tendency to play down business as a theme, focusing instead on labor market and governmental policy (economic policy-making), and only strengthening their orientation towards business themes after 1980. *Helsingin Sanomat* diverges from the general pattern, with several shifts in thematic orientation and a very strong emphasis on governmental policy and labor market issues.

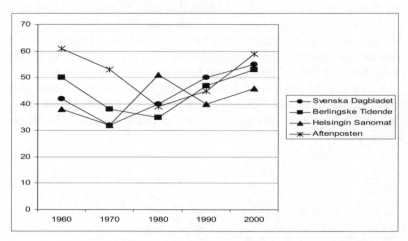

Figure 5.8: Share of Business Themes, General-Interest Newspapers

The 'economic' theme has thus ceased to be a question of government policy and regulation and has become instead a question of 'business.' In the niche segment this change occurred during the 1970s, and in the general-interest segment somewhat later. It is interesting to note, however, that economic policy and the labor market remained serious thematic rivals to business until the 1980s at least, and there was in fact a decline at first in the emphasis on business as a theme in many of the studied outlets. However, by the time the situation was checked in 1990 and 2000, the hegemony of 'business' seemed to have been secured.

Business became a major focus of attention during the 1980s and 1990s. The question now is whether business firms and their representatives were also being portrayed as important *agents and sources* in the news. As in the case of themes, any measurement of agents and sources in a quantitative and comparative context has its methodological difficulties. National conventions as well as shifting conventions regarding genre may affect the way journalists and others use speakers and agents in the news.[18] At the same time, media texts in general have grown more complex in terms of actors, and appear to be orchestrated

---

[18] In a Finnish context, journalists are generally less likely - for cultural or linguistic reasons - to identify actors clearly when they describe particular events or debates, preferring to use impersonal or indirect formulations, such as 'it was decided'.

by the journalists themselves to a greater extent. In other words, changes do not necessarily reflect – or do not only reflect – major changes in the way journalists and editors perceive 'economy' and 'business.' While we are thus unable to make any finely drawn inferences from our data, we can identify two general trends regarding the dominant entities – speaking or acting – that have appeared in the economic news since 1960.

Taken all round, the portrayal of agents and sources evolves in a way very similar to that applying to the themes. The number of articles in which the dominant agents and sources are business firms and/or their representatives has almost quadrupled between 1960 and 2000, from approximately 300 to nearly 1200 per year. The total number of articles with a political agent or source was on the increase up to 1990, after which it dropped rather abruptly between 1990 and 2000. Neither the total number nor the relative share of labor market organizations are ever high, and they decline from 1980 onwards. While there seems to be a fairly straightforward relation between the growth in business themes and the growth in business agents and sources in the news, it is interesting to note that by the year 2000 agents/sources have overtaken themes in this connection. In other words, it seems that even in some news stories that may relate to issues other than business and industry, business firms have become an important element.

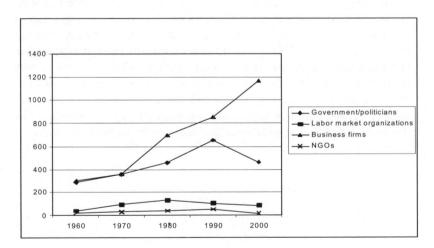

Figure 5.9: Dominant Agents and Sources in All Newspapers

Again we find several noticeable differences between general-interest and niche newspapers. Up to 1990 the emphasis on government actors remains remarkably stable in the general-interest newspapers, dominating in approximately 40% of all economic news articles. It is interesting to note that although business firms occupy a strong position to begin with, their importance had waned by 1970 and they experienced dramatic advances only between 1990 and 2000. Labor market organizations also stand relatively high, although their importance diminished steadily from 1970 onwards.

Among the niche newspapers we find a steady increase in the importance of business firms, with a share of about 40% rising to over 70%. This was at the expense of governmental and political actors, whose share dropped from about 50% to a little over 20%. Labor market organizations are much weaker in the niche segment, where they have played a very limited role during and since the 1980s.

Thus, as regards agents and sources, we find that up to the 1990s the general-interest newspapers maintained and even strengthened a political perspective in their coverage of 'the economy', while the niche newspapers tended to equate economy with business firms very early on. Further, it is worth noting that there seems to have been a little more variation regarding agents in the general-interest newspapers than in their niche counterparts.

The analyses of themes and agents both suggest that there has been an intensive 'corporatization' of economic news over the years. Up to a point this process has been going on since 1970, but it became more marked in 1990 and 2000. The process seems to have started earlier and more enthusiastically in the niche segment, while up to the 1980s the general-interest newspapers maintained a broader political perspective as regards the economy, so that today there is remarkably little difference between the two suggesting that representing 'the economy' as 'business' has become widely institutionalized in the business press.

Conclusion: The Contours of a Journalistic Sub-Field

In our analysis we have compared four countries and two platforms for the production of business news, and we have sought to show how changes in newspaper content support the claim that over the last 40 years a journalistic sub-field has in fact emerged. The analysis supports the general claim that the innovations in the business press that first appeared in the mid-1960s have had a significant and concrete impact on newspaper content.

First and most noticeably, there has been a dramatic expansion in the overall and the relative volume of business and economic news in all the outlets studied. We have also found a general pattern of expansion starting with a phase of gradual growth in the output of business news up to 1980, a second phase of rapid expansion during the 1980s and early 1990s, and a third phase of more moderate growth since 1990. We also found that this expansion started in the niche-outlets, after which it gradually came – to a varying extent - to involve the general-interest newspapers as well.

Secondly, we found that the expansion of business and economy news was accompanied by a process of professionalization and popularization. The professionalization of the field is reflected in the growing importance of feature news, at the expense initially of news briefs and economic information. However, after 1980 the analysis also revealed a renewed interest in news briefs and an increase in economic information, suggesting that professionalization came hand-in-hand with an orientation towards concrete audience demands. We also saw a strong tendency towards the visualization of business and economic news, suggesting a firm attempt to popularize business news with the help of new formats to rid it of its specialist connotations. It is interesting to note that we found popularization to be more evident in the niche segment than in the general-interest newspapers.

Thirdly, we found that the expansion of business and economic content also entailed a transformation in the evaluation of economic issues: what was to be regarded as important? In particular we found a great emphasis on the 'corporatization' of economic news. This showed itself in a dramatic increase in the appearance of business as a dominant theme in the news, and in the frequent references to business as a source of news and to the business agents involved – in both cases at the expense of wider political or economic issues. Not surprisingly, this emphasis on business proved to be much stronger in the niche press than in the general-interest newspapers, suggesting that these last have maintained a broader view of what and who are economically relevant. At the same time, however, it seems that niche outlets have developed a more comprehensive view of what is included in the concept of business, while the general-interest outlets sometimes tend to adopt a more specialized focus - on large and well-known enterprises, for instance.

So far our argument has suggested that the innovation of news platforms in the business press has had a significant impact on business and economic news in general. We have also found a number of distinctive features characterizing economic content in the niche and the general-interest outlets. For instance, the expansion and innovation process began in the niche platforms and only gradually spread to the general-interest platforms. Further, the niche platforms have shown themselves to be deeply ingrained with a business world view – in a sense indicating a high degree of specialization – while also going to great lengths to popularize their business content, which together suggest an orientation towards a very wide audience. The general-interest platforms on their part have maintained a broader economic perspective and have only gradually - and sometimes hesitantly - moved towards a stronger emphasis on business; they have also made less effort to popularize their content. In conclusion we can say that positions in the national media orders have been reflected in business and economic content of newspapers, as regards both its timing and the nature of its transformation.

Do national media orders exert an influence in a more general sense, i.e. by constraining or enabling the overall development of business and economic news in national contexts? Here our evidence is weaker, but we have found indications of national trajectories. Thus the niche/general-interest divide seems to be much clearer in Finland than in the other countries studied, perhaps due to the unique status of *Helsingin Sanomat* in the national media order. In our present context *Helsingin Sanomat* has maintained a very broad general-interest orientation throughout, while *Kauppalehti* maintained a distinct and specialized niche profile until it suddenly embarked on a strategy of popularization. This pattern is less marked in Sweden, where *Dagens Industri* started at a late stage as a rather technical newspaper with a focus on industry, and then gradually developed into a specialized business newspaper with a more popular orientation. In Denmark, there seems to have been greater convergence between *Børsen*, which was less specialized than its Finnish and Swedish counterparts, and *Berlingske Tidende*, which like *Svenska Dagbladet* has always had an interest in business issues. Norway, on its part, stands out as having the lowest level of specialization and the strongest trend towards popularization, which suggests that the pattern of niche versus general-interest in Norway is perhaps the least sedimented among the four Nordic countries.

A quantitative content analysis focusing on a limited number of outlets at particular times is bound to raise as many questions as it answers. In our case the present sample has made it possible to ascertain some general trends in the way the content has developed in the Nordic business press. However, many other issues need to be looked into in future content analyses. Here we will mention only a few. First, it is necessary to consider more outlets and platforms in the business press to get a more detailed picture of how positions emerge and become transformed in this field. Our analysis has focused on the specialized business newspapers and the national general-interest newspapers, but, as we noted in Chapter 2, weekly, bi-weekly and monthly magazines all seem to play an important part in the innovation of this field, at least in Norway and Sweden. Also, today web-based platforms constitute a major challenge to the 'old' business press in all four countries.

Secondly, it is necessary to look at the more detailed movement of platforms over time. With our emphasis on ten-year intervals, we get a smooth path of development without too many reversals or effects of the business cycle when we examine changes in content volume, formats or orientations. This may exaggerate the orderliness of the changes studied, as well as making it more difficult to identify critical turning-points in the history of the business press, for instance in connection with the first wave of expansion in the early 1970s or in the saturation phase in the business news market in the mid-1990s.

Thirdly and finally, we naturally need to move on from general content categories to the stories themselves to see how the qualitative features of business news content change and how, in conjunction with this, the dominant news frames and formats operate and change at the micro-level. But this is a question that will be addressed in the subsequent chapters.

Bibliography

Ainamo, A., E. Vaara, J. Tienari & N. Erkama (2004) The Rise of the Nordic Business Press. Some Preliminary Finnish Results, Unpublished report prepared for Nordic Workshop on the Business Press in Copenhagen, September 2004.

Barnes, F. (1998) The State of U.S. Financial Journalism. *International Economy*. Vol. 12 (4): 12-17.

Benson, R. (1998) Field Theory in Comparative Context: A New Paradigm for Media Studies. *Theory and Society* Vol. 28 (3): 463 – 498.

Benson, R. & E. Neveu (2005) *Bourdieu and the Journalistic Field*. Cambridge: Polity Press.

Bourdieu, P. (1993) *The Field of Cultural Production*. Cambridge: Polity Press.

Bringert, L. & B. Torekull (1995) *Äventyret Dagens Industri: Historien om en tidnings födelse*. Stockholm: Wahlström & Widstrand.

Cook, T. (1998) *Governing with the news. The news media as a political institution*. Chicago: Chicago University Press.

Davis, A. (2000) Public relations, business news and the reproduction of corporate elite power. *Journalism* Vol. 1 (3): 282-304.

Ekonomiska Samfundets Tidsskrift: Ekonomiska Samfundets Seminarium 15.1.2003, 2003, Vol. 56 (1).

Gavin, N. (Ed.) (1998) *The Economy, Media and Public Knowledge*. London, New York: Leicester University Press.

Goozner, M. (2000) Blinded by the Boom. What's Missing in the Coverage of the New Economy? *Columbia Journalism Review* November-December: 23-27.

Grafström, M. (2005) The Expansion and Change of Business News Content in Sweden, 1960-2000. Working Paper, Center for Business and Politics, Copenhagen Business School.

Grafström, M. (2006) The Development of Swedish Business Journalism. Historical Roots of an Organizational Field. Doctoral Thesis No. 121. Department of Business Studies, Uppsala University.

Henriques, D. B. (2000a) Business reporting. Behind the Curve. *Columbia Journalism Review* November/December: 18-21.

Henriques, D. B. (2000b) What Journalists Should Be Doing about Business Coverage--But Aren't. *The Harvard International Journal of Press/Politics* Vol. 5 (2): 118-121.

Herskedal, L. M. (2004) Research memo on Norwegian content analysis. Unpublished report prepared for Nordic Workshop on the Business Press in Copenhagen, September 2004.

Keat, R. & N. Abercrombie (1990) *Enterprise Culture*. London: Routledge.

Kjær, P. (2005) The evolution of business news in Denmark 1960-2000: context and content'. Working Paper, Center for Business and Politics, Copenhagen Business School.

Kjær, P. & R. Langer (2005) Infused with news value: Management, managerial knowledge and the institutionalization of business news. *Scandinavian Journal of Management* Vol. 21 (2): 209-233.

Lindhoff, H. (1998) Economic Journalism of the 1990's: The Crisis Discourses of Sweden. In Gavin, N. T. (Ed.) *The Economy, Media and Public Knowledge*. Leicester: Leicester University Press.

Mazza, C. & J. L. Alvarez (2000) Haute couture and prêt à porter: The popular press and the diffusion of management practices. *Organization Studies* Vol. 21 (3): 567-588.

Mazza, C. & J. S. Pedersen (2004) From press to E-media? The transformation of an organizational field. *Organization Studies* Vol. 25 (6): 875-895.

Parsons, W. D. (1989) *The Power of the Financial Press. Journalism and Economic Opinion in Britain and America*. Aldershot: Edward Elgar Press.

Powell, W. W. & P. J. DiMaggio (Eds.) (1991) *The New Institutionalism in Organizational Analysis*. Chicago: Chicago University Press.

Roush, C. (2004) *Show me the Money. Writing Business and Economic Stories for Mass Communication*. Mahwah: Lawrence Erlbaum Associates, Inc.

Scott, W. R. (1995) *Institutions and Organizations*. Thousand Oaks, CA: Sage.

Slaatta, T. (2003) *Den norske medieorden. Posisjoner og privilegier*. Oslo: Gyldendal Akademisk.

Vaara, E. & J. Tienari (2002) Justification, legitimization and naturalization of mergers and acquisitions: A critical discourse analysis of media texts. *Organization* Vol. 9 (2): 275-304.

Volden, K. (1996) Seddelpress i tabloid og rosa. In Gustafsson, Karl-Erik (Ed.) *Dagspresstrategier: För och nu*. Gothenburg: Mass Media Research Unit, School of Economics at Gothenburg University.

Welles, C. (2001) Writing About Business and the Economy. In Thompson, Terri (Ed.) *Writing About Business*. Colombia: Colombia University Press.

155

Appendix: Code Sheet for Coding of Newspapers

1 Identification
1.1 Article number (generated automatically)
1.2 Date
1.3 Newspaper name
1.4 Page
1.5 Front page?
   a) *Front page of newspaper*
   b) *Front page of section*
   c) *Not front page*
1.6 Text type (a)
   a) *News article*
   b) *Editorial comment*
   c) *External comment*
   d) *Economic information*
   e) *Reviews*
   f) *Other entertainment*
   g) *Formalia*
   h) *Picture*
   i) *News briefs*
   j) *Advertisements*
   k) *Announcements*
   l) *Other*

2 Text type (b) (Coding of specific text types within general text type categories)
2.1 News article
   a) *Feature*
   b) *Interviews*
   c) *News analysis*
2.2 Editorial comment
   a) *Editorial*
   b) *Internal expert analysis*
2.3 External comment
   a) *Reader's comments etc.*
   b) *External expert analysis*
   c) *Letter to the editor*
2.4 Economic information
   a) *Figures/statistics*
   b) *Charts*
   c) *Indexes*
   d) *Stock exchange comment*
2.5 Critics, reviews
   a) *Review articles*
   b) *Consumer tests/advice*
2.6 Other entertainment
   a) *Crosswords*
   b) *Humor*
   c) *Curiosa*
2.7 Formalia
   a) *Personalia*
   b) *Other*

3 Economic Article?
3.1 Economic article?
   a) *Yes, definitely economic article, article in economic section*
   b) *Yes, economy most important sub-theme*
   c) *No, economy only mentioned as minor sub-theme*
   d) *No, economic aspects not involved*

4 Economic Indicators (non-economic articles only)
4.1 Are there economic indicators in the article?
- *a)* *No, no economic indicators*
- *b)* *Yes, money and numbers*
- *c)* *Yes, agents*
- *d)* *Yes, products*
- *e)* *Yes, words such as prices, market, profit, management, etc.*
- *f)* *Yes, other*

5 Non-economic theme (non-economic articles only)
5.1 Non-economic theme
- *a)* *Politics*
- *b)* *Culture*
- *c)* *Sport*
- *d)* *Society*
- *e)* *Other*

6 Size and illustration (economic articles only)
6.1 Width
6.2 Length
6.3 Size 'As width x length (generated automatically)
6.4 Photo
- *a)* *Photo*
- *b)* *No photo*

6.5 Illustrations
- *a)* *Drawing*
- *b)* *Graph, numerical representation*
- *c)* *Other graphs*
- *d)* *Other visuals*
- *e)* *No illustration*

7 Dominant Theme, Sources, Agents (economic articles only)
7.1 Dominant theme (economic articles only)
- *a.* *Economic*
- *b.* *Non-economic*

7.2 Source number: (count 1 each time a new source is mentioned)
- *a)* *No sources*
- *b)* *1 source*
- *c)* *2-5 sources*
- *d)* *More than 5 sources*

7.3 Agent source number: (count 1 for each time a new agent or source is mentioned)
- *a)* *No agents*
- *b)* *1 agent*
- *c)* *2-5 agents*
- *d)* *More than 5 agents*

7.4 Agent source type
- *a.* *Governmental*
- *b.* *Private (firms etc.)*
- *c.* *Employer organization*
- *d.* *Employees organization*
- *e.* *Other NGOs*
- *f.* *Consumers*
- *g.* *Other ordinary people*

8 Theme and Sub-theme (economic articles only)

8.1 Theme:
- a) *Capital/investment*
- b) *Markets*
- c) *Production*
- d) *Labor*
- e) *Economic policy/regulation*
- f) *Legal affairs, crime*
- g) *Morals, ethics, responsibility, culture, personality etc.*
- h) *Health, environment*
- i) *Public policy, administration*
- j) *Portrait*
- k) *(Edit – add themes)*

8.2 Sub-theme:
- a) *No sub-theme*
- b) *Capital/investment*
- c) *Markets*
- d) *Production*
- e) *Labor*
- f) *Economic policy/regulation*
- g) *Legal affairs, crime*
- h) *Morals, ethics, responsibility, culture, personality etc.*
- i) *Health, environment*
- j) *Public policy, administration*
- k) *Portrait*
- l) *Politics (non-economic)*
- m) *Culture (arts, history, human sciences)*
- n) *Sport*
- o) *Society*
- p) *Other*
- q) *(Edit – add themes)*

9 Non-economic Main theme

9.1 Dominant non-economic theme
- a) *Politics*
- b) *Culture*
- c) *Sport*
- d) *Society*
- e) *Other*

9.2 Economic sub-theme
- a) *Capital/investment*
- b) *Markets*
- c) *Production*
- d) *Labor*
- e) *Economic policy/regulation*
- f) *Legal affairs, crime*
- g) *Morals, ethics, responsibility, culture, personality etc.*
- h) *Health, environment*
- i) *Public policy, administration*
- j) *Portrait*
- k) *(Edit – Add themes)*

10: Discourse

10.1 Discourse type (defined through correlation of audience target group/theme/agents)
- a) *Business, trade*
- b) *Macro economy (national/international economy trends etc)*
- c) *Owners/investors/finance/stock exchange market*
- d) *Public economy (government/public spending etc)*
- e) *Wages/labor/tariffs/conflicts*
- f) *Consumers, customers etc.*
- g) *Other, cannot be subsumed*

CHAPTER 6

Changing Constructions of Business and Society in the News

PETER KJÆR

Introduction

In mid-November 1960 the biggest business story in the Danish daily *Berlingske Tidende* was entitled 'It's all about carrots'. The article celebrated the 85th anniversary of the reclaiming of the Lammefjord coastal area some 75 kilometers west of Copenhagen:

> *Lammefjord first became famous a couple of generations ago in connection with the draining and transformation of the seabed into fertile arable land. Lammefjord then achieved nationwide fame for its fine asparagus, which has remained an important line of production. Then came the large-scale production of onions. And now, at last, carrots have become a major product of Lammefjord, commanding not only the Copenhagen market but even catering for carrot consumption throughout Denmark – in addition to a sizable export.*

Photographs of various aspects of carrot production - harvesting, storing, washing and quality control - accompanied the article, which included interviews with a carrot farmer, with the chairman of the local carrot producers' association, and with a Copenhagen vegetable wholesaler.

In mid-November 2000 the biggest business story in *Berlingske Tidende* was about the expansion into the Swiss market of the Danish telephone company, Tele Danmark (now TDC). The story generated several articles, the biggest of which, under the heading of 'Dyremose's billions', consisted of an interview with CEO Henning Dyremose. The article was introduced thus:

> *Next time there is a meeting of the Danish Federation of Industry, Tele Danmark CEO and DFI-board member Henning Dyremose will be able to tell the story of the biggest acquisition ever made by a Danish company. The readers of Berlingske Sunday can read the story here.*

Illustrating the article were two almost identical extreme close-ups of Dyremose. The caption for one of them read:

> *'Of all the telecommunications companies in Western Europe, Tele Danmark has shown the best development in earnings. But, sadly, this cannot be read from the stock market quotation', says Henning Dyremose.*

These two articles illustrate the main theme of the present chapter, namely the qualitative changes that have occurred in the way business is represented in the news. The articles differ not only in terms of their subject matter and the style of writing but also in the perspective adopted. Thus the 1960 article positioned its story as part of a long historical narrative of progress, pitching it among other things as a story of man's struggle against nature and depicting an entire community devoted to the development of its carrot production. The 2000 article, instead, positioned its story in a contemporary or perhaps even a future context, focusing on the relationship between management decisions and the market, and emphasizing the CEO and the stakeholders with whom he engaged himself on behalf of his firm. A communal approach to work and economic progress seems to have been replaced by a more individualistic approach and an emphasis on performance.

One way of capturing the changing perspective in the news about business and the economy is to note the increasing dominance of 'finance' (Parsons 1989, Lindhoff & Mårtensson 1996, Davis 2000, Kjær & Langer 2005, Doyle 2006). After a period during which news reporting on the economy was concerned with broader economic issues, 'economy' has come to be equated not only with business, but also increasingly with the financial aspects of business, while other more 'social' aspects of the economy - labor market relations, industrial policy, social policy and so on – have been marginalized (see also Kjær, Erkama & Grafström in the present volume).

This observation has led many critics to conclude that business journalism today is remote from the traditional ideals of journalism, since business journalism is no longer concerned with the description and interpretation of current events on behalf of the public, but has come to target a far more select audience and a particular set of issues and interests (Davis 2000, Slaatta 2003). While such a conclusion may be justified, it also begs the question of the actual nature of the financial perspective on business and the economy. What is a financial perspective, how did such a one evolve, and how does it affect business journalism? Has it managed to turn away from 'society' in the process of becoming the dominant perspective in business and economic news? These are the questions that the present chapter will attempt to answer.

Conceptions of Control and the Practice of Business Journalism

My analysis is inspired by Fligstein's notion of 'conceptions of control'. This concept was introduced in Fligstein's book *The Transformation of Corporate Control* (1990) which describes the historical emergence and institutionalization of different conceptions of the business enterprise in America. Fligstein identifies four conceptions of control, the most recent of which is the finance conception:

> *The finance conception of the modern corporation, which currently dominates, emphasizes control through the use of financial tools which measure performance according to profit rates (...) Firms are viewed as collections of assets earning differing rates of return, not as producers of given goods* (Fligstein 1990: 15).

In contrast to earlier conceptions of control – 'Direct Control', 'The Manufacturing Conception of Control', 'The Sales and Marketing Conception of Control' (Fligstein 1990: 12ff) – the finance conception focuses strictly on financial performance; it is concerned with financial assets, not with production sites or places of work, nor with particular products or the relations within a particular industry. While earlier conceptions emphasized problems of integration (direct control), productivity and planning (manufacturing) or market expansion (sales and marketing), the finance conception emphasizes financial returns.

Fligstein's historical analyses of how conceptions of control become institutionalized suggest that while conceptions of control are to be seen as ideational constructs, they do have significant social implications. They inform state regulation, they contribute to the organization of particular organizational fields, and they become widely diffused, affecting what are conceived as legitimate organizational and managerial practices in concrete organizations.[1]

Focusing on the way business journalists have come to draw upon a financial conception of control, we become aware of two important aspects of journalism. First, journalists represent a variety of phenomena, and in doing so they draw on particular perspectives that allow them to make sense of events and situations. Thus, in the context of conceptions of control, the expansion of business journalism does not only put 'business' on the agenda, it also becomes informed by a particular conception of business that involves specific notions of what a firm is, how it relates to its environment and what constitutes good performance on its part. Second, the act of representing is also constitutive of what it represents. Journalism is a discursive practice, and as such it is 'constitutive of society, not only in the traditional sense of reproducing established power relations, but in its socially constructive role' (Ekecrantz 1997: 393). While journalists may be predominantly concerned with events, with reporting and interpreting current affairs, in the course of doing so they also construct society.

Business journalism is a practice that contributes to the definition and legitimization of particular social identities, relations and practices (Fairclough 1995, Gavin 1998, Vaara & Tienari 2002, Risberg, Tienari & Vaara 2003, see also Tienari, Vaara and Erkama in the present volume). While the finance perspective in business journalism may have marginalized other perspectives that are conventionally regarded as 'social', a 'society' is still being produced on the business pages. The Tele Danmark article cited above identifies certain actors as legitimate, certain ways in which problems and issues are resolved among these actors, and certain ideas about the past and the future of the actors and the relations described. The question is not thus whether a finance perspective has come to ignore society; rather, it is what conception of society has it put in place of those that preceded it?

To answer this question, we must subject the discourse of business journalism to empirical analysis.

Fairclough (1995) has proposed a multilevel approach to the analysis of media discourse, one that distinguishes between texts, discursive practices and social practices. According to this approach, a communicative event, such as a particular news item, should be analyzed as a single text, as a 'moment' of discursive practice, i.e. as an element in a chain of texts defined by theme, genre or similar, and as being consti-

---

[1] See also DiMaggio (1991) and Kjær (1996) for similar analyses of the historical development and institutionalization of conceptions of management and organization. See Meyer and Rowan (1991 [1977]) for an early contribution to the debate.

tutive of and constituted by broader social practices. Fairclough thus attempts to span textual analysis, discourse analysis and cultural-social analysis while maintaining a particular focus on communicative events.

Following Foucault (1972), Fairclough is interested in discerning the 'order of discourse' which he defines as 'the totality of its discursive practices, and the relationships (of complementarity, inclusion/exclusion, opposition) between them' (Fairclough 1993). In other words, media discourse analysis allows us to identify the constitutive effects of the discursive practices of the mass media in terms of the way they order representations of reality and constitute particular social identities and define the relations among them.

In my present analysis, the order of discourse of journalism will be defined as the *perspective* drawn upon and produced by a discursive practice. Orders of discourse may involve a multiplicity of discursive distinctions and relations, but the present analysis will focus on the 'society of the news', that is to say how a chain of news texts make particular distinctions that constitute social identities and relations in particular ways. I will focus on three sets of distinctions, namely distinctions pertaining to social change (e.g. concerning past, present and future), distinctions pertaining to the nature of social relations (e.g. whether relations are harmonious or conflictual) and, finally, distinctions pertaining to social identities (e.g. who are the key social actors and entities).[2]

In contrast to Fairclough's insistence that media texts are both constitutive of and constituted by broader social practices, my emphasis will be on the constitutive effects of business journalism itself. The question of how broader discourses and institutional arrangements make their imprint on the practice of business journalism is thus beyond the scope of the present analysis (but see earlier chapters and the following chapter in this volume, and Tienari, Vaara & Björkman 2003).

Methodology

The present analysis will not engage in a detailed linguistic analysis of individual news texts but will take the discursive practice of business journalism as its object of analysis. Empirically, the analysis examines

---

[2] These analytical distinctions are inspired by Ekecrantz and Olsson's analysis of time, agency and order in journalistic texts in Sweden from the 1920s onwards (Ekecrantz & Olsson 1994, Ekecrantz 1997), and by Pedersen et al.'s analyses of events, time and actors in political news narratives in Denmark (Pedersen, Kjær, Esmark, Horst & Carlsen 2000).

a collection of news texts broadly concerned with business and economy in order to capture historical changes in business journalism.

The database for the analysis is a sample of news articles published the Danish conservative newspaper *Berlingske Tidende*. As a business-oriented newspaper *Berlingske Tidende* is a newspaper 'in the middle' (Kjær 2005). Unlike *Helsingin Sanomat* in Finland, for example, *Berlingske Tidende* is not dominant in the general-interest segment as a whole, and unlike some of the niche outlets, it was not a first mover in the recent development of business news. However, during the 1970s and since, it has employed several outstanding business journalists and has earned a reputation as a solid, albeit somewhat conservative, producer of business news.

The sample consisted of 105 articles from seven issues of *Berlingske Tidende* from 1960, 1980 and 2000 respectively (the second week in November each year). The 5 longest news articles dealing with 'business and economy' were selected from each issue.[3] Since the meaning of 'Business and economy' has changed over time, the selection has encompassed articles on 'business', 'economy' 'trade', 'commerce', 'industry' or 'finance' etc. identified by the name used in the heading of newspaper sections, pages or articles concerned. The 'news article' category covers features, news briefs, news analysis, background articles, stock market reports, shipping reports, but not editorials, commentaries, letters to the editor etc., which belong to rather different genres.

The material was first coded with the help of a simple qualitative code sheet that recorded how the individual articles referred to events, themes, actors, contexts or roles of business and journalists.[4] This first coding made it possible to group the articles in three broad thematic clusters, 'Danish business and economy', mainly concerned with events involving Danish firms, industries or sectors as actors or objects of attention; 'International business and economy', dealt mainly with events involving foreign countries, international organizations or large companies, and 'Economic policy and regulation' dealt mainly with policymaking within the framework of the Danish government while

---

[3] Estimates of size including illustrations. The selection procedure obviously entails a certain bias, since the total number of articles on business and economy was much smaller in 1960 than in 1980 and 2000. Thus, in a few cases, the material from the 1960s includes newsbriefs, while the material from 2000 contains a significant share of background articles and news analyses, which tend to be longer than the average feature news article. The sample is not representative of news articles as such, but does represent the articles that seem to have been prioritized by the newspaper on given days.

[4] The code sheet can be found in Appendix A.

also taking labor market negotiations into account. In each group I have noted whether the coverage of business and economy seemed to embrace a finance conception of control. Here I used two indicators of a finance conception: the extent to which the coverage was oriented towards financial institutions as opposed to other economic actors, and the extent to which there was an interest in financial performance as opposed to other measures of performance such as productivity, employment or market shares.

On a basis of this first analysis, ten stories from each year were subjected to a second analysis based on a closer reading to identify conceptions relating to change, conflict or identity. This sub-sample consisted of longer articles from the 'Danish business and economy' group that concerned business.[5] The sub-sample represents the largest group of articles each year. The reading of these articles focused on the three following sets of questions:

- What is the notion of *change* in the text? Any news text must position its news story in a particular temporal context whereby the specific events make sense as part of a greater sequence of events. In concrete terms this entails considering how the text brings in notions of development, change, progress, crisis, etc.
- What is the notion of *order/conflict* in the text? Empirically, the emphasis here is on whether events are construed as conflicts, and if so how these conflicts are described and how they are resolved.
- What is the notion of social *identities* in the text? Who are the actors involved in or affected by a particular event or issue and how are these actors and their actions described?

Given the limitation to only three periods of time - during 1960, 1980 and 2000 - the analysis does not allow for a detailed analysis of any more subtle developments (or reversals) over time, but it does enable us to develop an extrapolated portrayal of the way the constitution of 'society' has been transformed in the news with the advent of a financially oriented type of news journalism.

Below I present the results of these two analyses. The first which is built on the larger text sample is organized diachronically and concerns the different conceptions of control in the coverage of business and economy since 1960. The second builds on the smaller sample of busi-

---

[5] These articles are listed in Appendix B.

ness-oriented texts. It is organized synchronically and describes changes in the three analytical categories - change, conflict and identity - described above.

Business and Economy News in 1960, 1980 and 2000

The three thematic groups - 'Danish business and economy', 'International business and economy', and 'Economic policy and regulation' – have all developed in significant ways over the last five decades. However, the 'Danish business and economy' theme has been the most prominent throughout the years, and has even grown in importance over time.

In 1960, the articles concerned with Danish business and economy represent more than half the articles sampled. Two types of article appear. On the one hand we have news articles concerned with development and planning in specific firms, industries or regions for instance in exports or industrial development, as exemplified by the 'It's all about carrots' story. On the other hand there are routine reports on the stock exchange, etc., which stick to a regular formula, describing the 'mood' of the market, detailing the major deals and prices of the day (or week), and listing rates etc., all using a lot of technical jargon. The articles concerned with international business and economy that constitute roughly one-fifth of the sampled articles also contain two types of articles. Most are them are concerned with news about international trade policy or international business events, such as events connected with 'The Seven' (The European Economic Community), East-West relations or big multinational corporations. But there are also routine reports on international commerce, perhaps about shipping rates or fuel prices, similar in style to the stock exchange reports mentioned above. The articles on economic policy and regulation answer for another one-fifth of the articles, and are mostly concerned with the labor market or government policy in Denmark.

Almost all the stories focus mainly on work, production and trade, thus apparently informed by a manufacturing conception of control. Most of the very numerous articles concerned with particular firms and industries take up problems connected with product or process development or with domestic and foreign trade, while the regular reports are devoted to trading in goods or stock. The foreign news reports are concerned primarily with various aspects of international trade. News about economic policy and regulation are also concerned with work, production and trade, perhaps about how a new labor market settlement will improve the efficiency of Danish industry, or how tax laws affect investments in 'our' industry. Finance only surfaces in routine reports about trading on the Danish Stock Exchange and, in a few instances, about the level of investment in industry.

In 1980 articles on business and economy in Denmark also represent about half the sampled articles. Whereas the typical 1960 story on Danish business and economy wrote of expansion and modernization, the typical 1980 story exuded a much more pessimistic mood. One of the big stories of the week was concerned with the restructuring of the food industry, and about the fierce resistance of the independent retailers to various attempts at merging meatpacking firms and creating a new and more centralized distribution system. Other articles describe the crisis in the fishing industry, and the search for alternatives. The number of articles concerned with international economic affairs has become relatively small, comprising a mere 3-4 articles describing international economic forecasts and economic policy developments in the United States and Sweden. Articles on Danish economic policy and regulation now represent about one-third of the articles, and these include articles on new legislation regarding mortgage loans and taxation, on the negotiation of oil concessions in the North Sea and on the struggle among local political actors to secure the survival of a Danish ferry-line.

Most stories now concentrate on competitiveness, employment and wages, emphasizing macro-economic balance in addressing concrete issues. To a manufacturing conception of control a sales and marketing conception of control now seems to have been added with an emphasis on market shares, competitiveness and demand management. The numerous articles dealing with the crisis in particular industries and firms and the associated restructurings thus take up the question of competitiveness – whether it is lacking or has been acquired – while also looking at the way in which particular economic and political decisions affect production and employment locally or nationally. Similarly, articles on public policy and labor market relations are concerned with the implications of policy decisions and settlements on factors such as income levels, the employment level or the national balance of payments. Once again finance is a marginal concern. None of the sampled articles are concerned with the Stock Exchange. A few articles look at mortgage loans and pensions, but they focus either on the need for consumer protection or the concerns of the mortgage and real estate business as an industry. Ownership issues are considered in a few instances, for instance in stories on mergers and acquisitions but then only as a means for enhancing industrial competitiveness.

In 2000, articles on Danish business and industry constitute almost two-thirds of the sampled articles. Most articles in this group describe the development and strategies of particular firms, and how various external actors, usually stock analysts, evaluate their performance. There are several articles on Danish firms 'going abroad', i.e. acquiring foreign subsidiaries, establishing partnerships or attempting to enter financial markets abroad. The main story of the week is the expansion of Tele Danmark into the Swiss market. There are also several articles on the Danish financial sector. About one-sixth of the sampled articles deal with international business and economy. These articles are mainly concerned with issues relating to international trade regulation (WTO) and international business trends. Another one-sixth of the articles are about Danish economic policy, regulation, etc. Articles in this category describe changes in state subsidies to subscription medicine, changes in the tax system and liberalization of shopping hours.

Finance is a key concern in more than half the sampled articles, especially in the big group of articles dealing with individual firms. Some articles are specifically concerned with financial institutions such as banks or insurance companies, but finance appears mainly when a firm's decisions are being viewed in relation to their owners/shareholders or to stock market expectations. There are many articles on market opportunities, mergers and acquisitions or new management appointments, but now – unlike the 1980-articles - the initiatives, decisions, reactions, etc. are no longer seen primarily in relation to competitiveness, employment or the national economy, but instead to returns on investment, risks or new players in the field of financial investment. This concern with finance is revealed in the articles on individual firms that now regularly include graphics depicting the financial standing of the firm in question in terms of its annual turnover, its capital base, its stock market performance and even in some cases surveys of the sell recommendations of stock market analysts. As indicated, not all articles are geared towards finance. There are still articles on new products and new markets, and others on public regulation and international trade, that are concerned either with market expansion or production or consumer protection, or with social responsibility and the environment. However, compared to the articles on finance, such articles are less numerous and generally appear singly, whereas finance stories often entail a series of news and/or background articles.

Thus, taken as a whole, the overall content of business and economic news has changed dramatically since 1960. Not only has the share increased for articles dedicated to Danish business and industry, and in particular for those articles dealing with individual firms, but more significantly from our point of view is the observation that between 1980 and 2000 finance has become an important concern in a majority of the sampled articles. Interpreted in terms of Fligstein's notion of conceptions of control, the transformation in content suggests that the coverage of business and economy has shifted from a 'manufacturing' and 'sales and marketing' conception of control, towards a finance conception. While the first two conceptions were concerned with efficiency, market expansion (e.g. market shares), and competitiveness, the latter is preoccupied with the financial returns generated by firms regarded as financial assets. In 1960 and 1980, most of the news stories about business and industry were concerned with industrial development, productivity, employment and competitiveness in the domestic and the international markets. Finance was a peripheral issue dealt with in routine stock market reports or treated as a minor aspect of stories concerned with other issues. In 2000, most news stories about business and industry regard financial performance as a key concern, even when writing about other issues.

Notions of Change, Conflict and Identity in Business News

We will now examine the discursive practice of business news journalism, in greater detail, using a smaller sample of 30 lengthy articles on business and economy and looking especially at the way in which business news has changed over time with the advent of the finance conception of control.[6] The analysis is organized synchronically, first describing how articles deal with change, then how they deal with conflict, and finally how they look at the various social actors and the relations between them in each of the three years studied.

Change

> *In a few years time, a new industrial city is going to be built on a reclaimed two-square-kilometer area in the middle of the Bay of Køge. In a few months time, excavators and bulldozers will start shifting the embankments about one-and-a-half kilometers into the sea and wrest valuable building sites from it (1960).*

---

[6] An article-by-article reading of the discursive transformation of business journalism can found in Appendix B. It should be noted that articles characterized by a finance conception of control constitute 8 out of the 10 articles in the sample for 2000. The two remaining articles were concerned with consumer issues.

Through the closer cooperation that is coming, the slaughter-houses can help to improve the current crisis economy in Denmark's extensive pork production (...). Hans O. Kjeldsen, president of the Danish Agricultural Council, had just been emphasizing that slaughterhouses and dairies must abandon their internal quarrels and raise their compensation to the farmers, if the current crisis is to be dealt with (1980).

Carlsberg's one-year action plan now seems to be bearing fruit. The collaboration with Orkla [a major Norwegian investor], which has created a solid growth platform, is approved of by analysts all over the world, who regard Carlsberg as one of the few breweries that will survive in the beer business of the future (2000).

The notion of change in business news shifts from an emphasis on more or less uninterrupted progress through the rationalization of business and on towards a much more troubled conception of change in 1980, followed in 2000 by a view emphasizing the strategic pursuit of business opportunities.

Every business news article in our 1960 sample is a testimony to progress. In stories about individual businesses – for example a small aviation firm, a large shipbuilder or a giant consumer cooperative - the firms are portrayed as vigorously pursuing a strategy of technical development, specialization and rationalization. In stories about groups of firms or other actors such as chambers of commerce or business associations, there is an emphasis on the constant quest for rationalization and expansion, for overcoming obstacles by way of planning and rational decision-making. Such quests are usually successful, in the end. Just a few articles address rather more problematic situations: falling exports, weak demand for particular products, or industrial conflict. In the first two cases the causes are depicted as externally given, simply calling for a rational adaptation to altered circumstances, whereas industrial conflict necessitates another type of response (see below), since rationalization itself seems to be part of the problem here.

Almost all the articles in the 1980 sample describe the struggle for survival in a profoundly depressed economy. In contrast to the 1960 stories of progress, the future here is bleak and resistance to change is strong. Agricultural producers turn to concentration as a survival strategy, but they face austere market conditions and internal opposition.

Retailers issue credit cards to counteract moves on the part of the banks that would entail new costs in the retail sector. A small factory struggles to get new orders, but faces unfair international competition, while a large IT-producer desperately needs public procurement. Meanwhile the government is introducing new legislation that only increases the uncertainty in the affected industries. Admittedly there are some successes as new business opportunities arise - wood-burning furnaces, corporate head-hunting or private pension schemes for instance - but every such opportunity seems to involve new potential for opportunism or conflict.

In 2000, the idea of growth seems to have been securely re-installed, but quite often without the more general promises of progress that marked 1960. In 2000 all firms in fact do their best to develop and exploit market opportunities, usually measured in terms of stock or shareholder value. Some market opportunities were triggered by new ideas among entrepreneurs, while others emerged with structural changes in particular industries where mergers and acquisitions became a profitable strategy for expansion. New opportunities were also created by political decisions. In 1980, political decisions had largely been a hindrance to business development, while in 2000 political decisions were creating new opportunities by changing property rights or sanctioning specific types of behavior.

Conflict

There are strikes or slowdowns at several cooperative slaughterhouses. They began at the Odense Export Slaughterhouse [Odense Eksportslagteri] almost a week ago. Work stopped because people were dissatisfied with the piece rates. Yesterday the Standing Court of Arbitration discussed this strike and gave a preliminary verdict that it was illegal and that work was to recommence immediately (1960).

Conflicts between agriculture and groceries over the principles for the distribution of perishable goods are behind the struggle about [the firm of] Lund & Rasmussen. A struggle, the result of which may have great implications for many groceries and for the consumers (1980).

Bioscan, which produces systems for transforming manure into water and energy, is now considering going on the stock exchange

*in the USA and Japan within the next three to five years.
'Unlikely', says analyst Peter Falk Sørensen from Danish Stock
Analysis [Dansk Aktieanalyse]* (2000).

It would be premature to conclude from the stories of progress in 1960 that there was no conflict. However, conflict was rarely an explicit feature. Several stories indicate the obstacles that can hinder rationalization and progress. In the story of the aviation firm, the entrepreneur had to convince people about the potential for aviation in a modern society; in the cooperative movement story, the highly decentralized structure seemed to be an obstacle to planned change. Other stories show traces of a more mythical conflict between man and nature, for instance in stories about how coastal areas were reclaimed from the sea or how the B&W Shipyard was testing a new diesel engine. In each case conflict was overcome by rational argument, planning or scientific experiment. As we have noted, conflicts are rarely overt, except in a few spectacular cases. In the story about industrial conflict in the meat-packing industry, the article refers to a series of direct confrontations regarding rationalization, working hours and management. However, the article also mentions how the conflict can be resolved by the institutions of the labor market. Even the story of the carrot producers mentions a series of conflicts between the local producers' association and the fishermen, or between wholesalers and the authorities. Things seem to have been resolved either by reinforcing local cooperation or through intervention on the part of the authorities.

In 1980 conflict is everywhere. Whereas most conflicts in 1960 could be regarded up to a point as irrational – as obstacles to progress or the persistence of the 'past' – conflicts are a pervasive feature of the news in 1980. Almost every news story involve a conflict of interests – between large and small producers, banks and retailers, new and old producers, domestic and foreign producers, the interests of firms and those of individual managers, or the interests of banks and those of consumers. The problem, however, is that there are no straightforward solutions. Most conflicts have to be fought out in the market or, sometimes, politically. But there is no guarantee that a resolution is at hand, even in the long run. Thus even when there is political intervention, the outcome may be new conflicts – as when the government attempts to reform the legislation regarding mortgage loans.

In 2000 there is also an abundance of conflict, but now it is less a question of conflicts of interest so much as conflicts of interpretation. Several stories about individual companies describe in detail how the

expectations of management collide with views held by 'the market' -
almost always a metaphor for stock market analysts or, more rarely,
for key investors: the Bioscan bio-tech firm is thus criticized for its 'intransparency', while Tele Danmark's move into the Swiss market trig-
gers a reluctant market reaction. Sometimes the conflict is not a conflict only between firm and market but also between entrepreneurs
(amateurs) and experts (professionals), whereby the entrepreneur
represents visions, innovative ideas, etc., while the experts either are
insightful or just plain skeptical. How are such conflicts to be resolved? In most cases they aren't, and it is simply assumed that 'the
market' - in this case the investors - will prove who was right or who
was wrong. Sometimes other options seem possible: in the case of a
large utility company facing consumer criticism and in the case of the
controversy over an attempted take-over in the real estate business,
further negotiations, court settlements or government intervention
seem to offer possible resolution. In the case of 'intransparency' in the
insurance market, resolution is to be found not through government intervention but through negotiation between the Minister of Economic
Affairs and representatives of the insurance industry. Generally, however, conflicts of interpretation remain open – to be resolved through
the financial markets.

Identities

*On Wednesday Burmeister & Wain will conclude the trial run of
the first out of six 10-cylinder diesel engines of the 84-VT2BF-180
(...) While the '84, which is its pet name among the Christian-
shavn professionals, is being packed and shipped to one of the
leading personalities in Norwegian shipping, shipowner Sigval
Bergesen JR, B&W has now seriously inaugurated its new 28-
meter high and, 23-meter wide and 90-meter long testing hall
(1960).*

*Many of the firms that saw their chance of getting out of financial
difficulties in the fall of 1979 by throwing themselves into the production of wood furnaces have already closed down, and the rest
are seriously threatened. Wood furnaces did not become the life-
saver that the distressed manufacturers had hoped for when the
great demand for them opened a year or so ago (1980).*

> *Play off. ['] Without a crown in his pocket and equipped only with a god-given talent for sales, the totally unknown photocopier salesman John Rasmussen Troll created in seven years a business worth billions, and known as Memory Card Technology. With his life's work now in pawn to the banks Trolle seems to be finished as a salesman – perhaps a victim of his own inflated sales talk (2000).*

The 'subject' of the 1960 articles is often some kind of collective: a group of concerned actors developing industrial plots; a group of engineers testing a large engine; the cooperative movement; the fishing industry; the Lammefjord carrot producers; Denmark as a whole. Even in the case of the aviation-entrepreneur, pronouns such as 'one' or 'we' are frequently used to signal the communal nature of the enterprise. In most cases these collectives engage in grand projects of industrial modernization. Similarly, the article on the Danish chamber of commerce in Belgium goes into detail about the individual life story of the Danish consul, but also refers persistently to 'Denmark', 'Danes' and occasionally 'Scandinavia' as actors desiring to export, to expand and so on. There are exceptions, however: the article on the meat-packing strikes refers not to a single collective, but to conflicts between collectives: the collective of workers confronting the employers.

In 1980 we find collectives being challenged in various ways. Whereas the 1960 articles occasionally mention outsiders, opponents of the current process of modernization, the struggle in 1980 between big and small is predominant. Big business entities driven by grand schemes for expansion and concentration clash with (usually) smaller entities representing a wide range of interests: individual firms struggling to survive, established businesses seeking to maintain quality standards, or ordinary people enticed by the promise of 'easy money'. In a few cases the roles are reversed: sometimes the state is pictured as the Leviathan that – perhaps unwittingly - is damaging business and the general public with its bureaucracy or its inattentiveness. The only actor seemingly representing society as a whole is the occasional expert who speaks out against some particular development trend.

In 2000 stories usually revolve around the 'strategist', be it an entrepreneur or an established business corporation that is seeking to exploit some business potential. Strategists of this kind are not lone players, but are always faced by challenge from 'the market': investors,

---

[7] The Danish term is 'slutspil' which in a literal translation also means 'final game' or 'game over'.

competitors or consumers. It is interesting to note that stock analysts, albeit used extensively as expert commentators, are also sometimes regarded as part of the game - particularly if they have proved to be wrong. Finally, the state is no longer seen as a barrier to the workings of the market, but as an agent in creating or expanding it, or even representing the interests of 'the market', as in the case of the insurance industry and its lack of transparency. Whereas the actors' problem in 1960 lay in overcoming obstacles to modernization and in 1980 of surviving in an unjust world, the problem in 2000 seems have been one of communication: of demonstrating to 'the market' one's own credibility as a strategist. Communication seems to have assumed a variety of forms: direct negotiations, public displays of responsiveness, or simply 'transparency', i.e. opening oneself to scrutiny by 'the market'.

Discussion: The order of Business News Discourse

In the previous sections I first identified the changing content of business news, and showed how reporting on business and economy has changed over time as regards its predonderent perspective: from a manufacturing or sales and marketing perspective in 1960 and 1980 to a finance perspective in 2000. Articles in the first two of these years tended to emphasize efficiency, employment, market shares and macro-economic performance, while the majority of articles in 2000 - and certainly most of those concerned with business issues - emphasized financial performance and financial institutions.

I then attempted to identify changes in notions of change, conflict and identity between 1960 and 2000 in order to describe how the 'society' to which the news belonged had been transformed as a financial conception of control became more evident in the news. The following Table summarizes the main findings of this second part of the analysis:

	Change	Conflict	Identity
1960:	The modernization project	Obstacles to progress – resolved through planning, authority or education	Collectives in pursuit of modernization
1980:	Struggle for survival in a hostile environment	Conflicts of interest – with no immediate resolution in sight	Challenged collectives
2000:	Strategic pursuit of business opportunities	Conflicts of interpretation to be settled ultimately by the market	Strategists and markets

Table 6.1: Society in the News, 1960, 1980 and 2000

In 1960, business news articles position business as part of a collective pursuit of industrial modernization, where obstacles are typically associated with the past or with something outside the direct control of the agents involved (the world economy), and where conflicts are rarely explicit and are usually relegated to particular arenas outside the business world or are simply resolved through rational argumentation, planning, or scientific experimentation. In 1980, business finds itself in the tragic position of having to pursue its interests and attempting to survive in a hostile environment characterized by fierce opposition, unjust competition and arbitrary regulation, and where small actors seem to be fighting a losing battle against big business and, sometimes, against the government. Finally, in 2000 business news articles are concerned with business strategists in conflict with 'the market' on questions of interpretation, which compels them to communicate via negotiation, by symbolic action, or by assuming transparency.

The analysis allows us to consider some of the implications of an increasingly financial conception of control in business news, and it shows that although financial markets and financial activities did get some attention in the news in 1960 and 1980, the notions of change, conflict and social identities at the time were not associated with finance. In 2000, however, the notion of change and of conflict, and the depiction of (business) identities, were all typically informed by a finance perspective: growth is considered mainly in terms of share prices or revenues, and obstacles to growth are interpreted in light of the financial situation of the firms concerned. Similarly, conflicts are depicted as a game of confidence between firms and possible investors (although other actors may also take part in it), and the main expectations to which firms are exposed are connected with market strategy, responsiveness to investor interests and transparency in face of external (financial) scrutiny.

The emphasis on 'the market' is indicative of a change in the order of discourse of business news, that is to say the way in which it constitutes social relations and social identities. In 1960, society was largely represented as an unquestioned (national) community in which all the main actors were embedded, each one playing their own part. The main conflicts were either part of the struggle between man (society) and outside forces (nature, other countries, etc.), in which case firms and entrepreneurs simply represented the side of society, or in the case of industrial or legal conflicts they were conflicts of interest, where it was generally assumed that a joint solution restoring social order to everybody's benefit could be found. In 1980, we find innumerable conflicts between competing versions of social or industrial order. Social order was something that was hoped for, but the hopes were often frustrated. In 2000 we find islands of 'negotiated order' around firms within a state-secured market framework.[8] 'Society' as a national community had largely disappeared from view, while the 'market' had come to represent the environment in which firms and other actors are compelled to engage, and within which particular communities of interest and particular social relations are defined and enacted. However, the problem seems to be that the market does not speak for itself, so that the main challenge becomes that of giving voice to 'the market'. In a world where firms-cum-strategists are constantly launching their interpretations of market opportunity, or of demands or challenges, business journalists have to look for those who, like stock analysts or anonymous investors, speak for the 'market'.[9] At the same time, it might be added, the challenge to firms and organizations becomes one of managing interpretations, i.e. helping to form organizational images, corporate reputations or legitimacy.[10]

Davis (2000) described the financially oriented business journalism as now largely an insiders game, acted out in the news but largely irrelevant to the general public. This may have a certain element of truth to it, but the analysis in this chapter has perhaps also shown why it is important to pay close attention to how the discursive practice of business journalism still impacts the current state of 'society', albeit in a more limited, negotiated and perhaps fluid fashion than might be expected.

Thus journalism informed by a financial conception of control is oriented towards financial performance, financial evaluations of markets and assets; it also tends to regard economic actors as strategists in financial markets. Here finance represents a particular lens through which business issues are seen. Davis may be right in observing that this entails a reduction of business and economy news, since the 'society' implied is no longer a broad (national) community concerned with the public good, but a financial community with a much more particularized range of interests. Given the widespread presence of financially

---

[8] See also Kjær & Pedersen (2001).
[9] Research on the roles of various groups in giving voice to 'the market' is just beginning to emerge in a variety of contexts. Pollock & Rindova (2003) thus analyse the role of the media in shaping expectations regarding newcomers in financial markets, and Rindova, Pollock & Hayward (2006) analyse how the media help to produce 'celebrity firms'. Grafström et al. (2006) discuss the role of financial analysts in the production of business news, while Beunza & Garud (2004) look at the role of financial analysts as makers of 'calculative frames'.
[10] See e.g. Deephouse 2000, Morsing 1999, Hatch & Schultz 1997, Elsbach 1994.

oriented journalism it is important to look in greater detail at the worldview of financial journalism, and future studies could perhaps even pay closer attention to shifts within a specific financial conception of control. The present analysis has been based on the broad definition suggested by Fligstein, but - as Zorn et al. (2006) have noted - a more recent development can be observed in connection with the finance conception of control, namely the ideal of shareholder value that focuses on the relationship between stockholders and management. In this context it might also be interesting to consider the implications of the recent interest in 'corporate governance' (Engwall & Sahlin in the present volume) for the practice of business journalism and for the discursive order that it constitutes.

Equally important is that finance even becomes a way of re-articulating other concerns: environmentally safe products can be regarded as objects of financial investment, production plants can be seen as financial assets, consumer complaints can become a liability in communication with concerned shareholders, and state regulation can be evaluated in terms of analysts' perception of its effects on the market, rather than on the basis of the principles of government on which it builds. Thus the financial conception of control is not necessarily limited to financial institutions or business corporations, but may apply even in new and 'alien' contexts. Risberg (2005) describes how debates on public health care have been reconstituted as financial journalism has developed (see also Byrkjeflot and Angell in the present volume), but it seems equally possible that a financial conception of control may have been adopted in other sub-fields of journalism such as sports, arts and entertainment.

Lastly, in view of the diffusion of a finance conception of control and its many permutations, it should be noted that the analysis also speaks of *other* conceptions of control apart from the one that currently seems to be informing business journalism. The finance conception of control is one of the most recent in a line of such conceptions, and it therefore seems relevant to ask ourselves whether new conceptions are emerging in the wake of those we have noted here. The present analysis provides no clear indications, but even among the major business-oriented articles in our 2000 sample, there are some that are *not* informed by a finance conception but seem to be oriented more towards consumer interests. Whether consumption is emerging as a new conception of control, and whether it involves social relations and identities of a broader and perhaps more open-ended kind, remains to be discovered in the future analysis of business news.

Bibliography

Beunza, D. & R. Garud (2004) Security analysts as frame-makers. *UPF Economics and Business Working Paper No. 733.* Barcelona: Universitat Pompeu Fabra.

Davis, A. (2000) Public relations, business news and the reproduction of corporate elite power. *Journalism* Vol. 1 (3): 282-304.

Deephouse, D. L. (2000) Media Reputation as a Strategic Resource: An Integration of Mass Communication and Resource-Based Theories. *Journal of Management* Vol. 26 (6): 1091-1112.

DiMaggio, P. J. (1991) Constructing an organizational field as a professional project. US Art Museums 1920-1940. In Powell, Walter W. & Paul J. DiMaggio (Eds.) *The New Institutionalism in Organizational Analysis.* Chicago: Chicago University Press.

Doyle, G. (2006) Financial News Journalism: A Post-Enron Analysis of Approaches towards Economics and Financial News Production in the UK. Journalism: Theory, Practice & Criticism Vol. 7 (4): 433-452.

Ekecrantz, J. (1997) Journalism's discursive events and socio-political change in Sweden 1925-87. *Media, Culture and Society* Vol. 19 (3): 393-412.

Ekecrantz, J. & T. Olsson (1994) *Det redigerade samhället - om journalistikens, beskrivningsmaktens och det informerade förnuftets historia.* Stockholm: Carlssons.

Elsbach, K. D. (1994) Managing Organizational Legitimacy in the California Cattle Industry: The Construction and Effectiveness of Verbal Accounts. *Administrative Science Quarterly* Vol. 39: 57-88.

Fairclough, N. (1993) Critical discourse analysis and the marketization of public discourse: the universities. *Discourse and Society* Vol. 4 (2): 133-168.

Fairclough, N. (1995) *Media Discourse.* London: Edward Arnold.

Fligstein, N. (1990) *The Transformation of Corporate Control.* Cambridge MA: Harvard University Press.

Foucault, M. (1972) *The Archaeology of Knowledge.* New York: Pantheon Books.

Gavin, N. (Ed.) (1998) *The Economy, Media and Public Knowledge.* London, New York: Leicester University Press.

Grafström, M., J. Grünberg, J. Pallas & K. Windell (2006) *Ekonominyhetens väg. Från kvartalsrapporter till ekonominyheter.* Stockholm: SNS Förlag.

Hatch, M. J. & Shultz, M. (1997) Relations between Organizational Culture, Identity and Image *European Journal of Marketing* Vol. 31 (5): 356-365.

Kjær, P. (1996) The Constitution of Enterprise. An Institutional History of Inter-firm Relations in Swedish Furniture Manufacturing. Ph.D.-dissertation, Stockholm University.

Kjær, P. (2005) The evolution of business news in Denmark 1960-2000: context and content. *CBP-Working Paper* No. 15, Copenhagen Business School.

Kjær, P. & R. Langer (2005) Infused with news value: Management, managerial knowledge and the institutionalization of business news. *Scandinavian Journal of Management* Vol. 21(2): 209-233.

Kjær, P. & O. K. Pedersen (2001) Translating Liberalization. Neoliberalism in the Danish Negotiated Economy. In Campbell, John L. & Ove K. Pedersen (Eds.) *The Rise of Neoliberalism and Institutional Analysis.* Princeton: Princeton University Press.

Lindhoff, H. & B. Mårtensson (1996) Dagens ekonomi: 'Går Persson stiger räntan'. In Becker, Karin, Jan Ekecrantz, Eva-Lotta Frid & Tom Olsson (Eds.) *Medierummet.* Stockholm, Carlssons.

Meyer, J. W. & B. Rowan (1991) Institutionalized Organizations: Formal Structure as Myth and Ceremony. In Powell, W. W. & P. J. DiMaggio (Eds.) *The New Institutionalism in Organizational Analysis.* Chicago: Chicago University Press.

Morsing, M. (1999) The Media Boomerang: The Media's Role in Changing Identity by Changing Image. *Corporate Reputation Review* Vol. 2 (2): 116-136.

Parsons, W. D. (1989) *The Power of the Financial Press. Journalism and Economic Opinion in Britain and America.* Aldershot: Edgar Elgar Press.

Pedersen, O. K., P. Kjær, A. Esmark, M. Horst, E. Meier Carlsen (2000) *Politisk Journalistik.* Århus, Denmark: Forlaget Ajour.

Pollock, T. G. & V. P. Rindova (2003) Media Legitimation Effects in the Market for Initial Public Offerings. *Academy of Management Journal* Vol. 46 (5): 631-642.

Rindova, V. P., T. G. Pollock & M. L. A. Hayward (2006) Celebrity Firms: The Social Construction of Market Popularity. *Academy of Management Review* Vol. 31 (1): 50-71.

Risberg, A. (2005) The development of the Swedish health care media discourse during 1985-1995. Paper presented at the 23rd Standing Conference on Organizational Symbolism, Stockholm July 2005.

Risberg, A., J. Tienari & E. Vaara (2003) Making Sense of a Transnational Merger: Media Texts and the (Re)construction of Power Relations *Culture and Organization* Vol. 9(2): 121-137.

Slaatta, T. (2003) *Den norske medieorden. Posisjoner og privilegier.* Oslo: Gyldendal Akademisk.

Tienari, J., E. Vaara & I. Björkman (2003) Global Capitalism Meets National Spirit: Discourses in Media Text on a Cross-Border Acquisition. *Journal of Managent Inquiry* Vol. 12 (4): 377-393.

Vaara, E. & J. Tienari (2002) Justification, Legitimization and Naturalization of Mergers and Acquisitions: A Critical Discourse Analysis of Media Texts'. *Organization* Vol. 9 (2): 274-304.

Zorn, D., F. Dobbin, J. Dierkes & M-S. Kwok (2006) The New New Firm. Power and Sense-making in the Construction of Shareholder Value. *Nordiske Organisasjonsstudier* Vol. 8 (3): 41-68.

Appendix A:

Code sheet – qualitative analysis of 105 business stories from 1960, 1980, 2000

1. Title: *Main title of the article*
2. Event: *What seems to have triggered the article: a meeting, a report, a public statement*
3. Main actors: *Three main actors as they appear in the text as acting or speaking entities*
4. Place (arena): *Specific or unspecified. Domestic or international*
5. Main theme(s): *Keywords to the thematic content of article*
6. The role of the firm: *Keywords or quotes (if any) describing firms and industries*
7. The role of the journalist: *Critical/uncritical; use of sources; feature/background/analysis*
8. Other: *Use of visuals. Other observations*

Appendix B:

Coding of 30 large business-oriented stories from 1960, 1980, 2000

1960

Article	Change	Conflict	Identities
1.*Danfly expanding*	Specialization and rationalization.	Not prevalent. Making people realize potentials.	Entrepreneur. Initiative. Experience. (Hobby, philanthropic, business). 'One'.
2. *Industrial city in Køge Bay*	Expansion and planning.	Not prevalent. Man against nature.	Collective initiative. Plans. Decisions. Calculation. 'One'.
3. *Trial run of giant diesel engines at B&W*	Technical development. Rational testing. Planning.	Not prevalent.	Engineering plant. Overcoming difficulties. 'One'
4. *1500 mio turnover in Coop*	Expansion. Modernization. Rationalization.	Not prevalent. How to get small co-ops to modernize.	Movement.
5. *No new orders*	Shifts in the environment. Adaptation.	Fishing industry having industrialized but now face problems.	Industry. Carry on regardless. See what will be rational outcome.
6. *Roulund Factories sold to A.P. Møller Shipping*	Expansion and modernization. Historical origins.	Not prevalent.	Well-established firm. Corporation seeking objects for investment.
7. *Strikes and reduced tempo in a number of meatpacking factories*	Process of rationalization meets resistance.	Conflicts over piece rates, working hours and management. Partial settlement in Court of Arbitration. Peak organizations.	Workers, management. Management and privacy.
8. *It's all about carrots*	Progress. Overcoming difficulties.	Conflicts when local entrepreneurs meet resistance or opportunism from fishermen or wholesalers. Conflict between monopoly regulation and rational local initiatives. Authorities solve conflicts. Self-organization resolves conflict.	A community of producers seeing potentials and seeking a decent profit. Seeing housewives' preferences. For the good of Denmark. 'We'.
9. *Denmark affected by US cut down plans*	Change of policy abroad creates problems for expanding trade/exports	Denmark's need for exports versus American interests.	Denmark. An exporting firm.
10. *Good news for the Danish trade with the Belgians*	Expansion. Technical progress. Political environments may upset plans.	Not prevalent. National conflicts. Balance of trade problem: Denmark importing more Belgian goods than vice versa.	Denmark – and Scandinavia. An entrepreneur and manager pursuing opportunities internationally.

1980

Article	Change	Conflict	Identities
1. The game over the giant wholesaler	Search for efficiency through concentration and standardization meeting strong resistance.	Conflicting ideas and interests and a struggle for power in agricultural industry. Opposition from small retailers and some farmers. The conflict is to be resolved in the market place – and through M&A.	The creation of big business units – overcoming competition, reducing costs. Local resistance and protests. But defeatism on the side of the small businesses. The future of both sides is bleak.
2. Magasin and BP introduce new credit card	Search for market share through customer orientation. Piecemeal development of cooperation.	Conflicting credit card systems. Struggle between banks and retailers over administrative costs. Conflict to be fought out in the market and through strategic alliances.	A joint venture – on a limited scale with a clear strategic edge.
3. Furnace producers threatened after giant sales	Struggle for survival entails desperate search for market opportunities.	Conflict between consumer interests and the new producers. Old professional producers and retailers versus the new upstarts, plagiarizing, producing low quality wood-burning furnaces. Conflict to be resolved through organization.	The (professional/serious) industry and the need to organize to secure quality.
4. Small factory struggling for uniform orders	Increasing but unfair international competition.	Conflict between small Danish producer/supplier and international state-subsidized producers. Conflict between small supplier interest and national monopoly producer. Employment versus efficiency.	Small Danish firm, representing Danish employment in face of unfair competition. Appeals to political interests versus the need to consider costs.
5. Advice to Regnecentralen: Look after the money	Seeking expansion but meeting market resistance.	Conflicts between strategies of continuous investment in development versus 'looking after the money'. Conflict between having an important firm and public sector reluctance.	A large firm in a phase of reconstruction. The need for strategy. Public sector as asset in business development.
6. Meatpacker cooperation to handle crisis	A necessary process of concentration to overcome crisis – meets resistance. Export market development determines opportunities.	Conflicts with third countries, resolved by EC.	Agriculture. The new big agricultural corporation. Competition in home market must be stopped.
7. 100.000 kr. for a head	New business opportunities emerging.	Not prevalent. Ethical concerns about headhunting. But resolved by managers realizing value of contacts.	New industry and firm. Professionalization of top management selection.

8. Lack of concrete knowledge about new mortgage rules	Government passing new complex legislation creating uncertainty..	Conflict between need for clarity and government bureaucracy. Conflict between official interpretation of legislation and private interpretation (in publication). Some resolution through negotiation with associations. And frustration.	Expertise. People. Mortgage institutions. Government. Politics versus clarity for market actors.
9. Expert new chairman of B&W Shipyard	Crisis; stagnation – struggle for survival.	Not prevalent. Conflict between B&W Shipyard and the B&W Inc. Resolution is semi-legal.	Expertise. Old corporation. Public interests and investments (guarantees).
10. Professor: Banks mislead on pensions	The search for market shares leads to irresponsible behavior among banks and insurance companies.	Conflict between banks' behavior/interests and the interests of ordinary people. Need for political intervention in the pension field.	Expert. People. Banks/Insurance Companies/Pension Funds. The need for balanced information on economic opportunities.

2000

Article	Change	Conflict	Identities
1. The stock market is skeptical towards Bio-scan	A firm seeking to expand by being quoted in foreign stock markets. Growth in revenues and turnover.	CEO's expectations of success and potentials versus 'stock market', embodied as analysts. Resolution in the stock market.	The entrepreneur, with an idea and strong international ambitions. But 'intransparent'; hard to evaluate.
2. Nesa yields to customer criticism	Changing property rights in the electricity field leads major supplier to exploit customer uncertainty – perhaps.	Conflict between Nesa business strategy and consumer interests – but conflicting interpretations of strategy and interests. Resolved in part by corporate action and by authority intervention.	Customers. Large corporation being 'too smart', but then showing sensitivity to criticism.
3. The right idea	Individual business success by having the right idea and attitude and by focusing on essentials.	Not prevalent. Conflict between entrepreneur and skeptics – and Danish culture (the Jante Law). Resolved by personal initiative and financial investors – and in part government (award).	The successful entrepreneur who was proved right. The importance of honesty and trust.
4. Articles on Norden take-over (series of 4 articles)	Large corporations struggling over control of real estate firm.	Conflict between 'suitors'. Conflict between Codan and unlucky suitor. Conflict between Codan/Norden and a rival. In part resolved in the market place, in part through intense negotiation, in part through recourse to legislation/public authorities.	Financial investors – using all means to gain or maintain control. No mention of benefits.

184

5. *Articles on Tele Danmark take-over (series of 3 articles)*	A firm pursuing a bold merger strategy in an exploding market – but facing reluctant stock market.	Tele Danmark 'doing the right thing' versus stock market reaction. Expansion strategy versus price of existing shares. Resolved in part through corporate strategy; in part in the market.	The large corporation. Taking the offensive. Capacity to handle merger. Being sensitive to 'the market'.
6. *Dyremose's billions*	Markets expanding in part due to public initiatives (auctions); firms taking advantage of new market opportunities. Top-level negotiations.	Conflict with sellers – handled through negotiation. Conflict with 'market' – blamed on calculation principles and analysts. Resolved in the long run.	Professional top manager – with political experience. Personal but not private. Strong focus on ownership and returns.
7. *The last sale*	The rise and fall of an IT-entrepreneur. Rising against odds and good advice but misjudging market.	Conflict between CEO and 'experts' (analysts) – on bulletproof plan. Now resolved through market or courts. Personal and professional conflicts as 'foreshadowing' downfall.	The ruthless salesman – the nouveau riche of the New Economy. Public awards and public image. Business associates. Politicians and board members.
8. *Carlsberg's hectic year*	Carlsberg engaging actively in the consolidation process in the brewery industry.	Conflict with competitors – but also collaboration. Conflict between strategy and investor views of potentials. However, conflicting evaluations by analysts. Limitations created by competition authorities. Decided in court.	Large multinational brewery struggling to expand and consolidate in changing market. Formulation of strategy to create value through integration, R&D and branding.
9. *No view to transparency in the insurance market*	Government pushes for increased transparency in the market but insurance companies are slow in responding.	Government versus insurance industry. Resolved, in part, through continued negotiations. Insurance industry versus newcomer – and conflicting opinions of problems of industry.	Government representing 'the market' versus industry seemingly protecting vested interests. The foreign newcomer.
10. *Framfab going up*	Business success despite association with parent company in peril. Success through adjustment, focus and competency.	Framfab Denmark reputation versus Framfab Sweden reputation. Conflict between business reality and inflated ideas of dot.com. market.	The stable, old-fashioned dot.com firm in a wild market. The need to attend to basics and to rely on experience.

CHAPTER 7

The Gospel According to the Global Market
How Journalists Frame Ownership in the Case of *Nokia* in Finland

JANNE TIENARI, EERO VAARA
& NIINA ERKAMA

Introduction

Journalists are able to present complex and multifaceted business issues in particular ways, framing and reinterpreting common concepts in their texts. In this chapter, we look at the way Finnish journalists have framed the concept of ownership in the case of the telecommunications company *Nokia*, and note how these framings have altered over time.

National ownership of internationalizing companies has traditionally been of crucial interest to small nation-states (Katzenstein 1985). National or domestic ownership has been favoured in the Nordic countries, where export orientation and internationalization of economic activity have been combined with welfare-state nationalism at home. However, the ownership discourse has recently showed signs of change.

Through in-depth critical analysis of media texts, we shed some new light on the issues discussed in the preceding chapters of this volume. The transformation, growth and success of Nokia is the most significant corporate example that contemporary Finland can offer to a book on business journalism. Nokia has strong Finnish roots (Häikiö 2001). In the 1990s, however, the majority of Nokia's shares fell successively into the ownership of American and other non-Finnish investors (Tainio 2003). Nokia yet continues to attract a great deal of attention in the Finnish media.

The focus here is on texts published in *Helsingin Sanomat* (HS)[1], the daily newspaper that is arguably the most important press outlet in the contemporary Finnish media order. HS has the largest daily subscription rate of printed media outlets in the Nordic countries. Since the mid-1960s, it has been in the forefront when it comes to producing and disseminating economic and business news as well as developing business journalism in Finland (Tienari et al. 2002, Ainamo 2003).

We adopt a perspective of discursive framings in our analysis (Fiss & Hirsch 2005). Framing refers here to processes whereby specific versions of social reality are given meaning and articulation. Focusing on the Nokia case, we show how business journalists become protagonists of neo-liberalism,[2] that is to say, how the discourse of neo-liberal global capitalism – based on a glorification of the 'free' market – comes to dominate discussion in a given societal context. This discourse becomes dominant by way of numerous recurring framings. In connection with Nokia, these framings include *exemplarity* (using a single case as a powerful example), *historical reconstruction* (framing the past, present and future in particular ways), *authorization* (using specific 'experts' to legitimize particular interpretations) and, ultimately, *naturalization* (framing foreign ownership as inevitable).

We first briefly tell the story of Nokia. We then introduce our discursive framings approach, and go on to specify and illustrate how journalists in *Helsingin Sanomat* have framed ownership in relation to the Nokia case during the period 1998-2004. Finally, we summarize

---

[1] *Helsingin Sanomat* is the descendant of the newspaper *Päivälehti*, which was established in 1889. *Päivälehti* was founded by a cohort of Finnish-speaking, nationalistic entrepreneurs and politicians. Russian authorities closed the paper down in 1903, but it was re-established as *Helsingin Sanomat* ('Helsinki News') in 1904. In the 1930s, *Helsingin Sanomat* began to reinvent itself from its origins in the Finnish nationalist movement into an independent and neutral outlet. Today, it is considered liberally rightwing. SanomaWSOY, a media corporation grown up around *Helsingin Sanomat*, remains controlled by the descendants of Eero Erkko, the founder of *Päivälehti*.

[2] *Neo-liberalism* has gradually become the hegemonic post-Cold War system of economic and social relations (Friedman 1999). It is based on the removal of barriers to the 'free' movement of capital and goods around the globe, and on the extension of the market to virtually all areas of social life. This is in contrast to the form of Keynesian capitalism practiced in Finland and the other Nordic countries in the decades following World War II. While the Finnish business system was characterized until the 1990s by a regulated and relatively closed economy, it has since transformed itself towards a market-oriented model (Skurnik 2005). Specifically, while the Finnish economy was previously open-outward (relying on export revenue) and closed-inward (protecting the domestic market), it transformed itself in the 1990s to be open both ways (Tainio et al. 1999). Abolishing restrictions on foreigners to own stocks in Finnish companies in 1993 is one example of this. In all, during the process of deregulation, large Finnish corporations have shifted from being driven by production to being finance-driven; managers manage firms increasingly as investment targets rather than production units (Tainio et al. 2003).

our arguments, and offer some conclusions based on our analysis. The insights offered are not exhaustive, but reflect our own focus and framing of the research.

The Nokia Story

In 1917 Finland became an independent republic for the first time, having been a part of the Kingdom of Sweden between 1323 and 1809 and of Czarist Russia between 1809 and 1917. The Winter War in 1939-1940 represents a grand Finnish survival story that has been nurtured actively over the years. The Finns banded together to perform what has been described in heroic terms as a miracle. Under the leadership of Field Marshal Carl Gustav Mannerheim, the Finns repelled the attack of the vast Red Army. The Soviets had the quantity, the Finns the quality. With an efficiency based on mobility, initiative and quick decisions down the chain of command, the Finnish army survived and succeeded in keeping Finland independent.

There is a curious rhetorical parallel between the Winter War and the recent success of Nokia. 'The significance of Nokia to the Finnish identity can be compared with…the Winter War. It is a question of national stories of survival' (HS, 23 November, 2001). In the Finnish media the transformation and phenomenal growth of Nokia in the 1990s has been presented as the ultimate Finnish success story. The glory is there for all to see. As an industrial conglomerate, Nokia ran into deep financial difficulties in the late 1980s and early 1990s. The company struggled with its ailing commercial electronics business and the legacy of an ambitious but costly internationalization strategy. In 1992, 41-year-old Mr Jorma Ollila, whose background was in financial management rather than engineering, was appointed General Manager of the company, and later became its CEO. Ollila surrounded himself with a like-minded team of executives and began to realize a strategy focusing on telecommunications. Today, Nokia is a world leader in this expanding market.

The growth and success of Nokia has been interpreted by Finnish academics as the result of several elements. In an early study on the breakthrough of Nokia Mobile Phones, Pulkkinen (1997) emphasized the contextual nature of the process, that is, exploiting specific institutional traits in the home market and turning them into capabilities internal to the firm. Finnish society played an important part in this. Ali-Yrkkö et al. (2000), among others, emphasized Nokia's steady flow of investments in research and development. Ainamo and Pantzar (2000) picked out the product design aspects of the process. Häikiö (2001) maintained that due to the previous traumatic internationalization experience in the 1980s, the Nokia management of the 1990s was marked by caution and a bias in favor organic growth.

The vision launched by Ollila and his team in the early 1990s was condensed into a potent message: focused, global, telecom-oriented, high value-added products (Häikiö 2001). In 1994 Nokia's board of directors officially accepted the exit from cables, rubber, power and consumer electronics. In 1996 the restructuring of the business portfolio was completed when Nokia succeeded in selling off its consumer electronics business. Aunesluoma (2003) connects Nokia's rapid rise with the global prominence of technological change, which coincided with a successful focusing of business operations, efficient manufacturing and managerial capabilities – all in the context of the worldwide deregulation of telecommunications.

In addition to focus, management and technology, Tainio (2003: 61) places great emphasis on the capital and ownership aspects of Nokia's transformation, growth and success: 'A small Finnish conglomerate sustaining huge losses reinvents itself as a telecom company and in a few years dominates the world market for mobile phones. It was listed on the New York Stock Exchange in 1994.' This, according to Tainio, was the single most decisive moment in Nokia's success story. 'Since early 1997 the majority of Nokia shares have been in American hands.' Tainio describes the excitement of American investors and its consequences: 'it's been a wonderful ride for all concerned (Fortune, 01 May 2000).' In Tainio's words, it was the American investors' enthusiasm in particular that fuelled a virtuous circle for Nokia, providing the company's top management with capital with which to implement their vision and to fulfil their promises. Tainio (2003: 71) quotes CEO Jorma Ollila: 'Listing on the NYSE was a more important step than we thought. But the access to capital was less important than the presence as such (Ollila 2000).'

The story of Nokia since the early 1990s is an intriguing one. Due to its dramatic character, this story has attracted an overwhelming amount of attention from a wide range of stakeholders. It opens a door into business journalism – and into the public debate in general – in contemporary Finnish society. Nokia is a typical example of a subject for business journalists, but it is also an extreme case. Nokia is typical in the sense that in attracting foreign ownership, it is no different from a number of other Finnish companies in the 1990s and 2000s (Tainio et al. 2003). Nokia, however, is an extreme case in the Finnish context because of its unique growth and success.

All in all, Nokia's story reflects large-scale, global economic and social change, which affects people differently and arouses different opinions and interpretations. In theory at least it can be expected to become subject to a variety of discursive framings in the media.

Discursive Framings

Fiss and Hirsch (2005) argue that contemporary discourse on globalization is a struggle between different discursive framings. Globalization discourse may be conceived as a struggle about perceptions of the legitimacy of particular forms of economic and social change. The concept of framing captures the processes whereby societal actors influence the interpretations of social reality on the part of various audiences. Framing is the outcome of a process that combines both material change and symbolic construction (Fiss & Hirsch 2005, cf. Bourdieu 1998, Fairclough & Thomas 2004).

Framing[3] refers to processes of giving meaning and to articulations of particular versions of social reality. In a study of major US newspapers and company press releases, Fiss and Hirsch (2005) note the contradictory conclusions on globalization appearing in the various texts. They suggest that these conclusions illustrate the way in which diverse interpretations – positive, neutral and negative framings – can selectively cite and proclaim empirical support. Fiss and Hirsch claim that globalization has become a grand contest of social constructions. It has become an umbrella concept and, consequently, it requires substantial interpretation (Hirsch & Levin 1999). It also incorporates a temporal element. Fiss and Hirsch maintain that as globalization discourse spread through the United States between 1984 and 1998, its tone shifted markedly. Emergent globalization discourses were connected in part with macroeconomic fluctuations. Frame contests arose as various actors sought to influence the interpretation of changes in accordance with their own interests.

The mass media represent and contextualize economic news (Gavin 1998). Journalists, like other societal actors, are involved in the framing of concepts. They link interpretations to common ideas. They take part in the defining of concepts by making claims in the public realm. The media are powerful in that they promote particular versions of social reality, while marginalizing and excluding others (Fairclough

---

[3] The concept of framing has been used, for example, in the literature on social movements (Snow & Benford 1992) and rioting (Ellingson 1995) to capture processes whereby actors influence the interpretations of social reality among their audiences.

1995). This can be seen as a result of the continuous pressure of space and time under which journalists work and where their choices have to be made. Limited space in the media outlets means that individual texts have to be compressed. Time pressures mean that texts have to be produced rapidly.

Bourdieu (1998) argues that journalists think in clichés, relying on banal, conventional, common ideas or commonplaces that are generally accepted. Journalists write what everybody 'already knows'. They write what they think their audience expects them to write. In this way, journalists often reproduce commonly held views rather than act as opinion-leaders in relation to given phenomena. There are also controls that shape their work. The purpose of commercial media corporations is to make profits for their shareholders, and this is likely to shape media content (Herkman 2005).

Journalists frame issues and themes discursively. As a result commonplaces become part of the framing in media work (Fiske 1989). If the journalists choose to frame their stories with what everybody 'already knows', they reduce the uncertainty of how the story will be received and interpreted by the readers. Journalists need to be aware of earlier texts on given issues so that they can link the messages they wish to convey into a larger totality – because their readers will probably be doing the same. Journalists also rely on their sources, that is, on specific actors who provide them with information. This means that the journalists' framings are also infused with the viewpoints and interpretations of their sources.

Journalists can pursue various strategies to produce texts linking their interpretations to ideas common in a given context. Such strategies can be regarded as discourse practices that are available to journalists (Fairclough 1995, 1997). Hellgren et al. (2002) suggest that journalists can enact practices, factualizing (establishing facts), for instance, or rationalizing (justifying states of affair within a framework of economic rationale), or emotionalizing (appealing to the emotions of an audience) all in order to make sense of business issues for the benefit of their own audience. Further, the various genres of journalism such as editorials, news features or columns, have traditionally favored particular practices and excluded others. In recent years, however, a number of intermediary forms have appeared between 'pure' news reporting and opinion pieces such as columns, and it has become increasingly difficult for readers to distinguish between these intermediary forms or hybridized genres of journalism (Fairclough 1997).

In the present chapter, we focus on the ways in which Finnish journalists frame ownership in relation to Nokia. We analyze texts published in *Helsingin Sanomat* between 1998 and 2004[4] (see Table 7.1). As is evident from the preceding chapters of this book, the 1990s and early 2000s belong to a general phase of growth, professionalization and popularization of business journalism in the Nordic countries. The following account is based on our analysis of media texts, in the spirit of critical discourse analysis (Fairclough 1997). It is not intended to be – and it never could be – exhaustive.

How Journalists Frame Ownership: The Case of Nokia in Finland

Our account of how journalists in *Helsingin Sanomat* frame ownership in relation to the story of Nokia is divided into three sections. The first section covers the spring of 1998, focusing on the nascent debate on domestic versus foreign ownership in Finland. The second section is based on texts published in 1998-1999, illustrating the growing hegemony of a particular discourse within the ownership discussion. The third section covers the period 2000-2004, describing what we call the ultimate drying up of the discussion.

Does Ownership Matter...?

Mr. Ollila, Nokia's CEO, addressed the annual function of the Finnish Cultural Foundation on 27 February 1998. *Helsingin Sanomat* (HS) ran two news articles based on his address. The first appeared in the domestic section the following day, under the heading 'Jorma Ollila, CEO of Nokia: Connections between national culture and industry are significant'. The second article was published in the economy and finance section a few days later under the heading 'A nationalist spirit is awakening in companies'.

In the first article Ollila was reported as stressing the significance of nations and national culture before broadening his theme to discuss the role and fate of Finland in Europe. Ollila was reported as claiming that 'Finland will face a completely new international configuration next

---

[4] We searched the archives of *Helsingin Sanomat* for articles published since 1990 using the key words 'Nokia', 'omistus' (ownership) and 'kansallinen' (domestic/ national). This produced a sample of 56 articles, mainly editorials, news pieces and columns in the economy and finance section of the newspaper. Curiously, 48 of the articles were published during the period 1998-2004, which we then chose as our empirical focus. The three authors of this chapter first read the articles independently, and analyzed them in terms of content (what), actors (who) and style (how). From the sample of 48, we chose for closer scrutiny a total of 21 articles that were explicitly concerned with ownership in Nokia.

year when our country holds the presidency of the EU and hopefully becomes part of the EMU'. According to Ollila, HS reported, Europe should strike a balance between integration and a national approach. Ollila was said to have 'emphasized that the roots of business life and economy lie much deeper in the national soil than is apparent, and it will be beneficial for the Finnish economy in the future, too, to have strong domestic ownership.' Ollila went on to discuss the continuing importance of regions and local communities, 'presenting Nokia as an example of a company that has always relied on strong local communities. He quoted success stories from Oulu and Salo [towns in Finland] to exemplify the importance of cultural consciousness as a vital force.'

HS's interpretation of this message was recycled a few days later: 'The roots of business are much deeper in the national soil than is apparent on the surface.' Great prominence was given to the assertion that 'One of the most important explanations for the success of Finland and the Finns is, after all, the strength of the national culture, Finnishness.' The journalist then asked: 'Who said this and when? Wrong. It was Jorma Ollila, the CEO of Nokia, the largest and most international industrial company in Finland, owned 70 percent by foreigners.' The journalist went on to suggest that 'Questions about Finnishness have began to hover increasingly often in the minds of Finnish industrial executives. Many corporate executives are terrified, for example, about banks selling off their stakes in industry', because 'cross-ownership [between banks and industrial corporations] has become unfashionable'.

These texts display a curious mixture of stating 'facts' and of pandering to the nationalist sentiments and identification of the readers of HS. Two days later, on 6 March, 1998, HS ran an article under the headline 'A longing for domestic ownership has arisen'. The journalist reflected upon an American investment fund that had 'penetrated' as the single largest stockholder in UPM-Kymmene, a major Finnish forestry company. This was said to 'be reinforcing fears that have been simmering for some time. What if they come and take over the flagships of Finnish industry...'. Here, foreign ownership – 'they' – seems to represent a mysterious threat from outside; a force that may disturb the established ways of running businesses in Finland. Around a month later, on 10 April, the theme of domestic versus foreign ownership was taken up again in HS, also with direct reference to Nokia. In an article headed 'Nokia University Ltd', the opening words ran:

CEO Lars Ramqvist announced last summer that the telecommunications giant Ericsson is thinking of transferring its headquarters out of Sweden, because the company's markets are elsewhere. Jorma Ollila, CEO of Nokia, quickly confirmed that the Nokia headquarters will stay in Finland.

'We need Finland,' Ollila maintained.

What on earth does Nokia need Finland for? Nokia's markets are also elsewhere. 75 percent of the ownership of the company is abroad.

'The people, the atmosphere, education and economic policy decisions are all right in Finland,' Ollila listed the reasons why Nokia feels comfortable in Finland.

The journalist concluded: 'It is worthwhile for Nokia to stay in Finland, because Finland needs Nokia more than Nokia needs Finland.' The point was that 'Keeping the company in Finland is in the national interest, as the beneficial operational environment that has been created for Nokia confirms.' Nokia had by now become the favourite child of Finnish journalists – and of society in general. The company's well-being and satisfaction had become a question of national interest now that a 'beneficial operative environment' had 'been created' for its existence (see also Pulkkinen 1997). At this stage assumptions about Finnishness as a source of advantage to Nokia also appeared in the general discussion. Up to a point Ollila's address served to fuel such ideas. Against this background it is worth noting that the journalist quoted above was already expressing doubts about the nationalist argument. In the text the company has now risen above the nation in the hierarchy of contemporary society, and the link between companies and nations is becoming increasingly ambiguous.

Mr. Asko Schrey, Chief Operating Officer of the Helsinki Stock Exchange, wrote a guest column in HS on 19 May, 1998. Schrey applauded foreign investors who since 1993 (when restrictions on foreign ownership were lifted) have 'believed in our recovering national economy and in our companies quoted on the Stock Exchange; in their dynamism and innovativeness.' Schrey reminded his readers that 'the HEX-index, which measures the average development of stock prices, indicates that Finnish companies have been worthy of the trust placed in them.' Schrey then added a few words apparently aimed at Finnish investors: 'Investors must get used to the fact that you cannot put restrictions on capital in an efficient market economy. Domestic ownership in Nokia is now about 20 percent and domestic sales about five percent.' In effect, Nokia had ceased to be Finnish. Mr. Schrey went on to fine tune his message:

> *Discussion about the ownership of Finnish companies has begun to sound rather weird. The nationality of owners is hardly the most important thing. Rather, it's a question of how well the company fulfils its mission as part of the economy. For the investor, it's the profitability of the investment that is always most important, seeing that the company is successful and is showing good results.*
>
> *We're on the wrong track if we call for more domestic ownership, trying to force companies to adopt strategies detrimental to competitiveness, or burdening them with social obligations stemming from an outmoded welfare state model. This way of thinking would mean going back to the 'era of cementing' [i.e. regulation], the sins of which have not yet been fully atoned.*

So, ownership matters, but its nationality does not. This is an argument at the center of contemporary neo-liberalism, an ideology geared to breaking down barriers to the movement of capital or goods around the globe, and to extending the market to virtually all areas of social life (for criticism of this view, see e.g. Fairclough & Thomas 2004, Bourdieu & Wacquant 2001). When Mr. Schrey declares that companies must fulfil their 'mission as part of the economy' efficiently and profitably, it is clear that 'the economy' is no longer national, but interconnected and global. It is dominated by professional owners – in other words, by investors.

As the text above exemplifies, the discourse of neo-liberalism proclaims its own inevitability and the outmoded nature of its alternatives. 'Domestic ownership' is belittled and represented in the text as the opposite of 'competitiveness'. From this perspective, the discussion begins to 'sound rather weird' when people still dare to talk of 'burdening' companies with the 'social obligations stemming from an outmoded welfare state model.' The text presents regulation as the mother of all evils, apparently taking the great recession in Finland in the early 1990s as an example. The 'sins' that are claimed to have led to this recession 'have not yet been fully atoned.'

The day after Schrey's column had appeared, in an editorial article under the headline 'Who cares about Finland?', HS commented on a study undertaken by researchers at ETLA (The Research Institute of

the Finnish Economy; like the Stock Exchange, another institution infused with the neo-liberalist agenda):

> *ETLA has made a study of companies that have fallen under for-
> eign ownership. Foreign ownership has been growing rapidly.
> Foreigners already own one in three of the 500 largest companies
> [in Finland].*
> *The research undertaken by Mika Pajarinen and Pekka Ylä-
> Anttila dissolves any fears about foreigners coming here only to
> over-exploit [the opportunities for investing in Finnish stocks].
> According to the study, foreign ownership has introduced market-
> ing and internationalization competence into Finnish companies.
> Also, return on investment is greater in companies owned by for-
> eigners.*

Again, comments such as 'foreign ownership has introduced marketing
and internationalization competence into Finnish companies' and 'return on investment is greater in companies owned by foreigners' are
typical of the neo-liberal market discourse, which seeks to set specific
criteria and time-frames for assessing the value of social action. On the
other hand, it could be argued that the origins of competence are im-
possible to measure in practice and that the time-frame was still too
short for assessing the impact of foreign ownership on Finnish companies.[5] The above text can be seen as another example of an attempt by
certain actors to glorify unrestrained global capitalism. It is interesting,
though, that the journalist reporting on ETLA's study did not seem to
be totally convinced. He concludes his article with a comment on the
time-frame set by the researchers (the following oracular last sentence
is worth noting):

> *However, this research does not answer the important question:
> what happens in the long term to companies that come under for-
> eigner ownership? What will happen to Finland when more and
> more core companies are in foreign hands? It's impossible to an-
> swer such questions yet, because too little time has passed to al-
> low for reliable answers.*

---

[5] Apparently, in April 2006, Ylä-Anttila and Pajarinen published a study indicating that
companies owned by Finnish families had been more profitable than the subsidiaries of foreign
companies operating in Finland in 1986-2004. Their study was based on companies' financial
statements. 'According to Pekka Ylä-Anttila, the present study is the first in Finland to
investigate the impact of ownership structure on company profitability. Degree of solvency and
growth were also studied', HS reported on 4 April, 2006. (Sic!)

> *Opening borders is part of internationalization. But the line has to be drawn somewhere.*

Despite reflections of this kind about the appropriate time-frame for judging the costs and benefits of foreign ownership in companies, the neo-liberal bandwaggon continued to roll on. 'According to Talous-sanomat [a daily business newspaper from the same publisher as HS], it is "anachronistic" or outmoded to worry about securing domestic ownership' (Editorial, 18 April, 1998). 'The Economist has recently maintained that "economic nationalism" delays cross-border unions between companies in some countries' (Editorial, 17 March, 1999). In an interview with HS on 31 May, 1998, Mr. Vesa Vainio, Chairman of the Board for the financial services company MeritaNordbanken (the outcome of a Swedish-Finnish merger in 1997), 'declares that it is stupid to slam foreign ownership. There is no sense in it, either, from the company point of view or that of the so-called business economy, because foreigners are as good owners as Finns, or even better.' The punchline in Vesa Vainio's commentary was that 'talk about restricting foreign ownership belongs to another era.'

The Gospel According to the Global Market

Alongside the triumphant discourse of neo-liberalism, a rhetoric of helplessness seems to emerge in the texts published in *Helsingin Sanomat* in 1998 and 1999. On 16 September 1998, for example, the economy and finance section of HS ran an article under the headline 'The power in Nokia slips abroad: Half the voting rights soon in foreign hands'. The journalist noted that 'Foreigners already possess over 40 percent of the voting rights in Nokia. Foreigners' voting rights have increased over the last year, parallel with the growth in their share of the company's market value.' Non-Finns already accounted for and owned some 80 percent of Nokia's market value. In this way, 'power has fragmented into the four corners of the world.'

The metaphor of 'slipping' seems to reflect a sense of powerlessness. It is a metaphor that recurs in texts published in HS during 1998 and 1999. The question of voting rights came up because at the time Nokia had two share series. The voting rights of K-shares were tenfold in comparison to A-shares. Maintaining such a distinction used to be common as a safety measure in Finnish companies, mainly to prevent hostile takeovers and to bolster the power of longstanding Finnish owners.

Financial analyst Lauri Rosendahl (Aros Securities) was interviewed for the article quoted above. At the time Rosendahl was one of the best known Finnish analysts specializing on Nokia. He was frequently quoted in the media. He declared that 'growth in the market value of the share must exceed all national interests.' According to the journalist, Rosendahl says that 'this attitude is beginning to be delightfully common in Finland, too.' Rosendahls's message was clear. It reinforced the neo-liberal argument:

> *Sometimes people still say that national ownership should be defended. I wonder what on earth they mean. The goal of a company cannot be to maintain jobs at the expense of undermining the profitability and of reducing shareprices.*

Again, a note of inevitability can be detected in this comment. Finland, 'too', is catching up with the inevitable global development, although some ignorant people apparently still question this. Some time later, at the beginning of 1999 the debate about selling shares in Finnish companies to foreigners flared up again in HS, triggered by the annulment of the traditional cross-ownership in Finnish companies. Several Finnish companies had recently merged across national borders. Merita, the financial services company, is a case in point. In October 1997 Merita merged with Sweden's Nordbanken. An editorial article under the headline 'The gate was opened', published on 10 January 1999, began as follows:

> *It's hard to describe something of vast proportions – a great emotion or a big issue. The words can so easily sound grossly inflated or very flat.*
> *On Thursday at 4 pm, MeritaNordbanken sold its Pohjola shares to the Swedish insurance company Skandia. At a stroke, a hundred-year-old bastion of Finnish wealth was available to the Swedes.*
> *"Skandia inquired about the shares just before Christmas, and we've responded to their inquiry," said MeritaNordbanken chairman, Vesa Vainio, commenting on the sale.*
> *Back in 1808, on 5 May, Vice-Admiral Carl Olof Cronstedt surrendered the Viapori fortress to the Russians without much of a fight.*

The basic underlying issue discussed in the HS article is domestic versus foreign ownership or, more specifically, the sale of stocks in Pohjola, a major Finnish insurance company, to foreign buyers – here represented by Skandia, a Swedish insurance company. The journalist talks about 'surrender' and refers to events that occured some 200 years ago. Historical reflection is used to frame the text in a particular way, and Nokia was once again a factor in the argument. First, 'Merita had three very important holdings: shares in Nokia, Sampo and Pohjola.' Next, 'The Nokia shares were sold to international investors, scattered to the four winds.' And, finally, came 'the sale of Pohjola, the last major Finnish holder of Nokia shares.' Once again a sense of helplessness in face of global capitalism is apparent.

Meanwhile, in the spring of 1999 the Nokia board put a proposal before the annual general meeting whereby the various share series in the company were to be combined. This proposal was accepted in March and the tenfold voting rights of K-shares in comparison to A-shares ceased to exist. In anticipation of this, HS speculated on 2 February that 'the traditional Finnish owners slip into the line-up of regular owners [i.e. they no longer have special privileges], in addition to American and British funds.' The comment in HS sounds rather deterministic: 'Share series with powerful voting rights were created to protect the company from a hostile takeover. However, Nokia has grown too big for Finland.'

The journalist drew parallels with domestic owners in other countries, in particular, with the Wallenberg dynasty in Sweden: 'National ownership is vanishing elsewhere, too.' The writer (whose name was not given) went on to reflect:

> *Globalization appears to lead to a situation whereby world trade in all industries is dominated by about ten major companies with which other companies have to become associated in some way or another. These worldwide companies, including Nokia and Ericsson in their particular industry, are so expensive that their ownership becomes increasingly fragmented.*
> *The traditional owner role vanishes and faceless investors running after the highest yield take their place.*

The point is that ownership is becoming increasingly 'faceless'. The journalist quoted above continues: 'When steady owners disappear, the executives' position gets stronger.' After this, though, the wording becomes ambiguous: 'So, in the end, there's nothing but the emotions of the investors to oppose corporate executives. Even the most mighty corporate executive is powerless when a hurricane of hope or fear rages among a scattered collection of owners.' The metaphors of slipping and disappearing recur, and a sense of puzzlement appears in the text. Two days later, *Helsingin Sanomat* published an article under the headline 'The pain of losing power' (Editorial, 2 February 1999):

> *In Finland, as in other industrialized countries, companies that are regarded as national property slip away into the hands of foreign investors as internationalization spreads. Disputes about the privatization of state-owned companies then fan the emotional flames. [...]*
> *In the case of Finland, one might ask whose power is taken away exactly. Theoretically there are two parties in particular that lose out: the people and what is known as the blue-and-white capital.[6] This notion is based, however, on mythical conceptions of power: who has had it, and who is genuinely losing it. In the real world, the idea of the power of the people over its own property, in particular, has become a remote illusion.*

Opponents of privatization are deemed to be emotional, that is to say, not rational. The concept of 'internationalization', which has positive connotations in the context of the Finnish economy and Finnish business (typically to a small, export-driven nation-state), is used to frame this point in a particular way. It is interesting to note that in this line of argument, 'the real world' appears to have taken power from 'the people'. The article goes on:

---

[6] *Blue-and-white capital* refers here to a specific Finnish 'economic power bloc', which was now crumbling. Until the 1990s, Finland was characterized by highly centralized governance structures. A manifestation of this was the formation of economic power blocs, two of which centred on the Union Bank of Finland (UBF) and the Kansallis Banking Group. UBF was established in 1862. It was the first commercial bank in Finland (then under Russian rule). During the early decades of its operation it was known as the bank of 'Swedish-speaking money' in Finland. Kansallis, established in 1889, was a specifically Finnish countermove against this concentration of bank financing. Pohjola, the insurance company, became a key part of Kansallis' Finnish-nationalist, blue-and-white power bloc (Kuusterä 1990, Vihola, 2000, Kuisma, 2004). Eventually the centralized governance structures in Finland began to disintegrate. The two largest Finnish commercial banks, UBF and Kansallis, merged in February 1995 to form Merita Bank. In October 1997, Merita merged with Nordbanken, the fourth largest Swedish bank at the time. The initial domestic Finnish merger and the subsequent cross-border mergers (see Björkman et al. 2003) were extremely crucial events in the restructuring of the financial services industry in Finland and in the Nordic region.

> *The blue-and-white capital has created degenerate cross-*
> *ownership, and opportunities have been missed. Personal disputes*
> *between and within the different camps took over and the results*
> *have not stood to the challenges of time. [...]*
> *Nokia is an example of a company that has escaped the hands of*
> *the traditional Finnish power apparatus and become a worldwide*
> *company; its operations pander to the needs of the modern world.*
> *This situation is pleasing for economic reasons; billions in tax*
> *revenues and jobs are more than welcome.*
> *The Nokia example is also important in that it restores the right*
> *marching orders and division of labour in our country. A com-*
> *pany that is well looked-after takes care of itself and its own busi-*
> *ness, and the State is at its best when it, too, looks after its own*
> *business: governing the country, not companies.*

It is worth noting that in HS Nokia is constantly used as a radiant example of the virtues of deregulation and the 'free' market. It has 'es-
caped the hands of the traditional Finnish power apparatus' and now
manages to 'pander to the needs of the modern world' and, in this way,
to contribute to Finnish society by generating 'tax revenues and jobs'.
A sceptical reading of such comments might find that foreign ownership is being presented as the sole reason for Nokia's growth and success. Such a framing plays down the role of research and development
or of technological innovations and successful operative (as opposed to
strategic) management in making sense of Nokia's success. Nonetheless, the tone of the text is very optimistic.

In an article headed 'Bravery, capability and composure', published
on 6 December 1999 – the Finnish day of independence – HS made the
following claim: 'In the economy, independence is about buffers – financial and mental. These generate the strength to prepare and to act.
The paradox is that a company can be more independent, the more dispersed its ownership is throughout the world.' This rather abstract argument is then given concrete form: 'Nokia is a good example of this
as it is one of the largest companies in Europe in terms of market
value, and it is also one of the most independent.' Who enjoys this independence remains unclear in the article. Presumably, the reference is
to the top management of the company, which is curiously constructed
here as a counterforce vis-à-vis the owners.

Overall, 1998 and 1999 seem to have been marked in HS by a fairly
intensive debate about domestic against foreign ownership. Several
dramatic cross-border mergers and acquisitions involving major Fin-

nish companies occurred in 1997 and 1998, and the Nokia example could be linked to these events. In October 1997 Merita, the largest financial institution in Finland, merged with Sweden's Nordbanken. In June 1998 one of the major Finnish forestry companies, state-owned Enso, merged with Sweden's Stora. Commenting on the MeritaNordbanken merger, *Helsingin Sanomat* and other Finnish media drew on the nationalistic discourse alongside the dominanting neo-liberal one (Vaara & Tienari 2002, Risberg et al. 2003). The merger between Stora and Enso triggered similarly contrasting approaches. Due to the fact that Enso was owned by the Finnish state, the debate in the Finnish media was particularly intensive. However, the neo-liberal discourse emerged as the dominant tone in connection with the StoraEnso case as well (Vaara et al. 2006). When taken up in connection with Nokia, discussion on ownership clearly reflects the hegemony of the gospel according to the global market.

It is interesting to note that as regards cross-border mergers and acquisitions, Finnish business journalists could now deride actors in other countries for being overly nationalistic. For example, this showed in comments on the Norwegians in the Finnish media when MeritaNordbanken tried to acquire a Norwegian financial services company (Tienari et al. 2003). *Kauppalehti*, the Finnish business daily, wrote on 21 September, 1999: 'Although the importance of domestic ownership is declining everywhere else, it still appears to be a strong value in Norway, since that country has stayed out of the EU and the Euro zone.' In view of the public discussion in Finland described above, this seems rather a paradoxical comment. It is, however, a sign of the times.

When Domestic Ownership Becomes a Fantasy

On 24 July 2000, Dr. Pekka Ylä-Anttila, an economist in ETLA, wrote a column on the editorial page of *Helsingin Sanomat* with the headline 'The Finnish economy has benefited from its internationalization'. His opening words, which were picked up by the editing journalist, ran as follows: 'Economic nationalism in Finland emphasized protectionism. The debate on the risks of foreign ownership is now being toned down', writes Ylä-Anttila.

Ylä-Anttila drew on the neo-liberal discourse already specified above. 'Finland is a country that is very dependent on international markets and foreign trade. It was the opening of financial markets and European integration in the 1990s that revealed the weaknesses of the closed economy that had hitherto prevailed.' He then went on to hammer home his point: 'Internationalization was curtailed by the World Wars, with their restrictions on foreign trade and protectionism. In Finland, emphasis on economic nationalism gave an additional flavour to this. National ownership and production and the Finnishness of companies were regarded as crucial.' This, according to Ylä-Anttila, is both inefficient and outmoded:

> *Without widespread foreign ownership and foreign capital a phe-*
> *nomenon such as Nokia would not have been possible in a small*
> *country. Many defenders of blue-and-white capital seem to have*
> *forgotten this.*
> *Foreign ownership has made capital expenditure more efficient in*
> *companies operating in Finland. Foreign owners have been more*
> *demanding than domestic ones. In companies that have turned to*
> *foreign ownership, the yield on capital has been higher.*

Nokia is once again used as a positive example in support of deregulation and the 'free' market. Foreign owners – treated here as a group – are portrayed as more demanding than Finnish ones, and it is claimed that this has led to more efficient capital expenditure in the companies. There is no reference to the question of time-frames or to other measures for comparing the impact of domestic as opposed to foreign ownership in Finnish companies. 'Yield on capital' is everything that matters, but there is no mention that the 'yield' is now increasingly pocketed by non-Finns, and that this may have consequences for the Finnish economy and Finnish society in the long term.

Since 1998-1999, explicit mention in HS of the domestic-foreign ownership issue in Nokia seem to have become rare. A three-volume history of Nokia by Dr. Martti Häikiö was published in November 2001. The last volume was devoted to the period 1992-2000.[7] Mr. Max Jakobson, a well-known Finnish diplomat and right-wing lobbyist, reviewed Häikiö's book for HS on 23 November 2001 under the heading 'The history of a phenomenal rise'. The question that intrigued both Häikiö and Jakobson most was how to explain Nokia's rise 'to become one of the world's largest companies of the 1990s'.

According to Jakobson, Häikiö's answer was that 'the new management of Nokia bravely detached the company from its past. The

---

[7] As an industrial conglomerate, Nokia is the result of a major merger in 1966, although Nokia Ab was established already in the 1860s. The first volume of Häikiö's work covers the period up to 1982, while the second focuses on 1982-1991, and the third on 1992-2000.

company ceased to be a conglomerate and came to focus on telecommunications. This happened at exactly the right moment when international markets for telecommunications were opening up and when technological development was accelerating.' The ownership question fitted neatly into this picture: 'The internationalization of a bank-centred ownership structure, too, was a significant change. When the two share series were combined in 1999, the ownership of Nokia in its entirety came to be determined by the market. The result is that domestic ownership is now only a part of it. Private American investors represent the largest group of owners.' The nationalistic rhetoric then made a brief reappearance as if to reassure HS's readers that Nokia – despite its present ownership structure – was still Finnish:

> *Despite this Häikiö asserts that Nokia is still a Finnish company: "the significance of Nokia to the Finnish identity can be compared with Kalevala [Finnish national epic] and the Winter War. It is a question of national stories of survival." [...]*
> *These comparisons may be far-fetched but the fact is that Nokia is still a Finnish company: its headquarters are located in Helsinki, its management is almost entirely Finnish, and its research and development activities are to a large extent in the hands of Finns.*

By and large, in all comments and articles published in HS, Nokia seems to have been portrayed increasingly as a success story, and one that demonstrates the virtues of global capitalism generally. It also seems that the discussion has turned increasingly monolithic in this respect. In a curious article entitled 'The Russians are coming' on 20 May 2003, HS returned to the question of ownership on its editorial page. Historical reflection was again intrinsic to the framing in the text:

> *Foreign capital played an important part in the industrialization of our country, and the times when Finland has become wealthier have been times when its borders have been open. [...]*
> *There is not enough capital in Finland for us to seal off our companies from foreign ownership. [...] Finnish ownership is in the hands of individuals, wealthy families and trusts, and that is not enough.*
> *The fantasy of domestic ownership is thus increasingly an illusion.*

> *Closing our doors to foreign owners is impossible, and gives a
> false sense of security. A small country must find other ways of
> protecting itself.*
> *The only thing left is social policy: enhancing learning and com-
> petence, a wise tax policy and taking care of the service structures
> in society. [...]*

Domestic ownership, then, has finally become something that can be
called a 'fantasy'. The only function left for Finnish society is to secure a favourable operative environment for transnational corporations.
There is thus a moral element in the debate, separating society and
corporations from one another, and assigning different moral rules and
obligations to both sides. Comments such as 'The only thing left is social policy: enhancing learning and competence, a wise tax policy and
taking care of the service structures in society' do have a markedly
ambiguous air.

The next day, on 21 May 2003, HS commented on the merger between the Stock Exchanges in Stockholm and Helsinki. The heading
was 'Financing small companies becomes increasingly difficult' and
below it was declared that 'selling the Helsinki Stock Exchange to
Sweden arouses nationalist feelings.' Nokia popped up again as an example:

> *The Stock Exchanges in Stockholm and Helsinki and, in their
> wake, in the Baltic countries, have now been wrapped up as an at-
> tractive package for potential buyers. The titbit in the package is
> one of the most attractive shares in the world, that is, Nokia. The
> majority of Nokia shares are still traded on the Helsinki Stock Ex-
> change.*

The bottom line was that 'Only in Nokia, UPM-Kymmene and Amer is
foreign ownership purely investor-driven.' As a whole, Finnish listed
companies had not apparently managed to attract foreign investors, at
least not the 'right' active kind. It is interesting that the journalist
claims that 'the majority of Nokia shares are still traded on the Helsinki Stock Exchange', despite the fact that Nokia was listed in the
New York Stock Exchange (NYSE) as early as 1994, and that the vast
majority of the Nokia shares are held by non-Finns.

Nokia's financial performance then stumbled briefly in 2004, and
the Finnish nation sighed. 'Faith in Nokia is tested' was the title of an
article in the economy and finance section of HS on 18 August, 2004.

'Finns haven't sold their last Nokia shares, but they haven't started to buy shares back to Finland. Finnish investors presumably have similar doubts and desires about the future of Nokia as other investors.' The implicit message seems to be that Finnish investors are gradually becoming 'normal', as they focus more on the return on investment, and rely less on nationalistic emotion. Finally, then, it is business as usual in Finland in the neo-liberal mode.

Discursive Framings in Relation to Nokia

Our analysis of how journalists in *Helsingin Sanomat*, the major daily newspaper in Finland, have covered the topic of Nokia's ownership between 1998 and 2004 enables us to summarize some key elements in the short history of the neo-liberal global capitalism discourse in Finland. Our close critical reading of media texts raises several points about the discursive framings involved.

First, we have shown how a powerful single case like that of Nokia can be used by journalists to frame a more general issue, here, that of domestic as opposed to foreign ownership of corporations. This implies framing by *exemplarity*.[8] The Nokia case, which has undoubtedly been successful so far, has provided Finnish journalists with endless opportunities to argue in favour of the 'free' market characterized by the open flow of capital and, thus, by foreign ownership. Nokia could be used as a pretext and positive example to extend the argument to other corporate cases.

Second, *historical reconstruction* appeared in the media texts studied, and the past, present and future were framed in particular ways. The regulated past in Finland was presented as having culminated in the deep recession of the early 1990s. The past was frequently reconstructed as problematic, and then used to celebrate the virtues of deregulation. Although it could be argued that experience of foreign ownership in Finnish listed companies is still relatively limited (the last restrictions were abolished in 1993) and, consequently, the timeframe for assessing its consequences for Finnish society has been too brief, a questioning tone all but disappeared from the texts studied in the new millenium. This particular reconstruction of the recession is interesting, as a common earlier interpretation of its causes emphasized

---

[8] *Exemplarity* is a concept more common in philosophy than in organization or media studies. It concerns means for providing a transition from generality to particularity, or vice versa, in order to facilitate understanding of an idea or statement (Harvey 2002). In reference to management, exemplarity has been used in connection with the ability to set examples to enact change in organizations (Melkonian 2005).

the deregulation of the Finnish financial system (effected since the early 1980s), and the subsequent overheating of the economy.

Third, it is clear that personalities played a central role in the ways in which the neo-liberal discourse was framed in relation to the Nokia case. This can be referred to as *authorization*. Jorma Ollila (CEO 1992-2006) emerged as an authority whose comments were eagerly reported and interpreted. He even gained celebrity status (Fairclough 1995) as he enabled journalists to personify the drama in Nokia's phenomenal rise to global success. Significantly, positions of authority like this allow frequent opportunities for proclaiming the virtues of global capitalism and foreign ownership more generally. Other personalities-cum-authorities included business analysts and various 'experts' of a more general kind.

Fourth, historical reconstruction and authorization are connected with the final discursive framing in the studied texts, namely *naturalization* (Vaara & Tienari 2002). In the studied texts, this ultimately appeared in the form of a rhetoric of inevitability, often accompanied by a rhetoric of helplessness and powerlessness. Foreign ownership in Finnish firms was represented as a force of nature, which could not be questioned or resisted (Kuronen et al. 2005).

Overall, it can be seen how the notion of the 'national' in relation to ownership in Nokia has shifted by way of the journalists' framings, as it has become adapted to the neo-liberal discourse. The 'national' now seems to carry only a part of the meanings that it had in the 1990s. Nokia can still be discursively constructed by journalists as a Finnish company, although it is owned almost entirely by non-Finns, and an increasing part of its production and operations is overseas. It remains the successful flagship of Finnish enterprise.

Conclusions

In this chapter, we have applied a discursive framings perspective to the study of media texts in relation to corporate ownership (Fiss & Hirsch 2005). Our analysis gives rise to some general reflections on the rise of the Nordic business press. Particular interpretations of a complex issue can cite and assert empirical support selectively such that a particular discourse becomes dominant in the media coverage (Fiss & Hirsch 2005). The crucial point is that the dominant discourse justifies and legitimates particular moralities and principles, on the one hand, and downplays its alternatives, on the other (Vaara & Tienari 2002). The media participate in promoting particular versions of social reality, while marginalizing and excluding others (Fairclough 1995).

This is not altogether surprising. The findings reported by Fiss and Hirsch (2005: 47), for example, 'speak to a critical "project" conception of globalization as a political-economic construct promoted mainly by financial actors and institutions, with the idea of the free market at its center'. Our analysis shows that this conception is eagerly picked up by business journalists.

While we would like to believe that journalists covering business-related phenomena seek to act as neutral observers, it is clear that specific voices are privileged and others are silenced in the texts produced. Public debates on given issues become monolithic. Neo-liberal global capitalism becomes constructed as taken-for-granted and inevitable (for critique, see Bourdieu & Wacquant 2001, Fairclough & Thomas 2004). Business journalists emerge as protagonists of this form of capitalism as they frame specific social actions, for example, reworking of legislation, trading stocks and changing articles of association in corporations, or managing efficient and profitable business in general – all this usually *ex post* but sometimes in anticipation.

Our findings appear to support Herkman's (2005) claim that journalists may not be as self-dependent as is sometimes claimed; there are control mechanisms and journalistic practices that shape their work. Our analysis indicates that *Helsingin Sanomat*, despite its nature as part of the general media rather than a specialized business media platform, has done its share in celebrating neo-liberal global capitalism, that is, a particular political ideology. Blatantly nationalistic framings did appear sporadically in 1998 and 1999, but all but disappeared from later coverage of ownership in the Nokia case.

However, studies of other corporate cases in which the success of foreign ownership is not so apparent do show that the triumphal neo-liberal discourse can appear in a variety of contextualized versions. For example, journalists covering business issues continue to invoke nationalist sentiments in connection with dramatic events like cross-border mergers or acquisitions – *Helsingin Sanomat*'s journalists among them (Vaara & Tienari 2002, Hellgren et al. 2002, Risberg et al. 2003, Tienari et al. 2003, Vaara et al. 2006). The neo-liberal discourse prevails, but it may be challenged by or infused with banal nationalistic discourse (Billig 1995). While it would be easy to dismiss nationalistic framings as an example of the way in which journalists may 'merely' be narrativizing the economy and, in doing so, drawing on the popular discourse, we maintain that nationalistic framings may be serving a more fundamental purpose. Journalists appropriate the nationalistic discourse for particular reasons, while simultaneously reconstructing nationalism and keeping it alive as a potential counter-force to neo-liberal global capitalism.

Finally, our analysis begs the question of the specificity of the Finnish context. To what extent do particular national histories affect the way in which contemporary business phenomena are framed by journalists in the public debate? While there are no definite answers to this fundamental question, earlier studies have suggested that similar discursive dynamics are at work in the Swedish, Norwegian and Danish media.

For example, according to Hellgren et al.'s (2002) study on the merger between Astra (Sweden) and Zeneca (UK), a discourse based on an economic and financial rationale dominated the Swedish media coverage, although a discourse promoting nationalistic sentiments offered an alternative discursive frame. Tienari et al.'s (2003) study on Norwegian media texts reporting the attempts of a foreign company to acquire a Norwegian one also illustrates the dominance of neo-liberal discourse. At the same time, the same study shows how representations of economic nationalism continue to occupy a significant place in the Norwegian media. Peter Kjær's study of Danish media texts (Chapter 6 in the present volume) suggests that framings seen from a financial perspective and giving voice to the demands of the 'free' market (in what we would term neo-liberal discourse) are visible in Denmark, but again specific contextual references appear. We suggest, however, that over and beyond the similarities, the neo-liberal global capitalist discourse represented a rather more dramatic discursive turn-around in the Finnish media in the late 1990s than could be seen in the other Nordic countries. The neo-liberal discourse has hit Finland in a big way.

Bibliography

Ainamo, A. (2003) A Small Step for Insiders, Great Leap for Outsiders – The Case of the 'Tiger Leap' of SanomaWSOY. In Mannio, P., E. Vaara & P. Ylä-Anttila (Eds.) *Our Path Abroad: Exploring Post-war Internationalization of Finnish Corporations*. Helsinki: Taloustieto. Finnish Management Research Group / Taloustieto Oy.

Ainamo, A. & M. Pantzar (2000) Design for the Information Society: What Can We Learn from the Nokia Experience? *The Design Journal* Vol. 3 (2): 15-26.

Ali-Yrkkö, J., L. Paija, C. Reilly & P. Ylä-Anttila (2000) *Nokia – A Big Company in a Small Country*. ETLA / The Research Institute of the Finnish Economy, Series B-162.

Aunesluoma, J. (2003) Managerial Capabilities, Learning Base and Nokia's Fall and Rise in Electronic and Mobile Communications. In Mannio, P., E. Vaara & P. Ylä-Anttila (Eds.) *Our Path Abroad: Exploring Post-war Internationalization of Finnish Corporations*. Helsinki: Taloustieto. Finnish Management Research Group / Taloustieto Oy.

Billig, M. (1995) *Banal Nationalism*. London: Sage.

Björkman, I., K-O. Hammarkvist, T. Hundsnes, A-M. Søderberg, J. Tienari & E. Vaara (2003) The Nordea Case and the Nordic Context. In Søderberg, A.-M. & E. Vaara (Eds.) *Merging Across Borders: People, Cultures and Politics*. Copenhagen: Copenhagen Business School Press.

Bourdieu, P. (1998) *Acts of Resistance – Against the New Myths of Our Time*. Cambridge: Polity Press.

Bourdieu, P. & L. Wacquant (2001) NewLiberalSpeak: Notes on the New Planetary Vulgate. *Radical Philosophy* Vol. 105: 2-5.

Ellingson, S. (1995) Understanding the Dialectic of Discourse and Collective Action: Public Debate and Rioting in Antebellum Cincinnati. *American Journal of Sociology* Vol. 101: 100-144.

Fairclough, N. (1997) *Critical Discourse Analysis: The Critical Study of Language*. Second edition. London: Longman.

Fairclough, N. (1995) *Media Discourse*. London: Arnold.

Fairclough, N. & P. Thomas (2004) The Discourse of Globalization and the Globalization of Discourse. In Grant, D., C. Hardy, C. Oswick & L. Putnam (Eds.) *The SAGE Handbook of Organizational Discourse* London: Sage.

Fiske, J. (1989) *Reading the Popular*. London: Unwin Hyman.

Fiss, P. C. & P. M. Hirsch (2005) The Discourse of Globalization: Framing and Sensemaking of an Emerging Concept. *American Sociological Review* Vol. 70 (1): 29-52.

Friedman, T. L. (1999) *The Lexus and the Olive Tree*. New York: Farrar, Straus and Giroux.

Gavin, N. (Ed.) (1998) *The Economy, Media and Public Knowledge*. Leicester: Leicester University Press.

Harvey, I. E. (2002) *Labyrinths of Exemplarity: At the Limits of Deconstruction*. New York: State University of New York Press.

Hellgren, B., J. Löwstedt, L. Puttonen, J. Tienari, E. Vaara & A. Werr (2002) How Issues Become (Re)constructed in the Media: Discursive Practices in the AstraZeneca Merger. *British Journal of Management* Vol. 13 (2): 123-140.

Herkman, J. (2005) *Kaupallisen television ja iltapäivälehtien avoliitto: median markkinoituminen ja televisioituminen*. Tampere, Finland: Vastapaino.

Hirsch, P. M. & D. Z. Levin (1999) Umbrella Advocates Versus Validity Police: A Life-Cycle Model. *Organization Science* Vol. 10: 199-212.

Häikiö, M. (2001) *Globalisaatio. Telekommunikaation maailmanvalloitus 1992-2000. Nokia Oyj:n historia, osa 3*. Helsinki: Edita. [Globalization. The World Conquest of Telecommunications 1992-2000. Nokia's history, Volume 3.]

Katzenstein, P. (1985) *Small States in World Markets: Industrial Policy in Europe*. Ithaca, NY: Cornell University Press.

Kuisma, M. (2004) *Kahlittu raha, kansallinen kapitalismi: Kansallis-Osake-Pankki 1940-1995*. Helsinki: Suomalaisen Kirjallisuuden Seura. [Chained Money, National Capitalism: Kansallis-Osake-Pankki 1940-1995.]

Kuronen, M-L., J. Tienari & E. Vaara (2005) The Merger Storm Recognises No Borders: An Analysis of Media Rhetoric On a Business Manouver. *Organization* Vol. 12 (2): 247-273.

Kuusterä, A. (1990) Taloudellisesta vallasta Suomessa: Historiaa – käsitteitä – empiriaa. *TTT Katsaus* 4/1990: 31-40. [On Economic Power in Finland: History – Concepts – Empirical Evidence.]

Melkonian, T. (2005) Top Executives' Reactions to Change: The Role of Justice and Exemplarity. *International Studies of Management and Organization* Vol. 34 (4): 7-29.

Pulkkinen, M. (1997) *The Breakthrough of Nokia Mobile Phones*. Helsinki School of Economics and Business Administration, Acta Universitatis Oeconomicae Helsingiensis A-122.

Risberg, A., J. Tienari & E. Vaara (2003) Making Sense of a Transnational Merger: Media Texts and the (Re)construction of Power Relations. *Culture and Organization* Vol. 9 (2): 121-137.

Skurnik, S. (2005) *Suomalaisen talousmallin murros: suljetusta sääntelytaloudesta kaksinapaiseen globaalitalouteen*. Helsinki School of Economics, Acta Universitatis Oeconomicae Helsingiensis A-251. (The Transformation of the Finnish Business System: From a Closed Regulated Economy into a Bipolar Globalized Economy.)

Snow, D. A. & R. Benford (1992) Master Frames and Cycles of Protest. In Morris, A. & C. McClurg Mueller (Eds.) *Frontiers in Social Movement Theory*. New Haven, CT: Yale University Press.

Tainio, R. (2003) Financialization of Key Finnish Companies. *Nordiske Organisasjonsstudier* Vol. 5 (2): 61-86.

Tainio, R., M. Huolman, M. Pulkkinen, J. A-Y. & P. Ylä-Anttila (2003) Global Investors Meet Local Managers: Shareholder Value in the Finnish Context. In Djelic, M.-L. & S. Quack (Eds.) *Globalization and Institutions; Redefining the Rules of the Economic Game*. Cheltenham: Edward Elgar.

Tainio, R., M. P. & K. Lilja (1999) Economic Performance of Finland After the Second World War: From Success to Failure. In Quack, Sigrid, Glenn Morgan & Richard Whitley (Eds.) *National Capitalisms, Global Competition and Economic Performance*. Berlin: De Gruyter.

Tienari, J., E. Vaara & A. Ainamo (2002) The Emergence and Legitimization of Business Journalism in Finland. Paper presented to the European Business History Association (EBHA) 6th European Business History Congress, University of Helsinki, Finland, 22-24 August 2002.

Tienari, J., E. Vaara & I. Björkman (2003) Global Capitalism Meets National Spirit: Discourses in Media Texts on a Cross-Border Acquisition. *Journal of Management Inquiry* Vol. 12 (4): 377-393.

Vaara, E. & Tienari, J. (2002) Justification, Legitimization and Naturalization of Mergers and Acquisitions: A Critical Discourse Analysis of Media Texts. *Organization* Vol. 9 (2): 275-304.

Vaara, E., J. Tienari & J. Laurila (2006) Pulp and Paper Fiction: On the Discursive Legitimation of Global Industrial Restructuring. *Organization Studies* Vol. 27 (6): 789-810.

Vihola, T. (2000) *Rahan ohjaaja – Yhdyspankki ja Merita 1950-2000.* Gummerus Kirjapaino Oy, Jyväskylä, Finland: Gummerus Kirjapaino. (Steering Money – UBF and Merita 1950-2000.)

Table 7.1 Media Text Material

Title	Section (and date)
Jorma Ollila, CEO of Nokia: Connections between national culture and industry are significant	Domestic (1998-2-28)
A nationalist spirit is awakening in companies	Economy & finance (1998-3-4)
A longing for domestic ownership has arisen	Economy & finance (1998-3-6)
Nokia University Ltd	Economy & finance (1998-4-10)
Difference: the acid test of globalization	Editorial (1998-4-18)
Pension funds and savings into shares	Guest column (1998-5-19)
Who cares about Finland?	Editorial (1998-5-20)
Tauno, where's that boat of ours?	Economy & finance (1998-5-31)
The power in Nokia slips abroad Half the voting rights soon in foreign hands	Economy & finance (1998-9-16)
Jewels for sale	Editorial (1998-12-18)
The gate was opened	Editorial (1999-1-10)
Everyone manages for himself	Editorial (1999-2-2)
The pain of losing power	Editorial (1999-2-4)
Blue-and-white capital – does it exist?	Editorial (1999-3-17)
Bravery, capability and composure	Editorial (1999-12-6)
The Finnish economy has benefited from its internationalization	Editorial (2000-7-24)
The history of a phenomenal rise	Culture / book review (2001-11-23)
The Russians are coming	Editorial (2003-5-20)
Financing small companies becomes increasingly difficult	Economy & finance (2003-5-21)
Faith in Nokia is tested	Economy & finance (2004-8-18)
Vesa Puttonen: small domestic ownership is a problem for the national economy	Economy & finance (2004-9-3)

PART III

BUSINESS NEWS
AND
ORGANIZATIONAL CHANGE

CHAPTER 8

The Negotiation of Business News[1]

MARIA GRAFSTRÖM & JOSEF PALLAS

Introduction

How is the expansion of business journalism reflected in and handled by contemporary business corporations? According to the Swedish Public Relations Association the Swedish private sector together with governmental authorities and municipalities[2] invested more than 36 billion SEK in information and public relations activities in 2005 (SPRA and PRECIS 2005). In terms of personnel resources, the information and public relations sector includes almost fifteen thousand professionals and nearly fifty percent of those are assumed to work in private business (Larsson 2005: 131). These communicators are mostly organized in information and PR-departments that have witnessed a rapid growth in both size and organisational status. Research shows that more than seventy percent of the information and communication directors are standing members of senior management teams (cf. Cornelisen 2004, Larsson 2005). At the same time, the use of communication and media experts in corporations and corporate efforts to train and educate its employees in media management has increased (cf. Engwall 2006, Larsson 2005).

[1] This paper is partly based on an empirical study on business news production in four organisations carried out in collaboration with Jaan Grünberg and Karolina Windell. A special thank you goes also to Roy Langer from the Department of Communication, Business and Information Technologies, Roskilde University, Denmark, who worked on a first draft of this chapter and contributed with insightful comments and suggestions during the time of writing. We are also grateful to the editors who kindly read and commented various drafts of this chapter.
[2] Investments made in organizations with more than 100 employees. Investments made in professional and industrial organizations as well as in labour unions and associations are not included in this report as the statistics for these is not available.

Against this background, it becomes relevant to consider the nature of the relationship between business sources and business journalists. In this chapter, we therefore focus on this relationship and examine the interaction between media and sources through the concept of negotiation – conceptualised as a reciprocal process of interaction embedded in a field of practice. We apply this concept to the area of business news production which is an empirical field that has been largely neglected by researchers interested in media-source relations. More specifically, we focus on interactions between corporate communicators and business journalists.[1]

In the following we first outline the theoretical constructs of negotiation and institutional context, which then guide our theoretical understanding of relationships between media and business organizations. Our empirical study examines the Swedish business news field and media work in two Swedish business corporations. Following a brief characterisation of the field of practice, the analysis exemplifies inter-organizational professional practices in the two source organisations. In the final section of the paper, we discuss our findings and the fruitfulness of using the negotiation concept in the empirical field of business news, and emphasize the organised and institutionally embedded character of the news production process.

An Institutional Understanding of Business News

A common way to understand media-source interaction is through social and cultural arrangements as well as through organizational characteristics, conditions and strategies employed by media sources (Ericson et al. 1989, Gammal 1997, Cook 1998). Ericson et al. (1989: 377) put forward that the 'reality of news is embedded in the nature and type of social and cultural relations that develop between journalists and their sources, and in the politics of knowledge that emerges on each specific newsbeat.'

In these studies a key concept of understanding interaction between professional communicators and journalists is *negotiation*. For example, Cook (1998) argues that the negotiation of newsworthiness occur partly in the process of news making and partly in deciding the content

---

[1] The data we use is mainly derived from a Swedish study, conducted during the years 2003-2006, about the increasing importance of the media in the work of corporations (for a full description, see Pallas forthcoming). We also draw on two other Swedish studies: a study on how Swedish business journalism developed into a specific field of practice (see further, Grafström 2006), and a study on how quarterly reports are transformed into business news by both media and source organisations (for full description, see Grafström et al. 2006).

of the news. He claims that the sources have an advantage in the actual process, while journalists have more authority in deciding content, form, and presentation of the news. Ericson et al. (1989), however, argue that many source organisations influence not only the process of news making, but also the content and format of the news. But even if and when source organisations are able to influence the character of the actual news, they still remain dependent on the control media exercise on the final product. Consequently, the negotiation about newsworthiness is always an encounter between two groups of more or less autonomous actors – journalists and sources – each not only possessing key resources, but also being dependent on one another for success:

> *Each side relies on the other in the negotiation of newsworthiness, and neither fully dominates, because officials and reporters alike hail from at least partially independent institutions that command important and unique resources* (Cook 1998: 105).

In this way, sources and journalists depend on each other at the same time as they are in conflict.

Many of the existing studies of media-source relations have mainly been undertaken within the field of political journalism, while the field of business news has scarcely been studied. One exception, though, is Ericson et al. (1989), who analyse corporate interactions with the media. They use a model outlining different types of strategies available to sources in their interaction with the media (Ericson et al. 1989:9, figure 8.1).

Ericson et al.'s (1989) model assumes that source organizations are constantly managing what, when and how to release and present their information. The information provided can vary from being part of a variety of communication materials to media-specific interviews, video news releases or press-releases. The model captures four strategies used by the source organisation to either keep information private or to make information public through the media. The strategies are Publicity, Censorship, Confidence, and Secrecy. Publicity captures a company's efforts to openly distribute information or to create attention around its own activities, products, business deals, etc. Censorship addresses, on the other hand, the company's efforts to access and affect news production through editing the media material alongside its way to final news. Confidence describes situations where corporations use secret or sensitive information as means to create publicity covertly. Finally, Secrecy describes how organizations hide certain issues from becoming publicly known. Altogether, these four types of examples illustrate the specifics of media-source interactions as embedded in organizational routines and strategies.

But interactions between media and sources are not only organisationally embedded. Literature about the negotiation concept also stresses the role of institutional contexts – general norms and values permeating the practice of news making. Such a perspective suggests that the production of contemporary business news is organized according to shared norms about what is considered newsworthy and how news should be presented (Grafström 2006). Common norms about issues such as newsworthiness bear witness to the fact that journalists follow established rules and routines when producing news (Tuchman 1973, Cook 1998); norms that also – as we argue in this chapter – govern the news production work by other actors, such as analysts and corporate communication personnel. Hence, values and norms guiding business news production permeate not only media organizations, but also the work of corporate information departments (Pallas forthcoming) Moreover, former journalists often populate information departments, further strengthening a common understanding among a larger number of actors about what constitutes business news (e.g. Ericson et al. 1989, Slaatta 2003).

In the reciprocal interplay among various individuals and organizations – journalists, public relations officers, consultants, and media consumers – ideas about the nature of business journalism are constructed and re-constructed. This web of highly interconnected actors has been interpreted as a relatively 'small exclusive circle' (Davis 2000: 285). Those who are engaged in the production of financial and business news are usually part of the same corporate elite network, which includes 'financial PR practitioners (PRPs), City editors, analysts, institutions and top managements' (Davis 2000: 285). These individuals and organizations are members of a relatively exclusive and homogenous group, which promotes interaction among them. Routines for news production are, in this way, not dependent on individual organizations, but are formed and reformed in the interplay among several organizations engaged in news work.

Against this background, we suggest that business news production should be understood as a negotiation process within a particular institutional context, and hence governed by well established norms and ideas about what is, and what is not, appropriate and valued. From this perspective, we use the negotiation concept in the empirical field of business news production. In addition, we apply Ericson et al.'s (1989) conceptualisation of the media-source interaction from the perspective of the business corporations.

The Broader Context of Business News Production

How do business journalists and their counterparts on the side of business look at their work with business news? In our interviews we asked the informants to reflect on business-media relationships in their news work. The editor-in-chief of a business oriented media outlet summarizes his experience of the overall nature of the relationship as follows:

There are not so many information directors and press officers I work with on "private-basis", and most of the input to my work is coming through formal contacts. This used to be the case ten years ago where there was both time and resources. This is also a manner of professional attitude, not to be tied by personal relations when reporting on an issue or a company. In this context I believe that the sense of responsibility is very high, not only among my colleagues, but also among the business journalists in general.

The relatively formalized contact between media and large corporations dominating the contemporary production of business news is also supported by an information director at one of the major Swedish corporations reflecting on his role at the corporation:

Ten-fifteen years ago I acted more proactively. I contacted media more often and I was trying to deliver interesting stories and information about the company and its products. Often I wrote debate articles and got published by the major newspapers. These activities are rarer nowadays and I'm more reserved towards the media. However, I am always available and I try to treat media in a professional manner. My work is now more passive and reactive.

Despite the downsized role of personal and informal contacts between the parties both the journalists and their corporate sources stress the importance of such relations for news production. The importance and relevance lies in the access to the companies' sources and with respect to time and resources available for story research. According to the business journalists we have spoken with, the Swedish companies have become more difficult to access. One business journalist states:

> *There are two main reasons for a more limited access to relevant sources at the companies. Firstly, more and more companies choose to move their headquarters outside of Sweden. In countries like England the legislative regulations allow companies to keep press and media at a distance. The second, and more serious obstacle, facing journalists when investigating companies, are corporate "gatekeepers", i.e. information directors, press secretaries, corporate spokesmen, etc., restricting the accessibility to primary sources.*

Even if the access to Swedish corporations is relatively easy in comparison with other countries, the media seem to have only limited possibilities to meet the highest representatives of publicly listed companies. As expressed by another journalist the presidents and CEOs of large corporations are still relatively accessible, but it is obvious that conditions are changing and the journalists have to increasingly turn to information directors and press officers for information. Even in the work with quarterly reports access is of primary importance. The main focus of the business desks is directed toward the major corporations on the Stockholm Stock Exchanges. In this context the availability of CEOs and CFOs play a significant role for the newspapers' coverage as comments from these corporate representatives often 'constitute' the news.

During the periods of quarterly reports, the reporters' days appear as relatively scheduled and organised around the work with the reports, for example in relation to time and place for the reports' release, press conferences, analytical meetings, and media contacts (Grafström et al. 2006). These overall characteristics seem to be valid even for general business news coverage. A lot of the journalistic work is described as recurrent and routinized, not only with respect to whom and what topic to cover, but also how long the text should be and what pictures to use.

The role and importance of sources in business news production is also addressed by PR and media consultants we have talked to. One of the PR-consultants argues that:

> *The relation between business journalists and corporations is wrongly believed to be based on mutual commitment, i.e. negotiations between what journalists want to publish and what the companies deliver, and professional trust. But journalists generally find themselves in a weak position vis-à-vis large companies knowing that what is produced by the corporations (most often by*

their information departments) constitutes a significant part the final news.

Let us use this short background description as a base for understanding the empirical examples of how two large corporations handle their media work and what implications such work has for media-source interactions.

Corporate Media Work and Routinized Processes

What characterizes the corporate views on their media counterparts? Coming back to Ericson et al.'s (1989) typology presented earlier in this chapter, we organize our empirical examples[2] into four categories describing the specific patterns of interactions between corporations and the media.

Publicity

The first examples illustrate how companies use media contacts to generate publicity. Here one of the companies under study was involved in negotiations regarding the legitimacy of one of its projects in a Baltic country. As the issue had been noticed and well covered by the press of that country, the information director expected a 'spill-over effect' also in the Swedish media. Therefore, when he received calls from a journalist representing one of the major business dailies, the directors acted upon an already prepared strategy. The director commented:

> *There are relatively few business journalists that understand and cover our company, so I could assume whom I would talk to on this issue.*

---

[2] The study was conducted in 2004/2005 and includes two major Swedish companies. Both companies represent leading actors within their respective industries with annual revenues exceeding one hundred billion SEK and employing tens of thousands of people worldwide. Historically, these corporations belong to the most covered companies in the Swedish press (Observer 2005). The media interest results in annually more than one thousand articles, for each company, in the Swedish major newspapers. This study was based on two separate periods of observations in the respective companies' information departments, lasting two and half respectively three months. Media work of two information directors and two PR-managers was followed on a daily basis and documented in a diary-like form (cf. e.g. Barley 1996, Czarniawska 2004). The material was supplemented by individual interviews with people involved in the company's media work, ranging from members of senior management team to local PR-managers and non-managerial communicators.

During one of the incoming calls the information director tried to convince the reporter that the whole situation was entirely under control and that the present negotiations would be successfully completed within a couple of days. Therefore there was no need to exaggerate the news coverage by the country's domestic press. Rather, the focus could be directed towards other more relevant and interesting aspects of the project, the director argued. He described scope and complexity of the project as being very unique for the Baltic country, arguing that it required an enormous amount of planning and organizing capacity both from the company as well as from the country's different authorities. The information director mentioned the appreciated cost of the whole project and received an immediate positive response from the journalist. The director later explained:

The larger our projects are and the more money there is involved, the greater media attention one can expect.

By leading the interview into the new aspects of the project, the information director moved smoothly to other projects in the region. He gave the journalist 'inside' figures and facts about the successful development of these projects and offered several possible angles for interesting articles. The journalist got interested in these stories and asked the director for more detailed information. Eventually, as the interview continued, the director invited the journalist to attend a press conference taking place in one of the mentioned countries. At the same time he also opened up for further contact on the issue.

Another example of producing and distributing public material through the media is illustrated by one of the companies' work with non-commercial product information. Most of the media material was distributed to local and business press media. It was, however, interesting to observe how such 'local' activities occasionally also could become news at a corporate level. The production of these local press releases was described as relatively intensive compared to the amount of media material generated at the group level. Only a fragment of the 'local' texts made it to the corporate website's press-room because most were being 'driven out of business' by major corporate issues. In order to compensate for the relatively low attention at the group level, the marketing section of the information department worked along a 'payoff media strategy'. Instead of fighting for media attention trough the corporate channels, the department focused on distributing tailored media material adjusted to relevant customer groups, industry organizations and associations. One of the PR-officers argued:

> *The payoff strategy aims to persuade these organizations so they pass on the information. Media acceptance is much higher if the material is coming from a neutral and therefore, in their eyes, more reliable actor.*

Censorship

The first example concerning the use of censorship is taken from a press and marketing campaign lasting several weeks prior to one of the companies' participation in a large international work-safety program. The director of the information department suggested that they should pursue an active media approach in this context. The department prepared and provided the media with a short press release and ready-to-use statements about the project. The director motivated his decision:

> *In spite of the fact that there are internal attempts to avoid media publicity in certain issues, the company still needs to be active in its media work. The effects of positive media attention almost always outweigh possible negative consequences.*

As the media showed an increasing interest in the program, the information director decided to adopt a more restrictive approach toward the press. His decision was further reinforced when one of the large TV-channels showed interest in visiting one of the company's working sites in order to report about the program. After a meeting with the director for sustainable development, the information director finally agreed on the visit, but only on the condition that the company could examine and comment on the content of the TV-report. The information director also required that his PR-director and the company's own photographer followed the TV-team during its visit. The report was then shot under supervision of the PR-director.

Another example of corporate censorship of media material was observed in relation to one of the companies' release of a quarterly financial report. The information department was preoccupied with the preparation of the report's release for almost two weeks. Particular attention was paid to media-oriented activities, such as a telephone press-conference, press releases and specific interviews. The first thing to do was the production and distribution of an invitation press release. The following days were spent on handling and booking journalists for individual interviews and on the preparation of support material for these media meetings.

Many of the journalists wanted also preliminary comments from the information director, arguing that they needed to prepare for the release. Without revealing the specific content of the report, the information director met the journalists' requests in several cases and provided them with small bites of information. Reflecting on this, he said:

> *It is a matter of balancing between keeping the journalist interested in the report and, at the same time, not violating the disclosure regulations and policies prevailing during the silent period. However, you have to choose whom you trust and who is worth the extra information.*

At the release day the information director contacted the most important media and journalists in order to update them about the scheduled individual telephone interviews with the company's CEO. As these interviews were scheduled to take place before the telephone conference, the information director focused on major press agencies and on journalists from the most important dailies and TV-channels. He updated his list with the expected questions and prepared answers, and handed the list over to the company's CEO. The information director informed the CEO about the most important journalists and gave him a briefing on how to treat these in terms of time and amount of information.

The information director and the PR-director followed the interviews closely sitting next to the CEO and assisting him in critical cases. During the interviews the CEO refused occasionally to answer questions and was relatively restrictive in commenting others. However, the atmosphere was mostly positive and the journalists did not push the CEO into questions that he had marked - either *a priori* by the information director or during the interview - as undesired. The interviews were then followed up by the information director, who checked with the journalists whether there was any confusion or unclear points made by the CEO. The questions and answers from the interviews were also made available to other representatives of the management team in order to ensure they knew what to answer, if they had to deal with media requests on their own. The information director explained:

> *Even if we wish to reduce the spontaneous contact between media and people in the management to minimum, journalists always try*

to speak to the top managers directly in order to get the first-hand information and comments.

Confidentiality

In contrast to the earlier examples the following accounts illustrate more informal and covert forms of corporate media work. In cases where the information was perceived as sensitive or confidential, both the information and press directors preferred to communicate with media journalists directly over the telephone, rather than using e-mails or other communication channels. The information director in one of the departments explains:

> *The phone is probably the most important tool in my job. This is also true for the journalists, I assume, since almost all media requests are via phone.*

One example from this category was a planned sale of a company's business unit. The information director decided to wait with a press-release on the sale until negotiations with local labour union were completed. He revealed, however, some of the details to a journalist, who is specialized in covering the company for a major Swedish daily. The information director commented this:

> *It is better that news like this is brought by someone who has a long-term relationship with the company and can put the news in 'the right context'.*

He explained to the journalist that there would be a relatively extensive down-sizing related to the sale and made him understand that more similar structural changes were to be expected. The information director then advised the journalist to call the director of the unit and to conduct some background research on the prevailing changes. He also asked the journalist to write the proposed article without exposing him as his corporate source. The following day the journalist published a short article about the company's plan to adjust its prevailing structure to the main business activities. The article presented the unspecified changes as something positive due to the company's long-term obligations and goals. The information director was relatively satisfied with the presented angle:

> *Thanks to this article we can now send out the coming press re-*
> *lease without being especially concerned about possible negative*
> *reaction from the rest of the press.*

Another example of confidentiality was related to the release of quarterly reports. Here one of the companies prepared a press conference in
relation to a release of its quarterly report. The information director of
this company was contacted by a young local newspaper reporter, who
covered the company for the first time. As there was an obvious uncertainty in the questions she asked, the information director explained
the outline for the phone press-conference as well as routines and activities involved in the quarterly report release in general. The director
gave the reporter a brief background description of the different speakers, presented the agenda to be covered during the conference and argued that the report would touch upon several areas interesting from
the local point of view. The director presented also a number of specific issues he found relevant for the newspaper and the reporter was
encouraged to ask questions about these issues. Furthermore, the director offered a special treatment in form of an individual interview after
the release of the report.

Secrecy
Sometimes the companies also tried to avoid media publicity or to hide
their agenda by applying a variety of indirect media engagements. The
first example reveals how one of the companies tried to avoid publicity
with respect to a controversial political initiative taken by the company's president. Prior to an industry meeting, where the company's
president was expected to give a talk on the state of affairs in the
Swedish industry, an international business newspaper published an interview with the president in which he expressed his critical and controversial opinion about Swedish political authorities and declared his
concerns with regard to the company's future in Sweden. The interview was cited and commented upon in several Swedish newspapers
and the upcoming meeting was expected to receive intensive media
coverage. But the company's president expressed his wish to avoid
further media attention as he believed that this issue should not continue to be discussed in public. The information director and his department were therefore asked not to support and encourage the media
interest in the meeting and not to provide any specific information
about the president's appearance. Hence, there were no press releases
or media invitations prepared. When the information director received

a call from a journalist from one of the major business dailies asking for details of the meeting, the information director refused to comment both on the international article as well as the president's upcoming appearance. The journalist was kindly asked to wait for a formal corporate statement and official summary of the meeting signed by the company's president.

Another example for corporate secrecy vis-à-vis the media is the attempt of one of the companies to avoid direct public confrontation by redirecting the media's focus towards a third party. The CEO of this company asked the information director to initiate a public debate that would enable the company to exert influence on a recent decision made by the Swedish government. The decision was unfavourable for the company's future investments. The CEO was aware of how difficult it was to change the governmental decision, but hoped that an effective public/media debate could lead to consideration of alternative options and thereby also re-open the lost business opportunities. After discussing several alternatives with the company's PR-director, the information director decided on a strategy that aimed at a public discussion formally initiated by interest groups, industry organizations and academic experts. He motivated his choice of strategy as follows:

> *By the power of their authorities these professionals might initiate a public opinion that can 'prepare the land' and create pressure on the government to re-think its decision. We can then openly present our alternatives that will appear as more legitimate, without risking to be accused of serving our own interests.*

Hence, he contacted several organizations and academic experts and asked them to rewrite his 'story' based on their professional opinions. The following day the re-written articles were sent to a journalist at one of the major Swedish dailies in ready-to-use format, i.e. they were prepared for publication as they followed the standard format for journalistic articles. These articles were published on the front page as well as within the newspaper's business section.

Concluding Discussion

This chapter has aimed to unwrap and investigate media-source interaction in the production of business news. The theoretical concept of negotiation – previously used mainly in the field of political journalism – was brought into a new setting, the field of business news. The empirical study indicates that the term negotiation is relevant and useful also in analysing interactions between business media and corporate sources. In our characterization of the Swedish context of business news production we emphasized two types of professional players – business media organisations and corporate communication departments – and we suggested that interactions, while still being relatively unrestricted, had become more formalized over the last few years. Our study of media work in two corporations shows that corporate media work plays an important role in business news production. In the corporations, we found examples of all four media-source strategies, presented by Ericson et al. (1989), which indicates that communication work in news source organisations is highly organized and planned.

In this final section, we will elaborate on three key features characterizing the media-source interaction in the field of business news:
1) business news production as institutionally embedded negotiation processes between media and news sources, 2) corporate news sources 'running the show', and 3) intra-organizational structures of news sources and their effect on negotiation.

First, whereas earlier literature has stressed that the relation between media and news sources is characterized both by struggle and interdependence, the findings from the field of business news lead us to the latter feature of the relationships. Explicit 'struggles' over the news content are rare; rather, the production of news itself seems to work as a governing principle of interactions between corporations and the business media. The empirical findings describe situations in which business journalists and corporate representatives co-operate in the production of the news. Journalists want to produce business news, and corporations want to be in the news. Therefore, news production does not necessarily mean opposing interests between media and sources.

In this way, the interaction between business media and corporate news source is highly institutionalized and follows well established routines. Over the last few decades, practices of both business journalism and corporate communication have undergone processes of professionalization, which have made the two types of organizations adapt one another's practices. The corporate communication departments have largely learnt to talk the language of media. At the same time editorial offices of business news outlets, which are increasingly populated by business graduates, have to some extent also adopted the language and logic of business. In other words, differences in practices and organisational boundaries have become blurred, influencing the interaction of business media and business organizations. Actual negotiations between these two types of organizations, in the sense of overt bargaining over for example access and rights, are therefore rare because much of the interaction is based on established principles on how to interact and collaborate. The empirical findings presented earlier in this chapter support our ideas about corporate relations with journalists as guided by professional and occupational expectations where ongoing production of business news is a primary goal.

Second, the literature on negotiation suggests that news sources have an advantage in the process of news production and that the journalists have an advantage in finishing the final product, i.e. in deciding news format and content. In the field of business news, however, corporate news sources also play an important role in deciding news content. The examples of media work at corporate communication departments in Sweden presented in this chapter show that the interaction with journalists is guided by, and dependent on, the type of information, as it is defined by the corporations. Information directors and their co-workers edit, interpret and censure the news material through for example ready-to-use statements, prepared Q&A lists, press releases, co-optation of journalists, and communication strategies for addressing specific issues. Moreover, the corporate communicators can in advance assume and anticipate not only whom they would talk to on specific issues, but also what kind of questions and reactions they could expect from journalists. Similar awareness seem to also exist at 'the other side of the fence', in the media organizations, as for example has been shown in the previously mentioned study on quarterly reports (Grafström et al. 2006).

Third, the dominant role played by corporate news sources in the production processes of business news points to the importance of carefully examining the intra-organisational structures of corporate communication work. The four empirical examples in the present study – presenting four different media strategies used by the studied corporations – show how intra-organisational corporate routines and structures influence the characteristics of negotiation. As these structures constitute an organizational framework in which negotiations take place, they are of key importance for a comprehensively mapping of the relationships between media and news sources (cf. Gammal 1997).

In sum, our main conclusion is that the relations between journalists and corporate communicators are, to a large extent, based in a relatively stable context governing the mutual understanding of how to behave in specific situations. The chapter has shown that business news items are edited by both parties, but that this process is subordinated to common routines, rituals and norms supporting production of the news rather than negotiations of specific content. We have also addressed negotiations as being affected by the intra-organizational structures of the source organizations.

Finally, it is important to remember that the present study includes only business media and corporate communication departments. Previous studies in the field (see e.g. Grafström et al. 2006) point to a large range of actors, such as communication and public relation consultants, interest groups, analysts, engaged in business news production processes. Future studies should continue the work with identifying actors influencing the production of business news, and examine how they interact with one another and with business media.

Bibliography

Barley, S. R. (1996) Technicians in the workplace: Ethnographic Evidence for Bringing Work into Organization Studies. *Administrative Science Quarterly* Vol.41(3): 404-441.

Cook, T. (1998) *Governing with the News: The News Media as a Political Institution*. Chicago, Chicago: University of Chicago Press.

Cornelisen, J. (2004) *Corporate Communications: Theory and Practice*. London: Sage Publications.

Czarniawska, B. (2004) *Narratives in Social Science Research*. London: Sage Publications.

Davis, A. (2000) Public Relations, Business News and the Reproduction of Corporate Elite Power. *Journalism* Vol. 1 (3): 282-304.

Engwall, L. (2006) Minerva and the Media: Universities Protecting and Promoting Themselves. Paper presented at the 2nd Workshop on the Process of Reform of University Systems, Venice, Italy, May 4-6 2006.

Ericson, R. V., P. M. Baranek & J. B. L. Chan (1989) *Negotiating Control: A Study of News Sources*. Milton Keynes: Open University Press.

Gammal, D. L. (1997) *Relations Between British Government and the Media in Wartime. An Analysis of the Falklands War (1982) and the Gulf War (1991)*. Doctoral Thesis. Faculty of Social and Political Sciences. Cambridge, Cambridge University.

Grafström, M. (2006) *The Development of Swedish Business Journalism. Historical Roots of an Organisational Field*. Doctoral Thesis No. 121. Department of Business Studies, Uppsala University.

Grafström, M., J. Grünberg, J. Pallas & K. Windell (2006) *Ekonominyhetens väg: Från kvartalsrapporter till ekonominyheter*. Stockholm: SNS Förlag.

Larsson, L. (2005) *Upplysning och propaganda: Utveckling av svensk PR och information*. Lund: Studentlitteratur.

Pallas, J. (forthcoming) Talking Organizations: Corporate Media Work and Negotiation of Institutions. Doctoral Thesis. Department of Business Studies, Uppsala University.

Slaatta, T. (2003) *Den norske medieorden: Posisjoner og privilegier.* Oslo: Gyldendal Akademisk.

SPRA and PRECIS (2005) Informationsindex. Stockholm, The Swedish Public Relations Association and The Association of Public Relations Consultancies in Sweden.

Tuchman, G. (1973) Making News by Doing Work: Routinizing the Unexpected. *The American Journal of Sociology* Vol. 79 (1): 110-131.

CHAPTER 9

Dressing Up Hospitals
as Enterprises?
The Expansion and Managerialization of
Communication in Norwegian Hospitals

HALDOR BYRKJEFLOT &
SVEIN IVAR ANGELL[1]

*Organizations nowadays perceive anything they say and do as
communication – and in particular communication that can and
ought to be handled strategically* (Christensen & Morsing 2005:
21).

Introduction
It has become a standard exercise in political science and in the discipline of public administration to take note of the changes occurring in
the way the public sector is organized, in particular the shift towards
'New Public Management' (NPM). In this chapter we focus on the
hospital sector in Norway, which exemplifies the way in which market
and management oriented reforms can create identity problems for
public sector organizations. Following a series of reforms in the 1990s,
including the introduction of activity-based funding, stronger patient
rights, free choice of hospital and general management, a major reform
was undertaken in 2002 whereby the ownership of hospitals was transferred from the counties to the state. The hospitals were reorganised as
regional and local enterprises and merged into larger organizational
units with their own boards, missions and managerial hierarchies. Several of the new managers now argued that the organization had to think
more strategically about the way it used communication, since it was

[1] The research presented in this chapter is based on two projects at the Rokkan Center: 'Autonomy, Transparency and Management, three reform programs in healthcare: a comparative project', financed by The Norwegian Research Council and 'Freedom of speech for hospital employees', financed by The Freedom of Expression Foundation, Oslo.

necessary for each hospital enterprise to establish a specific identity. New information professionals were recruited into the managerial ranks and many of them were keen to develop communication strategies with such purposes in mind.

The questions asked in this chapter are, first, whether new communication roles have been developed, secondly, to what extent communication strategies have been adopted by these new hospital enterprises and, thirdly, is it possible to see a link between the content of such strategies and emerging concepts for the management of communication in the public sector; namely marketing management, media management and corporate communication.

We use four kinds of empirical material to document and analyze the recent expansion of strategic communication. First, we present survey data registering that information tasks are now being formalized, professionalized and integrated into the function of management. Secondly, most health enterprises now have communication strategies, which we have collected and analyzed.[1] Thirdly, we rely on several case studies of communication practices in healthcare enterprises (Johnson 2005, Johnson & Byrkjeflot 2006, Svendsen 2005, Holme 2006). Fourthly, we rely on interviews, documents and participant observation relating to the biennial meeting of the information workers in hospitals (IFS 2003-2005).

Why Do Public Institutions Develop Communication Strategies?

One might well ask why the hospitals together with several other public institutions set so much store today by developing strategic communication. In general, the act of institutionalizing strategic communication in public institutions has been understood as a response to an emerging 'audit society', i.e. a new governance regime associated with the development of a range of policy instruments dealing with performance control and monitoring of public institutions (Power 1997, Moran 2003). As a consequence, public institutions have to develop more strategic and 'auditable selves', selves that are transparent and

---

[1] We have collected and analyzed documents that present such communication strategies. Our sample contains documents that have been developed at various points of time and of shorter and longer durability. Most documents were written and adopted immediately after the hospital reform in 2002, while some of them were developed as late as 2004. One was even adopted prior to the hospital reform. We make use of these communication strategies and other empirical data to interpret the current communication landscape, and trace some of the possible paths into the future.

accountable to the outer world and which include mechanisms of monitoring and self-correction (Power 2005).

There are various ways to account for the process bringing forth such a regime. The first kind of developmental narrative puts emphasis on the idea that modern societies have become 'service democracies', which means that they move away from a traditional 'input' model of democratic legitimation associated with elections and political repre-sentation, towards an 'output' model, where it is increasingly the effec-tive production of services and performance in service production that count (Scharpf 1999).

A second narrative sees the development of strategic communica-tion as a response to a decline of trust in public institutions. Particu-larly in the USA it has been reported that there is a long-term trend to-ward a decline in public confidence in most public institutions. The same was the case with business institutions in the aftermath of the 'new economy' and the ENRON scandals. The slogans of transparency and accountability, that had become increasingly popular among busi-ness institutions that had been affected by the post-ENRON critique, were now translated also into public sector organizations and other countries than the UK and the USA. As they did this, however, the idea of strategic communication became associated with new kinds of problems and actors, and may for this reason have had unexpected consequences. It has not been documented that the confidence in pub-lic institutions in Norway has been plummeting in the same way as in the USA. One cannot exclude the possibility that the development of new concepts for organizing communication, may also lead to a de-cline in trust, rather than the opposite. Tsoukas (2005: 25), among oth-ers, has argued that expert systems are likely to become even less trusted when more information is provided on their inner working (Strathern 2000).

Another well-known narrative refers to the increasing differentiation of the public sectors and the knowledge systems that underpin them. This increased complexity relates to the expansion in information and also the increased demand for and access to information and expert knowledge among publics. Knowledge claims brought forward in sup-port of public reforms and public institutions are now contested on a regular basis. It may be for this reason that public firms have to make more use of strategic communication and knowledge management in order to convince their publics about the positive effects of reforms and in order to mobilize support for new reform agendas. One should also be aware of the role of the information professions, and the chang-

ing content of the concepts used by them in their strive for professionalization and as part of their ambition to be included in managerial
ranks. There are at least three alternative concepts for communication
management available; marketing management, media management
and corporate communication or reputation management.

Management Concept	Phenomenon Emphasized	Actors Emphasized	Ideal Characteristics of Communication
Marketing Management	New Public Management, competition, free choice, markets	Customers, top managers, governments	Establish a strong product brand in order to attract customers and employees
Media Management	Mediatization, expanding media, changes in public sphere and relationship between sources and journalists	Journalists, information professionals, top managers	Establish legitimacy in public sphere by developing stable channels into media. Control information flows from organization to media
Corporate Communication/ Reputation Management	Changes in corporate identities and communication practices. Reputation management as a necessary response	Information professionals, stakeholders, managers at all levels	Establish a corporate reputation through a unified organizational culture. Internal mobilization for two-way communication

*Table 9.1: Management Concepts Used in the Development of Com-
munication Strategies in the Public Sector*

New Public Management Reforms; the Rise of Quasi-Markets and Marketing

Since 1999 several reforms have been introduced in the Norwegian specialized healthcare sector, with a view to increasing effectiveness and
improving healthcare outcomes for patients and citizens in general. According to recent surveys of the internal organization of Norwegian
hospitals (INTORG) there has been a major increase in the use of instruments commonly associated with New Public Management in
Norwegian hospitals (INTORG 1999, 2001, 2003, 2005). Particularly
important in this context have been the development of activity-based
funding, patients' rights, free choice of hospital and the development of
indicators of quality and performance. In light of reforms such as these
the recently established state-controlled healthcare corporations can
justifiably be referred to as actors in a 'quasi-market' (Byrkjeflot 2005,
Bartlett & Le Grand 1993). For such quasi-markets to operate in a way

that is similar to 'real' markets, a lot of information is obviously needed. Thus we can expect a rush on the part of information professionals, and managers to produce the kind of information that the government may demand as a basis for well-informed political decisions and that consumers need for making rational choices. Also we can expect hospitals to start marketing themselves in order to attract patients (Table 9.1).

Mediatization - The Expansion of Journalism and Media Management

Mediatization refers to the media's potential for replacing other forms of communication - such as the interpersonal or place-bound – and to its capacity for expanding communication of such kinds (Schulz 2004). The mass media appear as an arena, that to a certain extent represents a challenge to established circles of power, such as 'club government' or medical societies (Cook 1998, Kristensen 2005, Moran 2003). A related effect of 'mediatization' is that practices and events have to be presented in a way that fits the media's own rules or codes. This means that the authors or presenters of any message directed at publics or customers have to take the media into account in the way they present their message. It is thus often pointed out that any manager or institutional representative has to be proactive and to think how to frame their own narrative and select the kind of events they want to have presented and reported in the media.

The mediatization argument is also connected with the idea that a more ideological, self-conscious brand of media professionalism - sometimes known as 'journal-ism' -has been institutionalized in the news media and in society in general.[2] This does not mean that journalism has become a more powerful profession in itself, but that it has become an ideology and a discourse that holds a fragmented occupational field together (Aldridge & Evetts 2003).

A recent Danish report on the relationship between public relations agencies and the media suggests that political and public institutions are particularly subject to influence by mediatization processes, since they are involved in democratic processes, where the public sphere occupies a particularly important position (Kristensen 2005). Public institutions like hospitals are now exposed to media even more than before, partly because they have become public enterprises that have to present their own strategies and visions, but also because of an increased

---

[2] The Nordic term 'journalisme' has been used to refer to the idea that journalists have developed their own self-serving ideology (Petterson 1994, Eide 2000).

emphasis on health consumerism and health as a key political issue in modern society. Reporting on healthcare issues has been and still is one of the major preoccupations of the modern mass media (Lund 1997, Møller Pedersen 2005, Seale 2004, Eide & Hernes, 1995).

The concept for managing communication referred to here as media management puts more emphasis on the relationship with the media, whereas in the marketing approach the emphasis is more on the economy. Both concepts of communication are mainly strategic with one possible exception: within media management there is also an emphasis on developing or maintaining a good relationship with journalists, and in this context one could discern an interest in a two-way dialogue.

A New Managerial Ideal: Corporate Communication

The new perception of communication that has emerged in business contexts during the last ten years or so is the concept of corporate communication and the associated practice of reputation management, which has now also been institutionalized in many public organizations.

Corporate communication is presented as a merger of several professional paradigms, including marketing and public relations (but not, it is interesting to note, journalism);

> *...advertising, public relations and marketing show a marked convergence these days in terms of preoccupation with identity. Within this expanding perspective.... virtually all dimensions of an organisation's life can be regarded as strategic communication, that is, communication that the organisation should actively seek to circumscribe, manage and control* (Christensen & Cheney 2005: 6).

The aim of the professional function associated with this new paradigm is to act strategically on behalf of 'the organization', not on behalf of the medical profession or any of the other stakeholders (Davis 2002). As in the earlier movement of organizational culture, there is in corporate communication a strong emphasis on integration and wholeness. Terms used include 'integrated communications' and corporate branding. The aim is to 'create a platform of symbols, a master brand, that can inform and shape all forms of market related communications' (Christensen & Cheney 2005: 7). It is thus suggested that there is no longer any difference between internal and external communication or between management and communication management. The same expertise is needed to serve employees and other stakeholders, and there should be consistency in the messages presented in the various contexts. A typical justification for this is that employees who speak out positively in favor of their workplace have more influence on would-be customers than advertising or distribution (Christensen & Cheney 2005: 9).

In the corporate communication literature the environment of an organization is considered in terms of various stakeholder groups rather than in terms of 'the market' (New Public Management) or 'the public' (e.g. as represented in the media). Cornelissen defines corporate communication as a management function 'that offers a framework and vocabulary for the effective coordination of all means of communications with the overall purpose of establishing and maintaining favorable reputations with stakeholder groups upon which the organization is dependent' (Cornelissen 2004: 23).

The concept of corporate communication provides the information professionals with a new and broader vision aiming at the integration of the previous paradigms of marketing and public relations. The view of communication favored by the protagonists of corporate communication is a dialogical-symmetrical one, but it can be claimed that this view is just as strategic as the other ones, and that it differs mainly in the way it seeks to legitimate itself.

Contrasting the Concepts for Communication Management

The three concepts may complement one another, but they also differ, in that they refer to different actors and development logics. The actors behind the development of quasi-markets in the public sector are governments, managers involved in the implementation and monitoring of policy instruments associated with New Public Management, consumers exercising their right to free choice, and so on (Table 9.1). The actors that have been most involved with mediatization are the journalists and the publics that consume media reports and participate most actively in the formation of public opinion. There is also a growing group of 'info-mediaries', public relations consultants, etc., taking part in the professionalization of the field of communication. The concept of corporate communication could probably not have been as easily adopted in the public sector, if it were not for the experiences made by the marketing and public relations professions with the previous New Public Management movement.

241

The concept of corporate communication aims at erasing the boundaries between management roles and the roles of communication professionals in the organization. Attempts to merge these two roles are bound to meet resistance, however (Christensen & Morsing 2005, Cornelissen 2005). If one of the aims of corporate communication is to develop loyalty to the organization and to avoid situations in which the organization speaks with many voices, then it also will have to use its power to establish a more unitary communication structure. Such structures may be seen by health professionals to challenge the ideals of free speech and the right of the public to be informed, however.

We have now presented some of the dilemmas, concepts and ideals associated with the current trends towards the institutionalization of strategic communication in the public sector. Against the background of this discussion we will now present the empirical data we have collected, consisting primarily of survey data, interviews, case studies and a sample of communication strategies.

The Expansion and Managerialization of Communication

It was reported in 2005 that a vast majority (95 percent) of Norwegian hospitals had engaged their own information managers. This meant an increase from 82 percent in 2003. In comparison, a similar investigation undertaken by the Forum for Hospital Information (FSI) in 2001 found that only 33 percent of the hospitals had employed their own information managers, and that only 20 percent of them included information managers in the top management teams. In 2005 it was reported that 50 percent of the hospitals had included the information managers in the top management groups.

We have no exact data regarding the number of information professionals or the diffusion of communication statements over time, but some trends can be traced by comparing FSI 2001 with INTORG's surveys of Norwegian hospitals in 1999, 2001, 2003 and 2005.[3] There is clearly an increase in the number of information workers and information managers in Norwegian hospitals, and we estimate that there was at least a 100 percent increase between 2001 and 2005. This trend is confirmed by several case studies that have been undertaken regarding four hospital enterprises in one specific region. The studies were

---

[3] The response rate for the FSI survey was 70%, 71 hospitals were asked. The INTORG surveys include a fairly complete sample of Norwegian hospitals. 63 public and 14 private hospitals were questioned in 2005. In 2003 59 hospitals were included in the survey. The response rate was above 80% in both 2003 and 2005.

based on interviews with information professionals, managers and journalists in each enterprise (Johnson 2005, Johnson & Byrkjeflot 2006, Svendsen 2005, Holme 2006). These case studies indicate that following the health reform in 2002 there was a rush among the enterprises involved to employ information personnel and to start issuing formal communication statements. The studies also revealed the many mergers between established hospitals that followed in the wake of the reform. All this meant that a new group of public relations professionals was being recruited to join the various staffs. The INTORG 2005 survey shows that 22 percent of the information workers came from a background in journalism, whereas 13 percent came from a marketing or public relations background. 49 percent had been recruited internally.

Some of the most high profiled of the new information managers came from careers in the media sector, often topped up by a brief period of education in marketing or journalism (Holme 2006, Svendsen 2005). The results of our case studies indicate that these externally recruited information professionals were those most active in developing the communication strategies discussed in the present chapter. In some cases external consultants had been involved in the development of strategies and visions.

Marketing

In the early period of the reform in particular there were expectations that a system would develop whereby the hospitals would compete for patients and resources. In this situation it was thought to be essential that the health enterprises should work at marketing and building up a good reputation in and outside their own region in order to attract patients. With this in mind the Forum for Hospital Information (IFS) thus held a meeting in November 2003, at which one whole session was devoted to one theme, namely 'How to make yourself attractive to the patients'. At this session some of the most successful cases of advertising in public hospitals were presented (Heldaas 2003, Johannesen 2003). Here it was emphasized that the Norwegian healthcare system had moved into a new age, the age of markets, and that marketing henceforth was the way to go in order to increase the number of patients and to generate more resources for the enterprises concerned. One of the cases revealed that a local hospital had raised the number of patients by 25 percent with help of modern marketing methods.[4]

---

[4] We have studied the agenda and presentations at the biennial IFS-meeting and have participated in some of the meetings (http://www.nsh.no/script/list.asp?show=old).

The increasing importance of marketing in Norwegian healthcare was also documented in the 2003 INTORG survey in which 52 percent of the hospitals reported that they had a strategy for marketing directed at patients. 46 percent had placed advertisements in daily newspaper in order to attract patients, and 69 percent had provided information to the media for the same purpose. Similar questions were asked in 2005, showing that slightly fewer hospitals had information strategies oriented specifically towards attracting patients, and that the number of hospitals providing newspapers with advertisements and information was slightly lower. However, those that had put advertisements in newspapers had advertised more intensively.

Media Management
Several sessions at the biennial meeting of the information workers in hospitals were devoted to media relations and media management. The 2005 INTORG survey shows that 40 percent of the hospitals regularly monitor the media, and that 61 percent had trained managers in media management. As noted above, 69 percent had provided information to the media in 2003, but no other questions about media management were asked that year. Some local enterprises have principles of their own when it comes to dealing with the media, and some of this had been developed before the current communication strategies came into being. The communication strategies also frequently outline the information routines, for instance how the media should be handled in specific situations, perhaps in connection with some major accident in the immediate neighborhood.

Corporate Communication
A topic that seems to have grown in importance, apart from the targeting of specific patient groups and the media, is corporate communication and reputation management. In November 2005 the major topic on the agenda at the IFS biennial meeting was the relationship between national, regional and local identities in the healthcare services. There was discussion as to the possible advantage to a hospital of developing its own logo, or whether they should all stick to the national standards developed by the Ministry of Health. It was reported that in three of five regions health enterprises were allowed to develop their own logos. It was discussed whether communication strategies and Internet presentations should be developed locally or in a more standardized way imposed from above. It turned out that most local enterprises, of which there were then 28 all together, had developed their own com-

munication strategies and presentations on the Web, as had the five regional health enterprises as well, but these five saw it as their job to adopt a coordinator role vis-à-vis the information managers in their regions.

Another indication of the growing emphasis on reputation management in the hospitals was the response to a question in the INTORG surveys about the use of visions and communication strategies and information personnel. In 2003 it had already been reported that a majority of the Norwegian health enterprises had adopted their own communication statements, and in 2005 we found that almost 100 percent had developed such documents. In 2003 nearly all health enterprises had adopted a vision formula. More than 80 percent of the enterprises also reported that they had one or more particular kinds of treatment known as their specialty ('flagship brand') (INTORG 2003, 2005).

Communication Strategies

In 2005 there were altogether 28 Local Health Enterprises and 5 Regional Enterprises in Norway. They all had a document of some kind to indicate their communication strategy. Our sample included documents from 24 enterprises - 19 local and five regional. The practice of adopting a communication strategy and a mission statement reflects the growing priority given to the management of communication. What is interesting about the communication strategies that we have collected is that they have been developed over a period during which hospitals were developing missions and visions of their own. Such documents, stating the visions, missions and basic values of the organization, have become more important in private firms as well as in public organizations in recent years (Bordum & Hansen 2005). The documents provide us with a self-description, indicating why greater emphasis on communication is considered necessary, and justifications for having a communication strategy. The communication statements may reflect the more prominent position occupied by communication personnel in contemporary hospitals. A communication strategy as defined in such documents seems to represent something between a guideline for action (instruks) and a mission statement.[5]

---

[5] All the documents state clearly that information is a managerial responsibility. This means that the responsibility may be delegated to the individuals who are in charge of particular divisions and units of the enterprise. This principle reflects a general objective that information activity ought to be integrated with the managerial activity in each unit. It is frequently stated in the documents that information and communication is a managerial tool, an indication of its high priority as well as its level of generalization.

However, there is a certain ambiguity in the very definition of communication: it is not only a managerial but also a technical skill, reflecting the previously predominant perception of communication work in hospitals, whereby the communication department was regarded a 'newsletter producer rather than a strategic unit' (Holme 2006: 79). Accordingly, some of the statements still describe in practical detail how internal newsletters are produced.

After the 2002 hospital reform most communication statements have become much more comprehensive, although not necessarily longer than the first strategies developed a few years before the reform. One communication plan, published in 2000 has 54 pages; another from 2002 has three. Due to the variation in format and content, it is still hard to find a 'typical' communication statement. The documents also have different titles. Examples are: 'Media – and communication strategy' (1), 'Information and communication strategy' (1), 'Communication strategy' (6), 'Strategy document (internal and external information)' (1), 'Communication and information plan' (2), 'Communication platform' (4 of the 5 regional health enterprises have a platform), 'Communication in xx hospital' (1), 'Communication policy' (1) etc. Some enterprises have several documents (e.g. one list of rules for handling the media and one general strategy including a communication strategy). There seems to be a trend toward developing a more standardized communication statement, however, and the most recent tend towards names like 'Communication strategy' or 'Communication platform'.

It is the impression from our interviews that in most cases the information manager in the enterprise has been responsible for developing the communication strategy, but that the top manager and members of the board may also have influenced the content before the board has accepted it. Against this background, a communication strategy can tell us several things about the ongoing attempts to define managerial roles and the relationship between communication activity and management in the health enterprises. The strategy documents naturally indicate the way in which the enterprises want to be regarded, rather than how they actually appear to the public. The fact that such statements have been produced at all indicates that the new information professionals have gained influence and that communication and management are now regarded as crucial to the establishment of a good reputation.

The Contents of Communication Strategies

If management is regarded as goal-oriented or strategic communication, then it is interesting to look at the way management philosophies are being affected by the new ideals associated with marketing management, media management and corporate communication. To what extent are these three concepts for the management of communication present in the communication strategy documents? A marketing perspective is oriented toward competition among individual institutions, and toward the transformation of institutions into enterprises. It is thus relevant to ask whether the communication statements reflect a private enterprise identity or an identity as public institutions. Do they identify themselves mainly as competitive units in a marketplace or as an integrated part of a larger national healthcare service? In the latter case, hospitals may turn more toward the government and the democratic institutions at various levels for guidance about what to do. In such a case, we may expect the hospitals more attuned to a view of communication as dialogue, while the marketing-oriented hospital may define its communication ideals on more strategic lines.

In terms of mediatization, the statements can be said to deal in particular with the media, and that the media is treated not simply as one among many stakeholders but as a particular stakeholder that has to be considered and influenced. What is particularly interesting in our present context is the extent to which the hospitals define their relation with the media in an active or a more passive way, i.e. how far do they seek to influence the way they themselves are presented in the media.

In terms of corporate communication the aim of the hospitals studied is to create a distinct identity of their own, not only with a view to establishing an image resembling that of a private organization or to attracting customers and employees, but also allowing them more power to manage and monitor their own relationships to a variety of stakeholders. We will analyze the extent to which the communication statements reveal an ambition to command reputation management, and the way in which this is to be achieved.

All three approaches emphasize the idea that communication is a managerial task, although it is clearly the corporate communication approach that is most ambitious on behalf of management and to the capacity of workers to adopt a managerial attitude. We thus analyze the extent to which communication is defined in the communication statements as a managerial task.

We explore five dimensions relating to these strategies.[6] First, to what extent is communication regarded as a tool for developing an identity for the hospital and what kinds of identity are presented in the communication statements? Do the enterprises see themselves as private enterprises, or do they reveal a public administration identity? Secondly, we want to find out whether the statements define an ideal way of communicating, and if so what does this actually consist of. Is it a dialogic or a strategic view of communication that the documents reveal? Thirdly, what kind of awareness of the role of the media emerges from the documents, and, to what extent do they express a desire to be proactive and to influence the media? Fourthly, what view of the relation between external and internal communication do the strategies reveal? To what extent is communication regarded as an explicit management tool? Finally, how far are the hospitals aware of the role of communication in their attempts to establish a positive reputation?

Communicating an Identity

Our first question concerns the kind of organizational identities that are revealed by these statements. This is a particularly interesting point, since it is generally claimed that the New Public Management movement usually heralds the private enterprise model as 'the more beautiful sister'.[7]

The statements are analyzed according to whether they reflect a private enterprise identity, a combination of private enterprise and a public administration identity, or a public administration identity, or whether it is difficult to tell whether they have an identity at all (Table 9.2).

	Numbers	Percent
Private enterprise identity	2	8
Mixed identity	7	29
Public administration identity	7	29
No explicit identity	8	33
N=	24	99

Table 9.2: Communicating an Identity

---

[6] We have coded the contents of the different statements according to the following main variables: communication and identity, communication ideals, communication and the media, communication and management, and communication and reputation, with sub-categories.

[7] Barbara Czarniawska, who made this claim, also says that 'Either the market or the state must understand organizational identity' (1997: 52). A public administration identity is oriented towards the state, whereas a private enterprise identity orients itself towards the market.

The communication statements reveal that there are noticeable differences in identity between the various enterprises. In two of 24 enterprises the communication plans reveal private enterprise values, expressing an orientation toward marketing, exhibiting commercial values and seeing patients as customers in a marketplace. In seven of the 24 enterprises such values appear in combinations with values reflecting a 'public institution' identity, which means that a certain awareness of being a part of public administration is present, and that this is thought to be relevant for the communication practice. In seven of 24 statements the communication activity is defined in accordance with a public administration identity. In eight of 24 enterprises the self-image is vague or not explicitly defined.

The private enterprise identity and the commercial values are most evident in the communication statement of the same enterprise that reveals an explicitly strategic communication ideal (see below). The development in the hospital sector in recent years is described in this communication strategy as a transformation from a 'public administration mentality' to a 'customer - perspective'. The communication statement of one of the other local health enterprises offers a striking – or illustrative – contrast:

> *The starting point for the information- and communication strategy of (the Health Enterprise) is the laws and regulations that govern public health service and the public sector in Norway in general. The strategy is the framework for the [health enterprise's] information policy…. As health institutions the hospitals and their staff have to act according to the norms of professional secrecy and personal protection that are also legally sanctioned. At the same time the hospitals are public institutions that have to act according to rules of public access.*

In some of the communication plans the private and public administration identities are combined, as in the plan of another of the local health enterprises:

> *The aim of the information from [the Health Enterprise] and the communication with its target groups is to contribute to the hospital's vision of being the most attractive hospital in Norway both for patients and employees.*

In the next section of the plan, however, the laws and regulation governing the communication policy of the enterprise are stressed.

As far as institutional identity is concerned, it is difficult to discern a clear pattern as to whether the hospitals consider themselves to be private enterprises mainly oriented towards providing information in order for the quasi-markets in healthcare to work properly or, public institutions still mainly seeking to satisfy the state and the public in their demand for information. Although the recent healthcare reforms, particularly the introduction of the enterprise form, were based on New Public Management ideas, it is not necessarily the case that a private enterprise identity has been established among the individual institutions.

The analysis of communication strategies reveals that the enterprises may prefer to dress up as part of the private sector, but that a public administration identity is still present in most health enterprises. Several researchers in the tradition of new institutionalism claim that such hybridism is a feature of New Public Management reforms in general (Brunsson 2002, Jespersen 2005).

Ideals for Communication
According to the corporate communication viewpoint the enterprises are mainly concerned about their reputation among their stakeholder groups, and communication is regarded as a tool for achieving an improvement in reputation among stakeholders. In such a case, one would expect to find a strategic communication ideal, which means that communication assumes an asymmetrical form rather than through the form of a dialogue (chp. Grunig & Hunt 1984). However, one may also expect that the enterprises maintain a view of communication in accordance with public policy statements that emphasize a more dialogical view of communication.

We have established four sub-categories for categorizing the communication statements. First, whether the communication ideal is explicitly strategic. Secondly, whether a dialogue between equal partners in a symmetric relationship is said to be the ideal. Thirdly whether the communication plan refers directly to the principles stated in the public communication policy conducted by the government (Arbeids- og administrasjonsdepartementet 2001) or whether no explicit communication ideal is presented. The results are presented in Table 9.3.

	Numbers	Percent
Explicitly strategic	1	4
Dialogue between equal partners	12	50
Public information policy	9	38
No explicit ideal presented	2	8
N=	24	100

Table 9.3: Communication Ideals

Perhaps surprisingly, strategic communication is revealed as an explicit ideal in one of the 24 cases only. Instead it is the dialogic ideals that catch the eye. In 12 of the 24 cases the communication ideal is defined as a dialogue between equal partners in a symmetrical relationship. In nine cases the communication activity is explicitly defined in terms of the government's communication policy. These statements too, could be said to rely on a dialogue perspective, since this is the expressed principle underlying the state communication policy (Arbeids- og Administrasjonsdepartementet 2001). The ideals for the communication practice could be characterized as ambiguous, or as not being defined at all in two of the 24 cases only. The fact that a communication policy is explicitly defined in so many of the statements suggests that it is regarded as important to have a policy. The mechanisms for the diffusion of such practices have been discussed frequently by neo-institutionalists, and it has been noted that it may either be a consequence of professionalization, which has been referred to as normative isomorphism, but could also result from mimetic and coercive processes (Dimaggio & Powell 1991).

The predominant way of defining communication in the communication strategies, then, is in the form of dialogue. This ideal, which is regarded as superior in the statements of the Norwegian Communication Association[8], is reflected in the communication strategies of several of the enterprises concerned. One of the local health enterprises can exemplify this. Here the given core value is that the transmission of information 'takes the needs of both the sender and the receiver into consideration'. The principles of trustworthiness, result-orientation and accessibility are also defined as core values, which could be said to be

---

[8] The association's objective is to 'work to promote the attitude that all information should be based on communication between equal partners and that it should be trustworthy, result-oriented, ethically defensible and easily accessible' (http://www.kommunikasjonsforeningen.no/).

in accordance with the principles defined by the Communication Association.

There is also an overlap among the ideals listed in the text-books that is in use at communication courses at Norwegian universities and colleges (Grunig & Hunt 1984, Ihlen & Robstad 2004) and those quoted in the communication plans. The statements of one of the regional enterprises, for instance, runs – in addition to the principle that the communication should rely on the dialogue approach – that communication should be undertaken in an active manner, that it should be coherent, and that it is the responsibility of the managers at the different levels in the organization. Symmetrical communication is 'the cornerstone of the strategic communication efforts' in the enterprise. In the next paragraph in the same statement it is stated that 'the health enterprise should be profiled as *one* coherent organization externally, and should contain a corporate strategy for dealing with the competition represented by other health enterprises.' Thus although only one of the communication statements reveals an explicitly strategic communication ideal, communication does appear as a strategic tool in most of the other statements too.

Communication and the Media

To what extent is the professionalization and institutionalization of corporate communication in the Norwegian health enterprises a response to the media? As noted above, mediatization can be described as a central process in society, and it is now our aim to examine the extent to which the influence of the media can be traced in the communication strategies of Norwegian health enterprises. All the communication statements contain paragraphs dealing with the media in some way. There are differences, however, in the extent to which the relationship to the media could be described as proactive (Table 9.4).

	Numbers	Percent
Proactive	10	42
Non-proactive	14	58
Non – existent	0	0
N=	24	100

Table 9.4: Communication and the Media

We consider that communication statements, which explicitly include a strategy for influencing the way in which the enterprise is presented in the media, can be described as proactive. As we can see from Table 9.4, 10 of 24 statements could be regarded as proactive, while a majority – 14 of 24 statements – could be characterized as non-proactive.

Among the proactive statements there is a difference as to whether or not the term 'proactive' is explicitly referred to. In the communication statement of one of the local health enterprises the proactive attitude is particularly visible. The statement contains a whole paragraph that is labeled simply 'proactive', and this attitude is linked to the reputation of the institution:

> *The Regional Health Enterprise is a prominent organization in the regional healthcare system and contains a great deal of medical and healthcare knowledge and knowledge about treatment. We want to achieve a more central position as regards the development of new medical knowledge and research on health treatment. It is important for the reputation of [the Regional Health Enterprise] that our competence is visible in the media.*

The need to be visible in order to maintain a good reputation is mentioned in several of the communication statements that we have categorized as proactive. One aspect of this is that the institutions want to influence the way in which they are presented in the media in order to avoid negative publicity. Some of the statements contain paragraphs that stress the importance of promoting a positive image of the enterprise in the media. The following extract from the statement of one of the local health enterprises is an example.

> *Journalists are important mediators of information to the population in the region, and they are also important spokesmen for the public vis-à-vis the hospital. The journalists' view of the hospital could be reflected in the news stories that they produce. In light of this a satisfactory contact with the media's coverage of the enterprise is essential.*

The same statement also includes several paragraphs containing exact prescription for dealing with the media. One important principle is that 'under any circumstances [journalists] must come to an agreement with the hospital before an interview is held. Any kind of photographing should be agreed upon in advance.' Furthermore, all employees have to come to an agreement with their managers or the communication department before talking to the press.

Relationship Inside - Outside

What is perhaps of greatest interest, however, is that so many of the health enterprises recognize the importance of adopting communication strategies in order to establish an identity for themselves. In this context communication is emerging as an important managerial tool and assumes an integrative function (Cornelissen 2004: 23). There is no difference now between the external and the internal. Corporate communication calls for full integration.

We have categorized the communication statements according to three criteria: whether the communications reflect an explicit awareness of the distinction between the external and the internal, whether they are mainly geared to the internal or the external, and the extent to which communication is emphasized as a tool for management (Table 9.5).

	Numbers	Percent
Explicit awareness of link between internal and external communication	13	54
Focus on internal or external link as a managerial tool	6	26
Less emphasis on communication as a management tool	5	20
N=	24	100

Table 9.5: Communication and Management

The most striking feature here is that a majority of the enterprises regard communication as a tool for organizational management. Sometimes they seem to have replaced the idea of having a management strategy by the idea of having a communication strategy. One example:

The communication strategy is a managerial tool that defines the measures and areas that call for the main efforts in the period in question. In addition it indicates who is responsible for and in charge of these efforts. The strategy is initiated and adopted by the board and senior managers of the health enterprise, and is intended as a dynamic tool available to managers at all levels in the organization. Communication must play a self-evident part in all kinds of planning in [the Health Enterprise].

More than half the communication statements recognize an explicit link between the way they manage and communicate internally and the way they manage and communicate with their environment. One of the regional health enterprises defines the aim of its communication activity as follows: 'Work proactively and to be on the offensive in the work with communication both internally and externally', 'Establish a harmonious and coordinated communicative effort for the whole of [the Regional Health Enterprise]'.

Against such a background communication emerges as a tool for developing a common organizational identity within an enterprise while also ensuring that this is consistent with the way in which the organization wants to be perceived by its external publics.

The Norwegian health reform set off a wave of mergers. Some of these naturally took place mainly on an administrative level, but we would also expect that in such cases management would set great store by developing a common organizational culture. The communication strategy of one of the larger local health enterprises, established as an amalgamation of a major hospital and two institutions in its vicinity, provides an example. It is stressed in the communication statement that, against the background of a merger like this, it is essential to ensure the coordination and development of a common culture among the units concerned:

A process is initiated to ensure coherence in visions, aims, strategies, different principles etc. between the various units. In addition, it is necessary to guarantee a satisfactory internal flow of information and communication among the different units.

Communication is thus regarded as a tool for the establishment of a common organizational culture that is to be reflected in the institution's external communication. The sample includes several other examples.

As is shown in Table 9.5, communication as a managerial tool is also stressed by several enterprises, even when there is no explicit reflection upon the link between external and internal communication. Here, too, communication is regarded as an instrument for developing a common organizational identity in the enterprises. The statement of one of the regional health enterprises can serve as an example of this.

This statement takes up the challenge represented by the 2002 enterprise reform as its starting point. The aim of the reform was to secure better treatment for the patients:

> *If this is to be achieved, then we have to work actively on our internal culture, starting with the transformation processes required. In this connection information and communication have a crucial part to play.*

The enterprise also has visions for its external communication activities, but without linking these directly to the role of internal communication within the organization, i.e. internal and external communication is not defined as an integrated managerial tool.

Communication and Reputation

Over the last ten years or so, several reforms implying harder competition for patients and resources among the different organizations have been introduced in the hospital sector. It has also implied a greater emphasis on autonomy at the institutional level. Some of the communication statements have claimed that in the present situation the reforms mean that hospitals have to act in the same way as other enterprises in a free market. It is no longer appropriate or sufficient to behave like a traditional public institution or only as an integral part of a national healthcare system. One communication statement says for instance that due to the introduction of free choice regarding hospitals, the 'customer perspective' has to be predominant in each institution's policy:

> *The patients or "customers" choose the hospital making the best offer. Because of a huge demand for health-workers, they will choose the hospital that provides the best terms of employment. In the struggle for patients and the most highly skilled workers, the hospitals have to market themselves to a greater extent than before in order to secure an adequate supply of patients and employees.*

Marketing as part of the communication policy is explicitly referred to in a minority of the communication statements only, and does not appear at all in the vast majority of the plans. It thus seems as though the statements are closer here to a corporate communication concept than to a marketing worldview. The reputation-promoting motif is evident in all the communication statements analyzed, although the extent to which it appears varies somewhat. In order to examine the variations among the communication plans we have classified these according to the emphasis placed on reputation management. The results are shown in Table 9.6.

	Numbers	Percent
Very much emphasized	16	67
Emphasized	5	21
Less emphasized	3	12
Not emphasized	0	0
N=	24	100

Table 9.6: Communication as a Strategy for Promoting a Good Reputation

In almost 70 percent of the strategies the reputation-seeking motif was preeminent. In 21 percent of the strategies this motif was present, but not in a very explicit way. In three of the strategies, the idea of using communication for reputation-promotion was less prominent, but there were no communication statements that lacked this motif entirely.

The analysis shows that the hospitals – or at least their communication managers and top administrators – are very much concerned with their reputations. But there is some variation when it comes to the way they seek to establish a reputation and upon which value reputation is supposed to depend. Some of the enterprises seek to build a reputation based on what could be called private market values. Not surprisingly, this is the case in the communication statement quoted above, for instance. This statement was imbued with a 'customer approach' as regards both patients and employees, and it also launched marketing as an integral part of its communication strategy. In this statement the idea of 'branding' is also introduced as a necessary part of the repertoire for improving reputation:

> *To create a reputation for this [Health Enterprise] as a hospital with satisfied patients and confident employees, we have to go in for what we call branding. An important prerequisite for this is to possess a product that is saleable. The 'product' in this case is ['the Health Enterprise'] – a hospital with satisfied patients and confident employees. Branding means reassuring people that the promises associated with the 'product' in communications with the stakeholders, are fulfilled. All the hospital's employees take part in the branding of [the Health Enterprise]. At every patient consultation, in every notice in the media, in every letter posted*

from [the Health Enterprise] and every conversation about our workplace, we are all involved in creating its reputation. Whether or not as employees, we take part in creating [the Health Enterprise] as a trademark will depend on the extent to which we manage to transform these 'moments of truth' into a positive experience. With the help of internal communication processes we have to make the employees conscious of their significance in the branding process.

This combination of reputation management and a clearly defined marketing strategy is exceptional, however. Such ambitions are less evident in other plans, although all the enterprises are concerned about their reputations in one way or another. The communication plan of one of the regional enterprises, for instance, defines the purpose of communication activities to 'ensure that [the regional enterprise] is seen as a region characterized by constructive cooperation between external and internal participants for the patients' best'. Reputation in this context should rest on the idea that the organization is able to adapt to its stakeholders, and that it is effective and competent.

Some of the communication statements reveal an eagerness to make visible the quality that the enterprise represents. One of the regional health enterprises, for instance, states that its core values are 'safety, respect and quality', and that this is what its communication statement must reflect: 'The Health Enterprise's ability to verify quality and to make it visible is a critical tool for success'. This could be said to demonstrate that new quality indicators and new demands for transparency put pressure on the enterprise to present itself as an auditable unit. One purpose of their communication activities is to ensure that the new tools introduced to measure the quality and efficiency of the sector are exploited to promote the reputation of the institution.

The communication plan of another of the regional enterprises, states its aim as being 'to develop trust in the public health sector and the activities that we perform'. This communication statement clearly considers the enterprise to be part of the public health service, and even regards the promotion of the reputation of the national healthcare services as one of its tasks. This is in striking contrast to some of the other communication statements, especially the one quoted above that defined market values as the guideline.

Conclusion and the Need for Further Research

The healthcare sector has emerged as one of the sectors most frequently referred to in news media, a fact that is connected to its status as one of the most economically expansive and politically contested sectors in modern societies. In Norway a major reform has recently established regional and local enterprises. Other reforms have also been introduced in the health sector with a view to transforming the hospitals from public administration agencies to become public enterprises in a quasi-market. The ideology of consumerism and free choice has acquired more influence, ideas that are reinforced by reforms to institutionalize patient rights and the free choice of hospital. The central state, which has taken over the ownership of hospitals from the Norwegian counties, emphasizes its intention to take control of the affairs of the hospitals, and also to leave more issues to the hospitals themselves.

Information tasks are being formalized, professionalized and integrated with the management function. There is thus an increase in the number of staff dealing with communication, and a trend towards including the chief information officer in the top management team. Information professionals with a background in marketing and journalism are increasingly being employed in the hospitals. Most health enterprises now have communication strategies.

Three perspectives have been presented here in seeking to clarify the communication strategies. These are marketing management, media management and corporate communication or reputation management. Some documents reveal a marketing approach, but more of them confirm expectations connected with media management and corporate communication. They all place great emphasis on communication as a management responsibility, but vary in their descriptions of the specific tasks of managing, in the emphasis they give to public against private identity, and in the importance they attach to media compared with other stakeholders.

In some statements the enterprises define themselves in terms of private enterprise language and as part of a traditional public administration. Thus the 'double standard' reflected in the reform, with its simultaneous emphasis on central control and decentralized autonomous enterprises, also seems to be reflected in the communication strategies of the hospitals. It is interesting to note that the enterprises which displayed a split identity (public/private) also emphasized the importance of reputation management as an aim for their communication activities.

Some enterprises display an ambitious strategy for developing a new identity and for transcending the distinction between external and internal communication. This is in line with recommendations contained in the corporate communication literature.

The two most predominant features in the communication strategies are the link between reputation-promotion and the conception of communication as an internal and external management tool. This combination appeared in seven of the communication statements. The enterprises concerned may thus be on their way to developing a self-identity that chimes with the corporate communication worldview described above.

Although several of the communication statements give coherency and consistency as norms, the statements themselves are not coherent. Some of them could even be regarded as self-contradictory, perhaps even hypocritical. This may not come as a surprise, given that many organizational theorists have referred to such inconsistencies as normal, or even as a prerequisite for contemporary organizations, particularly in the public sector (Brunsson 2002: 194-195).

To a certain extent, the coexistence of contradictory ideals may also reflect the fact that these organizations do not have much experience of strategizing. The communication strategies may be seen as part of a pioneering effort to establish such practices in the health sector, and they may, partly for this reason, still be decoupled from more established routines and standards (Llewellyn & Tappin 2003). The legitimacy of hospitals used to depend on the legitimacy of the public administration and medicine in combination. Now their legitimacy is perceived to a greater extent as depending on the way they communicate with markets and citizen-customers and the way they are managed and organized. However the health enterprise as an organizational form is still a recent phenomenon and it remains to be seen whether the prominent position attributed to communication management and information professionals will prove to be a lasting phenomenon in Norwegian hospitals.

In the introduction we posited several possible reasons for an increased emphasis on strategic communication in the public sector; first, a change away from input legitimacy and toward a greater emphasis on output legitimacy. Secondly, an expansion in knowledge and a development toward a more rational way to deal with knowledge in order to arrive at legitimate decisions. Thirdly, a general decrease in trust in public institutions. The empirical material presented in this study is not a sufficient base for addressing these questions, but some communication strategies mention the need to build trust as a motif for an increased emphasis on communication. The need for a more rational way to deal with knowledge is also mentioned, and there is clearly an awareness of the need to improve performance in order to improve legitimacy. In a further development of this study it would be useful to compare development patterns in hospitals that are of various sizes and that appear to have chosen different strategies, as well as to compare with development patterns in other sectors and countries. It remains to be seen whether strategic communication is mainly a response to a perceived 'crisis of trust' or whether it is in itself fuelling a long term process toward a less trusting relationship between healthcare workers and the citizens that depend on their services.

Bibliography

Aldridge, M. & J. Evetts (2003) Rethinking the concept of professionalism: the case of journalism. British Journal of Sociology Vol. 54 (4): 347-364.

Bartlett, W. & J. Le Grand (1993) Quasi-markets and Social Policy. London: Palgrave Macmillan.

Bordum, A. & J. H. Hansen (2005) Strategisk ledelseskommunikation. Copenhagen: Jurist- og Økonomforbundets Forlag.

Brunsson, N. (2003) The Organization of Hypocrisy –Talk, Decisions and Actions in Organizations. Copenhagen: Abstract, Liber, Copenhagen Business School Press.

Byrkjeflot, H. (2005) The making of a health care state? An analysis of the recent hospital reform in Norway. Rokkan Notat 15. University of Bergen.

Christensen, L. T. & G. Cheney (2005) Integrated Organisational Identities: Challenging The 'Bodily' Pursuit. Paper presented at Critical Management Studies Conference Cambridge, July 4-6 2005.

Christensen, L. T. & M. Morsing (2005) Bagom Corporate Communication. Copenhagen: Samfundslitteratur.

Cook, T. E. (1998) Governing With the News: The News Media as a Political Institution. Chicago: University of Chicago Press.

Cornelissen, J. (2004) Corporate Communications: Theory and Practice. London: Sage.

Czarniawska, B. (1997) Narrating the organization. Chicago: Chicago University Press.

Davis, A. (2002) Public Relations Democracy. Public Relations, Politics and the Mass Media in Britain. Manchester: Manchester University Press.

DiMaggio, P. J. & W. W. Powell (1991) The Iron Cage Revisited: Institutional Isomorphism and Collective Rationality in Organizational Fields. In Powell, W. W. & P. J. DiMaggio (Eds.) The New Institutionalism in Organizational Analysis. Chicago: University of Chicago Press.

Eide, M. & G. Hernes (1995) Død og Pine. Om massemedia og helsepolitikk. Oslo: Universitetsforlaget.

Eide, M. (2000) Den redigerende makt. Redaktørrollens norske historie. Kristiansand: HøyskoleForlaget/Norsk Redaktørforening/IJ-forlaget.

Grunig, J. E. & T. Hunt. (1984) Managing Public Relations. New Jersey: Thomson Learning.

Heldaas, J. (2003) Hvordan vi har skaffet oss flere pasienter. Paper presented at ISF seminar: Én million pasienter og 100 000 ansatte - kommunikasjonsutfordringer i kø. November 13. 2003, Quality Airport Hotel Gardermoen.

Holme, A. (2006) Det kommuniserende hospital - En studie av informasjonsfunksjonen ved sykehus. Master's thesis. Department of Administration and Organization Theory, University of Bergen.

IFS (2001) Kartlegging av informasjonsarbeid i sykehusene. Informasjonsforum for Sykehus (IFS).

INTORG 1999, 2001, 2003, 2005 –Organization and leadership structures in Norwegian hospitals (for full references see "Data" section).

Ihlen, Ø. & P. Robstad (2004) Informasjon & Samfunnskontakt – Perspektiver og praksis. Bergen: Fagbokforlaget.

Jespersen, P. K. (2005) Mellem profession og management. Copenhagen: Handelshøjskolens Forlag.

Johannesen, Ø. (2003) Hvordan gjør vi oss lekre for pasienten? Paper presented at ISF seminar: Én million pasienter og 100 000 ansatte - kommunikasjonsutfordringer i kø. November 13 2003, Quality Airport Hotel Gardermoen.

Johnson, H. K. (2005) Media- "vaktbikkje" og pragmatisk publikumsfrier? En studie av medias dekning av helsestoff og forhold til aktører i sykehussektoren før og etter sykehusreformen. Master's thesis. Department of Administration and Organization Theory, University of Bergen.

Johnson, H. & H. Byrkjeflot (2006) Media- public watchdog or hunting for news? How the interrelationship between media and hospitals in Norway were affected by recent reforms. Paper for the 22nd EGOS Colloquium 2006, Bergen July 6.-8th 2006.

Kristensen, N. N. (2005) Kommunikationsbranchens medierelationer - professionelle netværk, kommunikationsfaglige perspektiver og mediedemokratiske konsekvenser. Modinet Working Paper no. 19. www.modinet.dk.

Llewellyn, S. & E. Tappin (2003) Strategy in the Public Sector: Management in the Wilderness. Journal of Management Studies Vol. 40 (4): 955-982.

Lund, A. B. (1997) Smitsomme sygdomme i dansk journalistik. Copenhagen: Munksgaards Forlag.

Moran, M. (2003) The British Regulatory State: High Modernism and Hyper Innovation, Oxford: Oxford University Press.

Møller Pedersen, K. (2005) Sundhedspolitik: beslutningsgrundlag, beslutningstagen og beslutninger i sundhedsvæsenet. Odense: Syddansk Universitetsforlag.

Petersson, O. (1994) Journalistene som klasse. Journalismen som ideologi. In Edvardsen, Terje Steen (Ed.) Media og samfunnsstyring. Bergen: Fagbokforlaget.

Power. M. (1997) The Audit Society: Rituals of Verification. Oxford: Oxford University Press.

Power, M. (2005) Organizations and Auditability: A Theory. Paper presented at the SCORE Conference: 'Organizing the World', October 13-15, 2005.

Scharpf, F. (1999) Governing in Europe: effective and democratic? Oxford: Oxford University Press.

Schulz, W. (2004) Reconstructing Mediatization as an Analytical Concept. European Journal of Communication Vol. 19 (1): 87–101.

Seale, C. F. (Ed.) (2004) Health and the Media. Oxford: Blackwells.

Strathern, M. (2000) The Tyranny of Transparency. British Educational Research Journal Vol. 26 (3): 309 – 321.

Svendsen, T. (2005) Helseforetak og kommunikasjon - En studie av en kommunikasjonsstrategis betydning i et helseforetak. Master's thesis. Department of Administration and Organization Theory, University of Bergen.

Tsoukas, H. (2005) The tyranny of light: the temptations and the paradoxes of the information society. In Tsoukas, H. Complex knowledge: Studies in organizational epistemology. Oxford: Oxford University Press.

263

Data

Arbeids- og administrasjonsdepartementet 2001: Informasjonspolitikk for statsforvaltningen. Mål, prinsipper og konsekvenser, Oslo.

Communication statements from Norwegian health enterprises.

IFS (2001) Kartlegging av informasjonsarbeid i sykehusene. Informasjonsforum for Sykehus (IFS).

IFS 2002 – 2005. Agendas, presentations and communications at the biennial seminar for communication professionals in Norwegian hospital sector 2001 – 2006, (1. 4.-5.11. 2002, 19.5.2003, 13.-14.11. 2003, 22.4.2004, 21.4. 2005, 10. – 11. 11. 2005, 6 meetings in total).

INTORG 1999, 2001, 2003, 2005:

Kjekshus, Lars Erik, Sølve Mikal Nerland, Terje P. Hagen, & Grete Botten (2002) De somatiske sykehusenes interne organisering. En kartlegging av 58 somatiske sykehus, 1999 og 2001. Oslo, Center for Health Administration, HERO, University of Oslo.

Kjekshus, Lars Erik (2004) INTORG De somatiske sykehusenes interne organisering / En kartlegging av 50 somatiske sykehus i Norge i 2003. HERO skriftserie 2004: 6. Oslo: SINTEF Helse.

Harsvik, T. & L. E. Kjekshus (2007) INTORG – Organisasjon og ledelsesstrukturer ved norske sykehus. Oslo: SINTEF Helse.

CHAPTER 10

Corporate Governance and the Media
From Agency Theory to Edited Corporations

LARS ENGWALL & KERSTIN SAHLIN[1]

Introduction

In popular discourse the media is sometimes described as being everywhere, shaping and reflecting our lives, our tastes and our aspira-
tions. In contrast to this, theories of business and management leave
the media outside the core business of governance, control and management. We argue in this chapter that in fact the media have a powerful impact on the way corporations relate to their environment and the
way in which they are governed and managed.

We contend that conventional notions of corporate governance focus too narrowly on the owners' monitoring of managers, and that the
very centrality of media relations makes it urgent that we reconsider
and reformulate our notions of corporate governance. In this context
we identify two important roles for the media. First, the media fulfil a
monitor role. They report and investigate corporate activities and thus
provide the various stakeholders with in-depth knowledge and assess-
ments on which they can then act. Second, the media serve as *carriers*
of general models for conceptualizing corporations, management, governance and environments. In this way, the media contribute to the
shaping and spreading of management trends and fashions. In neither
of the two roles do the media act in isolation; rather, they mediate
among the many organizations that make up the densely populated
governance landscape (Sahlin-Andersson & Engwall 2002).

---

[1] This paper is based on research within the GEMS programme, which is supported by the Bank
of Sweden Tercentenary Foundation. See further www.fek.uu.se/gems.

In order to understand how the media, in these two roles, make an impact on corporate governance we need to look more closely at the working conditions of business media. In doing so we observe the continuous selection of information that occurs in media companies under time pressure of varying strength. We also stress the growing volume of activities that corporations devote to feeding the business media. Here we refer to studies of business-press and business-media relationships, which indicate that corporations have increasingly come to recognize the extreme importance of this aspect of the environment. Corporations have thus set up special information departments and have hired information directors (often former journalists, who thus bring with them knowledge from the media field) and, in many organizations, these information directors are appointed as part of the top management team.

Having painted this picture of a strong media influence in the corporate environment, we suggest further that this has implications for the way corporations are managed and organized. We therefore conclude by proposing that corporations will move toward a state of being that can be designated 'edited corporations'. This in turn can be expected to have consequences for corporate governance.

Corporate Governance Reconsidered

In the 21st century corporate governance has become a topic of crucial importance in both practice and the academic world.[1] Corporate scandals in several countries, like those at World Com and Enron in the United States (see e.g. McLean & Elkind 2003) and at ABB and Skandia in Europe (see e.g. Carlsson & Nachemson-Ekwall 2003, Nachemson-Ekwall & Carlsson 2004), have turned the searchlight on the whole issue of the governance of modern corporations. Legal processes have been launched and various measures undertaken to improve control over the top managers of large corporations. The Sarbanes-Oxley Act in the United States in 2002 (cf. e.g. Moeller 2004) is an example of this. The corporate scandals have also stimulated research in this area (cf. e.g. O'Brien 2005, Owen, Kirchmaier & Grant 2006).

Although we have noted a keen interest in corporate governance in recent years, the issue is not new to management scholars. As early as in the 1930s Berle and Means (1932) referred to the problem of growing diffusion of ownership in large corporations. In the 1940s Burn-

---

[1] A Google search on the web in the spring of 2006, for instance, gave more than 85 million hits.

ham took their argument further, stressing the rising power of the managerial class (Burnham 1941). In the 1950s and 1960s these authors were followed by a great many more scholars, who pointed out the rising power of the managerial class and the possible effect of this on business behaviour (Baumol 1959, Galbraith 1967, Marris 1964).

A common theme in these classical works concerns control as between owners and professional managers. More recently this has come to be known as the principal-agency problem, i.e. how principals (owners) can control agents (professional managers). Alchian and Demsetz (1972), Jensen and Meckling (1976) and Fama (1980) addressed this question theoretically in the 1970s and 1980s. Their work was followed by several influential studies of owner-manager relations (see e.g. Fligstein 1990, Roe 1994, Blair 1995, Monks & Minow 1995, Keasey et al. 1997, Barca & Becht 2001).

Although this research is important in helping us to understand the governance of modern corporations, it can in fact be challenged on three grounds. *First*, we have to remember that the owner-manager relationship does not consist of a one-way traffic. In other words it is not only owners who try to control managers, but the opposite also holds: managers try increasingly to convince owners of the need for financial resources for the company and for themselves, and to persuade them of the necessity of undertaking new projects – not least, mergers and acquisitions.

Second, the political aspects of corporate governance should also be taken into account. Although we have been experiencing decades of deregulation, the three branches of government (executive, legislative and judicial) still play a significant part in regulating and monitoring corporate behaviour. The scandals mentioned above were thus handled by the judicial branch according to laws established by the legislative branch; they also exposed corporate executives to political pressure. However, another important factor has been what Siebert et al. (1956) refer to as the fourth branch of government, namely the press, or, to use a more modern label, the media. And, in a modern society, a fifth branch of government must also be mentioned, that is to say: grassroot organizations such as Amnesty, Greenpeace, Oxfam and other organizations created by citizens who are dissatisfied with the effectiveness of the ordinary political system and who therefore want to take up certain specific issues (see e.g. Tsoukas 1999). Needless to say, the dual relationship mentioned above with respect to owners also applies to the five 'branches of government' (see Engwall 2006).

Third, the scrutinizing and governing of corporations is obviously not confined within the frames of established rules. The various governing bodies mentioned above all seek actively to influence or develop rules as and when things happen. Governing bodies and the corporations themselves are all active simultaneously as rule-setters, rule-followers and rule-monitors (cf. Ayres & Braithwaite 1992, Djelic & Sahlin-Andersson 2006). They all have the possibility of acting reactively and proactively vis-à-vis one another.

Of the five branches of government mentioned above, the fourth – the media – has come to play an increasingly important role in corporate governance in our modern societies. Various studies on the business press have thus shown that the volume of business news has been growing much more than other types of news. In Sweden, for instance, Grafström (2006) has shown that while other newspapers have faced stagnation, circulation in the business press has been growing. The same study shows that business news has also been extending its range within the media via special broadcasts, special newspaper sections and a growing number of news items about business life.

The expansion of business news has had a noticeable impact on the operations and organization of modern companies. Whereas thirty or forty years ago top managers were rather ill-prepared for meeting journalists, nowadays they have generally received professional training in how to handle the media. They now also get more protection and support from special information units. It has thus become increasingly common to appoint directors of information or communication as part of the top management team (see Davis 2000, Langer & Pallas 2006, Grafström & Pallas in this volume).

All this suggests that our present topic, the business press, is part not only of the broader context of corporate governance but also of the wider expanding field, of the media, which in turn includes not only the press but also radio and TV broadcasting, electronic newsletters, web pages, and so on. On a parallel track we have lively developments in the world financial markets, which in turn stimulate the demand for business information (Grafström 2006). And, affecting all these movements is the enveloping process whereby the centrally planned economies of yore have been reborn as market economies, markets generally have become connected across the globe and the world itself has been described as 'flat' (Friedman 1999, 2005).

The Media as Monitors

The role of the media, fundamentally, is to communicate news to the general public. Its identity as a vehicle of communication has deep roots, and even today represents an important part of what journalism is. There is thus a professional ambition to report continuously and in an adequate way on events considered to be of interest to the audience 'out there'. However, space is limited and sets its own restrictions on media coverage (Engwall 1978: Chapter 8). Editorial offices are thus always having to judge the newsworthiness of the information that pours in from all sorts of carriers: news agencies, other media companies, external informants, press releases, and so on. Out of this everlasting stream of information, media companies have to decide what to communicate and how much attention to pay each item. Through their selecting and editing the media organizations influence both the public and the political agendas. Even if the media are only relaying available information and intending to remain neutral and objective, the very selecting and editing process affects the communication of news. It is interesting to note here that, although these sifting processes are taking place in the editorial offices of many different media organizations, they tend to lead to astonishingly similar results. The reason for this lies in the professionalization of the media field, whereby journalists have been trained together, have been socialized by working together and keeping an eye on each other's editorial decisions (see Engwall 1981, 1985: Chapter 9, Cook 1998: Chapter 4).

Needless to say, business news follows the same logic as that described above regarding news generally, but came into the field later. Over the last twenty or thirty years or so, the business press has evolved into an organized field with common norms and organizing principles with its own structuring patterns of interaction and dominance (Grafström 2006). Business journalism used to be mainly a question of printing official information such as stock exchange quotations, and to some extent, executive appointments and other company news. As Grafström (2006) has noted, the space devoted to business news in the ordinary Swedish press was still limited as late as the 1960s and 1970s. Three factors lay behind this situation: first, information from companies was itself restricted; second, the capacity for evaluating economic information was scarce in the media; third, business was not considered to be of general public interest. Over a period roughly from the 1980s and onwards this changed as companies became more active and business journalism emerged as a field of its own as a result of interaction between business and the media (Grafström 2006). An increasingly important element in this has been the media's monitoring of the corporations and their activities.

Although the monitoring function may seem a relatively modern phenomenon in business media, it has a long tradition. US President Theodore Roosevelt thus coined the expression 'muckraking' for such activities a hundred years ago (Chalmers 1980: 4). Famous and more recent examples of such reporting include Günter Wallraff (e.g. 1970) on a variety of issues and Carl Bernstein and Bob Woodward (1975) on Watergate. Similar examples appear in the business media today, particularly since the above-mentioned scandals. However, in pursuing projects of this kind journalists appear to have a more difficult task in the corporate context than in the political. In the latter case, although information tends to be getting increasingly controlled, it is always possible to find alternative sources of information – the representatives of other parties, for instance, people who have not been re-elected, and so on. Corporations, on the other hand, are much more 'closed', with information policies that prevent many actors from communicating with the media. There are also good reasons for such policies, since the effects of 'naming and shaming' can appear immediately on the stock market and at a later stage can have a very negative effect on the company brand (see further Jonsson 2005).[2]

The importance of the media in relation to corporate governance can be exemplified by two cases, both from the Swedish truck industry and both occurring during the autumn of 2006. The first concerns Volvo. During August speculations began to appear in the media about who was behind the lively trading in the series A shares (shares carrying higher voting rights). Christer Gardell, a well-known risk capitalist, was named as the buyer, but uncertainty remained until Gardell's holding reached the level at which he had to reveal it according to the stock market rules. He then claimed a seat on the nominating committee for the board, a demand that was rejected by the Volvo leadership. The whole of this process, particularly the argument between Gardell and the Volvo chairman ran like a serial story in the Swedish business press. The composition of Volvo's board was thus no longer an issue for the shareholder's meeting, but became instead a subject of public

---

[2] It also happens that investigative reporters are threatened on account of what they write. An extreme case was the murder in July 2004 of the Editor-in-Chief of *Forbes Russia*, after publication of a profile of top Russian business leaders. For further information on this particular case, see: www.abc.neet.au/correspondents/content/2004/s1 155798.htm.

debate in the media (see e.g. *Affärsvärlden*, 34/2006: 16-23 and 37/2006: 26-29).

The second example concerns Sweden's other large truck manufacturer, Scania, for which German MAN made a bid in September 2006. This bid drew media attention long before any prospectus had become available. Further as the prospective bid was rejected by the major owners, the main actors − the leadership of MAN, the leadership of Scania and the owners − were frequently seen or heard delivering their views of the deal in the media. The takeover bid was thus no longer an issue between investment bankers and owners, but had become a hot media story that even triggered reactions among politicians of various shades regarding the danger of 'selling out' Swedish industry (see e.g. *Dagens industri,* from September 12, 2006 onwards).

The Media as Carriers

The second role of the media in modern society concerns the bearing or carrying of ideas. Here it should be borne in mind *first* that the organization, the management and the assessment of modern corporations are all powerfully shaped and influenced by the wide spread of management ideas. This point was made once and for all in Meyer and Rowan (1977), an article that has become a classic. The authors showed how, in order to acquire legitimacy and to appear modern, corporations adopted, and adapted to, myths of rationality that pervaded their environment. Although the flow and expansion of management ideas as rationalized myths is embedded in other more general institutional developments, there is nothing automatic about it. On the contrary, management ideas are actively shaped, transferred and transformed (Czarniawska & Sevón 1996). We have argued before (Sahlin-Andersson & Engwall 2002) that ideas of this kind are actively circulated, packaged and shaped by *carriers of management knowledge.* On the basis of the CEMP research (see Engwall 2004) we assigned particular importance to the media, together with business schools and management consultants, as carriers in this context. Media organizations are thus not only arenas for displaying the popularity of management ideas (e.g. Abrahamson 1996), but are also active carriers of the ideas themselves (cf. e.g. Jonsson 2005, Buhr & Grafström 2006, Windell 2006).

Second, it is also important to note that carriers are often interrelated in many more or less complicated ways: they collaborate, compete and run parallel with one another; a single carrier can be a creator, a mediator, and a user of management knowledge all at the same time. It can therefore be argued that this interactive character among carriers with their mixture of complementary and competitive roles and symbiotic development can explain the dramatic expansion of management knowledge and of management advice services. Thus, the role of the media as a prominent carrier of management ideas appears to involve carrying and mediating management ideas among other important carriers, as well as mediating between these groups and other stakeholders and the corporations.

The carrier concept strikes some as having rather passive associations, as of someone or something carrying a package, a passenger or even a disease. In our earlier analysis of the media as an important carrier of management ideas, however, we rejected this view, citing earlier findings particularly in the field of institutional theory (see Sahlin-Andersson & Engwall 2002: 9-11). We pointed out that the carrier concept has been used to convey a mixture of passivity and activity, of supporting, transporting and transforming (e.g. Jepperson 1991, Alvarez 1998). In analyzing the media as carriers of management ideas we thus envisage them as taking an active part not only in distributing but also in shaping the ideas in question. Moreover, when the media carry certain specific ideas they are also – more or less explicitly or implicitly – supporting and hence reinforcing certain specific ideals and taken-for-granted notions about how corporations normally act, how they should act and how they should be governed and managed (cf. Windell 2006).

Corporations can also be said to take an active part in the diffusion of management ideas, by boosting and publicising in various ways the solutions they have chosen.[3] Often, for example, top managers publish popular books, which are then promoted and cited in the business media. The publication of *Moments of Truth* (Carlzon 1987) by the then SAS CEO Jan Carlzon was a very successful such project. Former executives, too, quite often tell stories about the corporate success of their solutions, which are then widely circulated. The former CEO of General Electric, Jack Welch, represents a prime example of this (see e.g. Welch & Welch 2005).

---

[3] One Swedish example is constituted by the publicity around alternative production methods with autonomous groups introduced by the car manufacturers Saab and Volvo in 1960s and 1970s (see e.g. Sandberg, 1982).

Monitoring and Carrying – Two Interacting Roles

We can expect the media to take up ideas that corporations and other prominent actors consider to be relevant, topical and important – or simply popular. When the media are reporting and transferring ideas and news in their role as mediators and carriers, the messages and ideas themselves are subject to a certain amount of editing: an idea may be formulated slightly different, more clearly and/or explicitly or it may be contextualized in a new way. However, this reformulation may change not only the form of an account but also its focus, content or meaning. In other words the carriers who are spreading management ideas are also involved in their co-construction (Czarniawska & Joerges 1996, Sahlin-Andersson 2001). The media are thus active co-creators of the management ideas in circulation and of the accounts of specific corporations and what they are doing. And as the media spread and reconstruct messages and ideas, their editing is likely to be shaped by the general patterns that often appear as models become widespread and by the various logics and ideals that permeate the business media.[4]

The most common example of the media's role as monitor, and one where monitoring is particularly affected by the ideals to which they are subject, is the endless stream of reports on executive performance: reporting on companies is focussed to a very great extent on the actions of the various CEOs. Successful CEOs, together with their managerial solutions, provide role models for other managers, even though their success can often be attributed to favourable events in their environment. Thus, as a result of such 'monitoring', the business media also has an important role as a creator and carrier of corporate success models.

Altogether, then it can be said that the expansion of business coverage has helped to disseminate market solutions, and has affected economic control systems and financial markets. In this way the media have contributed to the creation of a Zeitgeist, which in turn has stimulated the demand for management education and paved the way for the acceptance of a variety of management ideas. Moreover, solutions originally developed for business firms have been increasingly introduced into the public sector under the banner of New Public Management (see e.g. Christensen & Laegreid 1996, McLaughlin, Osborne & Ferlie 2002). Methods such as Total Quality Management have been

---

[4] Cf. Sahlin-Andersson 1996, Strang & Meyer 1994, Greenwood, Hinings & Suddaby 2002, Sahlin-Andersson & Engwall 2002, Grafström 2006.

similarly spread via various channels (see e.g. Røvik 2002, Tiratsoo 2002, Walgenbach & Beck 2002).

The Management of the Media

Given the interpretation of governance as a two-way process and the role of the media as carriers and monitors it seems appropriate to look not only at the media's impact on business corporations but also at ways in which corporations influence the workings of the media. The flow of business information from corporations to media companies has intensified over the last fifteen years or so, which means in turn that business journalists are involved in the assessment, selection and editing of news much more than they used to be. They have to ask themselves whether or not the information obtained is news, whether it is reliable and how it should be presented. Here professional norms are an important factor. In addition, the way in which media activities and the interactions between different media are organized obviously affect the structuring, ordering and selecting of news. The decision to print depends to a very great extent on what competitors do and on the time available. An illustrative example in this context, discussed by Grafström et al. (2006), is the recurrent reporting of quarterly reports. Although questioned by many for their encouragement of short-termism and for their dubious journalistic value, these reports have become a significant part of business news in all the media.[5] Since they appear in clumps, it is difficult for the media to provide much more than a comparison of analysts' forecasts, and thus only to take part in a sort of recurrent ritual. As such they are very convenient for the media, who – although they do not know the content of the reports in advance – can prepare themselves because they know when the report will appear (see Engwall 1978: Chapter 6).[6]

The case of the quarterly reports reminds us of the great time pressure that prevails in the business media. This in turn may affect the possibility of critically examining the reports – something that is of course crucial to the whole issue of corporate governance that we are addressing here, as well as being fundamental to the media's monitoring function. All this means that getting behind the figures presented

---

[5] For a critique of quarterly reports, see www.darden.virginia.edu/corporate-ethics/, a report from the Business Round Table Institute for Corporate Ethics.

[6] These preparations can sometimes be very sophisticated. A Bloomberg news journalist thus revealed in a private conversation with one of us that for instance scheduled talks by the Chairman of the Federal Reserve Board is prepared in the company through the writings of five-six seven alternative articles based on different scenarios of what he could be saying. In this way the news agency can beat their competitors by being before them with comments.

by the companies requires time as well as the necessary analytical competence. As a result, the business media become increasingly aware of the necessity not just to train journalists to cover business adequately but also to take business graduates on to their editorial staffs (Grafström 2006).

The business media have thus come to play an increasing part in selecting and communicating business information, as well as in critically examining corporations. As a result business journalism has expanded considerably over the last twenty years or so, particularly as regards interactive processes between business and the media. It would not be fair to say here that the corporations are weak victims of the business media. Rather, they appear to have certain advantages due to their control over information – a position that has been reinforced by managerial strategies aimed at 'managing' the media.

The arguments outlined above have profound implications for the governance, organizing and management of corporations. Organization theory has long been emphasizing how environmental factors put powerful pressure on – and even helps to shape – organizations. Thus the corporate environment shape and influence corporate actors, and it is necessary for corporate managers and organizations to handle such environmental relations strategically. They do this in a variety of ways. One traditional way, noted in early open-system theories, was to protect the organization's technical core from the uncertainty resulting from the fluctuations and shifting demands of the environment (Thompson 1967). Organizations thus developed buffering techniques. Bridging strategies have also been examined (Scott 1987). Conceptual frameworks of this kind have been used as a way of understanding how organizations can deal with their resource environment, their task environment and their institutional environment. Due to the way in which they were originally formulated, theories about buffering and bridging have been interpreted primarily under the 'givens' of a resource view of corporations. Thus, what are buffered and bridged are resource flows. Under an institutional conception of corporations, we still find these concepts to be valuable (Scott 1995, 1987), but the implications for corporate structures and management are slightly different. Since institutional environments can be said to consist of regulative, normative and cognitive frames for the corporation (Scott 1995), the institutional environment to be bridged and buffered concerns information, accounts and conceptualizations of the corporation itself. This buffering and bridging is largely handled by setting up specific units and procedures within the corporations. Thus the 'media embeddedness' of corporations obviously has profound implications for their design and management.

As early as in the 1950s the concept of Public Relations began to appear in the Nordic countries (see e.g. Lindström 1958, Ihlen & Robstad 2004, Larsson 2005), and over the years a growing number of larger corporations have set up special units to send out news about their business. Today this is a very important part of corporate life, as 'managing' has become successively more of a performing art, with top managers working to construct a positive image of their companies. The discussion in Goffman (1959) about 'the presentation of self in every-day life' neatly applies today to corporations and their relations with investors, customers, governments and others. Consequently most large corporations have established special corporate information departments and have appointed centrally placed directors of information. By structuring information flows to and from the corporation, and largely handling or structuring its media relations (cf. Pallas 2005) such departments clearly serve as a buffer for management. The departments are partly staffed by former journalists as the corporation seeks to build a bridge to the logics and routines prevailing in the media.[7] Similar special units and positions have been created for investor relations, for government relations (lobbying units) and for Corporate Social Responsibility or community relations. Most large companies now have units or positions of this kind in a variety of combinations. The size and structure and of such departments and their position in relation to other key functions of the corporations do, however, vary (Pallas 2005). Routines and practices for handling media relations have also been widely established, so much so that they appear to be taken more or less for granted as something that is necessary and good. Media training and company presentations are two examples of this.

First, media training has come to be regarded as a natural or even necessary component of management training and the introduction of new staff to managerial positions. Many consultancy firms have started to sell training and other related products. Media training has thus become a widespread and, apparently a prosperous and appreciated form of consultancy in the corporate world and in the organizational world in general.

---

[7] Such movements between the media and corporate information departments, for which we have adopted the French expression 'pantouflage' (Engwall 2006), are clearly very important for in creating personal networks and establishing links between business and the media.

Second, there are various ways in which corporations present their financial results and handle relations with their shareholders regarding these matters. Most corporations have specially organized and staged events in connection with their annual and quarterly reports, including press releases, press conferences and special meetings with journalists and analysts (Grafström et al. 2006). Activities of this kind are designed by the individual corporations but are also regulated to some extent by law, stock exchange rules and so on.[8]

While it is clear that most corporations have established what can be called and analyzed as buffering and bridging units and procedures of roughly the same kind, there is still considerable variation in detail. This could be taken as a sign that corporate buffering and bridging activities have not yet become institutionalized to the extent that their form, and the expectations attaching to them, are the same in different corporations, industries or in addressing different stakeholders. However, there is nothing to say that such a development may not occur, which also means that managements will come to pay more attention to the editing of their corporate brand.

Edited Corporations

The corporate units and activities discussed in the previous section are all concerned with, and driven by, the importance attached to the way corporations are presented. They are all concerned with translating activities and operations into texts, speeches and events. In connection with this aspect of corporate management we introduce the concept of *the edited corporation*. The activities of the units in question are in fact geared to the *editing* of texts picked up by the corporation from the environment – management ideas, market information, news of competitors and so on – or texts about the company intended for its stakeholders or for other uses. Further, the term *editing* suggests the presence of reciprocal processes in which several individuals and units inside and outside the corporation interact with one another. Moreover, we want to emphasize the fact that such texts are often shaped – in fact, *edited* – according to more or less clearly established procedures and day-to-day routines or, to put it another way, according to certain sets of editing rules.

In describing the editing work of the corporation as a question of buffering and bridging, we are assuming the existence of a core requir-

---

[8] In addition to all this, quoted companies put on road shows at international financial centres to attract the attention of powerful investors.

ing protection from the pressures to which it is exposed by the media or by various governing bodies. While we have sought to demonstrate the merits of this conceptual framework, we should also point out that it only depicts one aspect – albeit an important one – of media embeddedness. In fact, media embeddedness probably has other even more fundamental consequences for governance, management and organization. Studies of corporate branding (Schultz, Antorini & Csaba 2005), of corporate expressiveness (Hatch & Schultz 1997) and of corporate reputation (Fombrun 1996, Deephouse 2000, Pollock & Rindova 2003), as well as daily reports on the way corporations are traded and valued on the stock markets worldwide, all seem to reveal the central importance of the way corporations are presented and conceptualized. In fact, many would claim that brands and presentations *are* the core of many modern corporations. The way in which corporations are presented and monitored by the media may thus have a direct effect on their finances, their development and even their survival (cf. e.g. Jonsson 2005).

The edited corporation, then, is a corporation that is clearly embedded in and dependent upon the media; it is a corporation in which a great many activities are devoted to managing and organizing for this media embeddedness, and to editing work. We noted one such example in the section above, the supply of information and routinely planned forms of reporting of quarterly and annual reports. To a great extent these corporations exploit the expected timing and rhythm of the media's news reporting as a means of controlling their own planned media-corporate events. We expect the edited corporation to become increasingly common in a mediatized society. The edited presentation of a corporation and its activities is not directed at an external audience only. The media also functions as a mirror, whereby the edited corporation appears in an auto-communicative process in which corporate activities are presented in the media, which in turn informs people in the corporation about their own situation and operations. The edited corporation is thus a corporation in which the very core of the corporate business is its brand, with the result that any presentation and report in the media have a direct and profound impact on the corporate business.

Increasing media embeddedness can be expected to have a significant effect on corporate governance, even if we look only at the traditional principal-agency model discussed above. We could expect that owners, and the search consultants whom they hire, will pay more attention in the future to communication skills in recruiting people for top management positions. On top of the three stages in top management recruitment as noted by Fligstein (1990), this would represent a fourth. To begin with, top managers were persons knowledgeable about production. They were people with a technical background, i.e. with the competence to organize and manage an efficient production flow. Secondly, as markets expanded it was increasingly necessary for the people at the top to have a marketing background. And, thirdly, as financial markets developed and advanced management accounting systems were introduced in divisionalized corporations, people from the finance side took over. The observations we have reported above may mean that a fourth group of executives will be taking over in the corporations in the future: the communicators. This would mean in turn that people with a background in journalism, the media or even entertainment may appear in top management positions. They would make their way to the top because the key function of the leadership group would be to present the corporation and its brand, and in a mediatized world such people are highly valued.

Conclusions

Starting from a traditional corporate governance approach and concluding with the concept of the edited corporation has led us to draw the following conclusions.

First, there is much to suggest that corporations are embedded in media relationships. Consequently the media have come to play a significant, albeit so far largely neglected, role in corporate governance.

Second, the media are important as monitors and carriers of ideas and information. In this capacity the media are active both in their continuous interaction with other organizations and in the selection and editing of information. They thus perform an important function as an intermediary in corporate governance relationships.

Third, as a consequence of media embeddedness corporations have created an increasing number of organizational units and developed new procedures for handling media relations. In doing so they have adopted buffering and bridging strategies that used to be common in earlier more resource-centred times.

Fourth, the creation and editing of corporate brands has emerged as a strategic task for modern corporations, which are consequently assuming the character of edited corporations. This in turn may mean that competence in communication will become an important criterion in selecting future managers as a result of the increasing role of media in corporate governance.

We can expect the many aspects of media embeddedness to provide material for possible future studies. We need to know more about the processes of selection and editing in the editorial offices of the business media and corporations. This in turn calls for in-depth studies of the media field and of media strategies in corporations. Other studies could also indicate the extent to which media embeddedness may impact on general models of corporations and corporate governance, and how they will do so. Our studies thus far have revealed a somewhat paradoxical pattern in the relation between the media and the corporate world and in the monitoring activities and corporate models attaching to the media. Although the media plays a significant role in the environment of corporations, and although the corporations take their media relations very seriously, this is not acknowledged in the media themselves. Rather the media generally seem to dispense a more traditional view of corporations as being led by their managers, governed by their owners and dependent on their customers. More studies are needed of the forms adopted by the edited corporation and the impact they make, so that we can develop theoretical models of corporate governance in a mediatized society.

Bibliography

Abrahamson, E. (1996) Management Fashion. *Academy of Management Review* Vol. 21 (1): 254-285.

Alchian, A. A. & H. Demsetz (1972) Production, Information Costs and Economic Organization. *American Economic Review* Vol. 62(5): 777-795.

Alvarez, J. L. (Ed.) (1998) *The Diffusion and Consumption of Business Knowledge*. London: Macmillan.

Ayres, I. & J. Braithwaite (1992) *Responsive Regulation. Transcending the Deregulation Debate*. Oxford: Oxford University Press.

Barca, F. & M. Becht (2001) *The Control of Corporate Europe*. Oxford: Oxford University Press.

Baumol, W. J. (1959) *Business Behavior, Value and Growth*. New York: NY, Macmillan (Revised edition 1967).

Berle, A. A. Jr. & G. C. Means (1932) *The Modern Corporation and Private Property*. New York: Macmillan.

Bernstein, C. & B. Woodward (1975) *All the President's Men*. New York, NY: Warner.

Blair, M. M. (1995) *Ownership and Control: Rethinking Corporate Governance for the Twenty-First Century*. Washington: Brookings Institution.

Buhr, H. & M. Grafström (2007) The Making of Meaning in the Media: The Case of Corporate Social Responsibility in the Financial Times. In Hond, F. D., F. G.A. De Bakker & P. Neergard (Eds.) *Managing Cor-*

porate Social Responsibility in Action: Talking, Doing and Measuring. Aldershot: Ashgate Publishing .

Burnham, J. (1941) *The Managerial Revolution.* New York: John Day.

Carlzon, J. (1987) *Moments of Truth.* Cambridge, MA: Ballinger.

Carlsson, B. & S. Nachemson-Ekwall (2003) *Livsfarlig ledning. Historien om kraschen i ABB.* Stockholm: Ekerlids.

Chalmers, D. M. (1980) *The Muckrake Years.* Huntington, NY: Krieger.

Christensen, T. & P. Laegreid (Eds.) (1996) *New Public Management: The Transformation of Ideas and Practice.* Aldershot: Ashgate.

Cook, T. (1998) *Governing with the News: The News Media as a Political Institution.* Chicago, IL: The University of Chicago Press.

Czarniawska, B. & B. Joerges (1996) Travels of Ideas. In Czarniawska, B. & Guje Sevón (Eds.) *Translating Organizational Change.* Berlin: de Gruyter.

Czarniawska, B. & G. Sevón (Eds.) (1996) *Translating Organizational Change.* Berlin: de Gruyter.

Davis, A. (2000) Public Relations, Business News and the Reproduction of Corporate Elite Power. *Journalism* Vol. 1(3): 282-304.

Deephouse, D. L. (2000) Media Reputation as a Strategic Resource: An Integration of Mass Communication and Resource-Based Theories. *Journal of Management* Vol. 26 (6): 1091-1112.

Djelic, M-L. & K. Sahlin-Andersson (Eds.) (2006) *Transnational Governance: Institutional Dynamics of Regulation.* Cambridge: Cambridge University Press.

Engwall, L. (1978) *Newspapers as Organizations.* Farnborough: Saxon House.

Engwall, L. (1981) Newspaper Competition: A Case for Theories of Oligopoly. *Scandinavian Economic History Review* Vol. 29 (2): 145-154.

Engwall, L. (1985) *Från vag vision till komplex organisation.* Acta Universitatis Upsaliensis. Studia Oeconomiae Negotiorum 22, Uppsala: Almqvist & Wiksell.

Engwall, L. et al. (2004) *CEMP — The Creation of European Management Practice.* Report EUR 20968 from the European Commission.

Engwall, L. (2006) Global Enterprises in Fields of Governace. In Djelic, Marie-Laure & Kerstin Sahlin-Andersson (Eds.) *Transnational Governance: Institutional Dynamics of Regulation.* Cambridge: Cambridge University Press.

Fama, E. (1980) Agency Problems and the Theory of the Firm. *Journal of Political Economy* Vol. 88: 288-307.

Fligstein, N. (1990) *The Transformation of Corporate Control.* Cambridge, MA: Harvard University Press.

Fombrun, C. (1996) *Reputation: Realizing Value From the Corporate Image.* Boston, MA: Harvard Business School Press.

Friedman, T. L. (1999) *The Lexus and the Olive Tree: Understanding Globalization,* New York: Farrar, Straus & Giroux.

Friedman, T. L. (2005) *The World is Flat. The Globalized World in the Twenty-First Century.* New York: Farrar, Straus & Giroux.

Galbraith, J. K. (1967) *The New Industrial State.* Boston, MA: Houghton Mifflin.

Goffman, E. (1959) *The Presentation of Self in Everyday Life*. New York, NY: Doubleday.

Grafström, M., J. Grünberg, J. Pallas & K. Windell (2006) *Ekonominyhetens väg. Från kvartalsrapporter till ekonominyheter*. Stockholm: SNS Förlag.

Grafström, M. (2006) *The Development of Swedish Business Journalism. Historical Roots of an Organisational Field*. Doctoral Thesis No. 121. Department of Business Studies, Uppsala University.

Greenwood, R., C. R. Hinings & R. Suddaby (2002) Theorizing Change: The Role of Professional Associations in the Transformation of Institutionalized Fields. *Academy of Management Journal* Vol. 45 (1): 58-80.

Hatch, M. J. & M. Schultz (1997) Relations between Organizational Culture, Identity and Image. *European Journal of Marketing* Vol. 31 (5): 356-65.

Ihlen, Ø. & P. Robstad (2004) *Informasjon & samfunnskontakt. Perspektiver og praksis*. Bergen: Fagbokforlaget.

Jensen, M. C. & W. H. Meckling (1976) Theory of the Firm: Managerial Behavior, Agency Costs and Ownership Structure. *Journal of Financial Economics* Vol. 3 (4): 305-360.

Jepperson, R., L. (1991) Institutions, Institutional Effects and Institutionalism. In DiMaggio, P. J. & W. W. Powell (Eds.) *The Institutionalism in Organizational Analysis*. Chicago: University of Chicago Press.

Jonsson, S. (2005) Naming Me and Shaming You: Inaccuracies in Mechanisms for Loss of Legitimacy. Paper presented at the GEMS workshop at Oxford University, August 2005.

Keasey, K., S. Thompson & M. Wright (Eds.) (1997) *Corporate Governance. An Economic and Financial Analysis*. Oxford: Oxford University Press.

Langer, R. & J. Pallas (2006) Negotiation of Corporate News: A Study of Source-Media Interaction. Paper to be presented at the 22nd EGOS Colloquium, Sub-theme 29: The Interrelationship of Media and Organisations, Bergen, Norway, July 6-8, 2006.

Larsson, L. (2005) Opinionsmakarna. En studie om PR-konsulter, journalistik och demokrati. Lund: Studentlitteratur.

Lindström, E. (1958) *Public relations: vad är PR: mål och medel: en bok om företagetskontakter inåt och utåt*. Stockholm: Forum.

Marris, R. (1964) *The Economic Theory of 'Managerial' Capitalism*. London: Free Press of Glencoe.

McLaughlin, K., S. P. Osborne & E. Ferlie (Eds.) (2002) *New Public Management. Current Trends and Future Prospects*. London: Routledge.

McLean, B. & P. Elkind (2003) *The Smartest Guys in the Room. The Amazing Rise and Scandalous Fall of Enron*. New York: Portfolio.

Meyer, J. W. & B. Rowan (1977) Institutionalized Organizations: Formal Structure as Myth and Ceremony. *American Journal of Sociology* Vol. 83 (2): 364-385.

Moeller, R. R. (2004) *Sarbanes-Oxley and the New Internal Auditing Rules*. Hoboken, NJ: Wiley.

Monks, R. A. G. & N. Minow (1995) *Corporate Governance*. Oxford: Blackwell Business.

Nachemson-Ekwall, S. & B. Carlsson (2004) *Guldregn. Sagan om Skandia.* Stockholm: Bonniers.

O'Brien, J. (Ed.) (2005) *Governing the Corporation: Regulation and Corporate Governance in an Age of Scandal and Global Markets.* Chichester: Wiley.

Owen, G., T. Kirchmaier & J. Grant (2006) *Corporate Governance in the US and Europe: Where are We Now?* New York: Palgrave Macmillan.

Pallas, J. (2005) The (Un)Mediated Organization – an Empirical Description of Two Information Departments and Their Media Work. Paper presented at the GEMS workshop in Oxford, UK, August 30-31, 2005.

Pollock, T. G. & V. P. Rindova (2003) Media Legitimation Effects in the Market for Initial Public Offerings. *Academy of Management Journal* Vol. 46 (5): 631-642.

Roe, M. J (1994) *Strong Managers, Weak Owners. The Political Roots of American Corporate Finance.* Princeton, NJ: Princeton University Press.

Røvik, K. A. (2002) The Secrets of the Winners. Management Ideas that Flow. In Sahlin-Andersson, Kerstin & Lars Engwall (Eds.) *The Expansion of Management Knowledge. Carriers, Flows and Sources.* Stanford, Stanford University Press.

Sahlin-Andersson, K. (1996) Imitating by Editing Success. The Construction of Organizational Fields. In Czarniawska, Barbara & Guje Sevón (Eds.) (1996) *Translating Organizational Change.* Berlin: de Gruyter.

Sahlin-Andersson, K. (2001) National, International and Transnational Constructions of New Public Management. In Christensen, Tom & Per Laegreid (Eds.) *New Public Management: The Transformation of Ideas and Practice.* Aldershot: Ashgate.

Sahlin-Andersson, K. & L. Engwall (Eds.) (2002) *The Expansion of Management Knowledge. Carriers, Flows and Sources.* Stanford, CA: Stanford Business Books.

Sandberg, T. (1982) *Work Organization and Autonomous Groups.* Lund: Gleerups.

Schultz, M., Y. M. Antorini & F. F. Csaba (Eds.) (2005) *Corporate Branding: Purpose, People, Process: Towards the Second Wave of Corporate Branding.* Frederiksberg: Copenhagen Business School Press.

Scott, R. W. (1995) *Institutions and Organizations.* Thousand Oaks: Sage.

Scott, R. W. (1987) *Organizations: Rational, Natural and Open Systems,* NJ: Prentice-Hall.

Siebert. F. S., T. Peterson & W. Schramm (1956) *Four Theories of the Press.* Urbana, IL: The University of Illinois.

Strang, D. & J. W. Meyer (1994) Institutional Conditions for Diffusion. In Scott, W. Richard & John W. Meyer (Eds.) *Institutional Environments and Organizations. Structural Complexity and Individualism.* Thousand Oaks: Sage.

Thompson, J. D. (1967) *Organizations in Action.* New York: McGraw-Hill.

Tiratsso, N. (2002) The American Quality Gospel in Britain and Japan, 1950-1970. In Sahlin-Andersson, Kerstin & Lars Engwall (Eds.) *The Expan-*

sion of Management Knowledge. Carriers, Flows and Sources. Stanford, Stanford University Press.

Tsoukas, H. (1999) David and Goliath in the Risk Society. Making Sense of the Conflict Between Shell and Greenpeace in the North Sea. *Organization* Vol. 6 (1): 499-528.

Walgenbach, P. & N. Beck (2002) The Institutionalisation of the Quality Management Approach in Germany. In Sahlin-Andersson, K. & L. Engwall (Eds.) *The Expansion of Management Knowledge. Carriers, Flows and Sources*. Stanford: Stanford University Press.

Wallraff, G. (1970) *Industrireportagen. Als Arbeiter in deutschen Grossbetrieben*. Hamburg: Rowohlt.

Welch, J. & S. Welch (2005) *Winning*. New York, NY: Harper.

Windell, Karolina (2006) *Corporate Social Responsibility under Construction: Ideas, Translations, and Institutional Change*. Doctoral Dissertation No. 123, Department of Business Studies, Uppsala University.

CHAPTER 11

Media Transparency as an Institutional Practice

PETER KJÆR & KERSTIN SAHLIN

The pursuit of transparency is an important factor in business and business journalism. Many handbooks concerned with business journalism or public relations observe that the business press has contributed to a dramatic increase in the visibility of business in society. Never before has so much attention been paid to the activities and ambitions of business, and never before has so much energy been devoted to the management of transparency. In this chapter we will look critically at the role of the business press and of business journalism in the pursuit of transparency.

The business press performs a variety of roles in society. One key role is still that of providing public information about business and economic events and of critically scrutinizing business activities. Ideally, the role of business journalists is not just to make business visible but to cultivate *transparency*, i.e. to make it possible for an observer to look beyond surface appearances and to scrutinize the inner workings of business corporations or of particular industries or sectors.

This role is as old as business news itself. Rosenberg, in his history of the *Wall Street Journal*, described how the *Journal* managed to discipline the flow of information on Wall Street in the late 1800s by providing reliable and transparent information about companies and trading at the end of each day, and by exposing dubious investment schemes (Rosenberg 1982: 11). However, the pursuit of transparency seems to have accelerated with the expansion and professionalization of business journalism. Many business journalists today, no longer satisfied simply to relay market information from established financial or commercial sources, instead engage in the intensive scrutiny of business operations, comparing official information with internal sources, with the judgement of experts, with international standards and so on. Business journalists have received many distinguished awards for investigative reporting, which is regarded increasingly as the hallmark of modern journalism (Schultz 2005).

There is both a heroic and a more skeptical interpretation of the pursuit of transparency. According to the heroic version, business journalists are the only remaining challenge to the power of business:

> *Today, the voice of labor has been reduced to a whisper, the consumer advocates and other nonprofit guardians are scattered and poorly funded, government regulation has become a dirty word, and Big Business stands alone on the stage, free at last from any meaningful countervailing social or civic power – except the power of the press* (Henriques 2000: 119).

The skeptical interpretation, which is the one that underlies our argument below, sees the pursuit of transparency as part of a broader societal trend and as embedded in new forms of social coordination. Writing in the field of accounting, Power has described the emergence of what he called 'an audit society' (Power 1997). As the result of an 'audit explosion' the logic of the financial audit has been replicated in other arenas in society and now constitutes a new system of governance that inculcates 'new norms and values by which external regulatory mechanisms transform the conduct of organizations and individuals in their capacity as "self actualizing individuals"' (Miller & Rose 1990, see also Shore & Wright 2000). The 'audit society' is a society where audits invade almost all aspects of social life, and where operations and organizations are being increasingly structured with their 'auditability' in mind (see also Strathern 2000, Shore & Wright 2000).

In examining the expansion of the business press below we will emphasize its audit society context. The development of business journalism is obviously closely related to changes in the media field as a whole – in technological platforms, professional projects and media markets. In organizational terms, however, the expansion of business news can also be regarded as part of a broader social transformation affecting, among other things the way in which organizational activities are observed, regulated and structured. Our ambition is to address the question of media transparency in this context, in order to pave the way for a further exploration of its organizational implications.

In the following pages, we first discuss the concept of transparency itself. We look at some of the dominant rationales for transparency and argue that it can best be analyzed as a social and institutional practice. We then describe the technological, organizational and institutional aspects of transparency practices, all in relation to the business press. Finally, we consider some possible organizational implications of media transparency in terms of organizational structure, identity and governance.

Transparency: From Ideal to Tyranny

'Transparency' - along with 'Governance', 'Flexibility', 'Quality', and 'Performance' - has become a lively concept of almost universal range. It turns up as an issue in fields as far apart as anti-corruption, corporate governance, architecture, health care policy and organizational learning. A wide range of beneficial - albeit not altogether compatible – outcomes are claimed for it. And although the meaning of transparency as a metaphor appears virtually self-evident (no barriers, full visibility, etc.), several more distinctive rationales for transparency do seem to exist. At least four such rationales for transparency can be identified.

1. Control. Transparency, as economists and some political scientists have used the term, implies a desire to be able to regulate interactions between certain actors. Today this problem appears in connection with corruption or agency problems. Corruption, it is claimed, arises when relations between government and business, for example, or within government itself, are not available for external scrutiny, for instance by independent regulatory bodies. Transparency is consequently a question of developing formal procedures and arrangements for third-party inspection, and of formal sanctions against illegitimate transactions (see http://transparency.org/). Agency problems can arise in relationships between, for instance, owners and managers in corporations operating under conditions of uncertainty or from information asymmetry resulting in opportunistic behavior on the part of certain agents. In such cases, auditing schemes and/or other regulatory arrangements may adjust the information asymmetry and get the agents (managers, workers, administrators, etc.) to conform with the goals of their principals (Clarke 2004, Monks & Minow 2004).

2. Efficiency. While efficiency is connected with control in indirect ways, there are also some links that are more direct. On the one hand, transparency has been connected with market efficiency, whereby 'information' is seen as a precondition for the efficient allocation of resources via the market. Economic historians have posited a close link between the expansion of markets and the development of reliable information systems allowing economic agents to make informed decisions beyond concrete localities and social spaces (North 1990: 126f, Babe 1995). On the other hand, according to a closely related approach, transparency is connected with technical efficiency, whereby standardized information is regarded as a precondition for optimal decisions in the marketplace and even in other context (cf. Miller & O'Leary 1987). Thus in engineering, management, medicine and elsewhere, standardization and the development of specific information systems are thought to lead to more scientific or rational decision-making by allowing for the systematic comparison and calculation of alternatives and consequences. Related to this idea is the idea that transparency facilitates collaboration among and between positions, organizations and occupational groups. As groups learn more about one another's work, they can be expected to be better equipped to collaborate and to coordinate what they do (see below).

3. Liberty. The development of the rule of law and various fora for public deliberations is connected with a third approach to transparency, whereby transparency is regarded as a precondition for liberty. According to one version, a transparent structure of rules and norms, in the form of positive law for example, allows individuals to form stable expectations and to engage in the rational pursuit of self interest, while other versions see transparency as involving the continued rationalization and illumination of society and selves, allowing for the continuous questioning of collective arrangements and individual behaviors, and the gradual elimination of arbitrary power and behavioral constraints. This notion of transparency is closely connected with the idea of a critical public sphere (Habermas 1991), but it also appears in the fields of architecture (Barnstone 2005) and management (Eriksen 1999). The more recent idea that the Internet, satellite TV, etc., constitute a global agora in which everything and everybody become visible to one another is based on a similar conception of transparency.

4. Trust. Finally, transparency has been interpreted as a precondition for the creation of social trust (and legitimacy), and for the development of shared knowledge and action. Thus in theories concerned with small-group learning processes, the development of transparent forms of interaction and communication are seen as the key to processes of collective knowledge production and innovation (Boud & Garrick 1999, Brown & Duguid 1991, Wenger 1998). Only when actors engage openly and succeed in removing artificial barriers to communication, will they be able to benefit from the synergies of small-group interaction and social learning. Here transparency has to do with the ways in which actors engage in social processes and how they expose their activities to outside scrutiny, often with the help of various information technologies. It is thus thought that transparency enables the free flow of information and ideas among a community of practitioners.

There are of course other conceptions and applications of transparency besides these, but for our purposes the above typology fleshes out what we regard as the main rationales for transparency. Each approach posits a particular interest in transparency, develops a particular ideal of transparency, and indicates specific means for creating or enhancing transparency. However, while the proponents of transparency within each group are eager to identify barriers and obstacles to transparency, rarely do they attempt to consider the notion of transparency itself in rather more critical terms.

In recent years a critical debate on transparency has emerged in which it is suggested that transparency is more than just the absence of something – of barriers, boundaries, restrictions and so on – but that it is a concrete and institutionally constructed *social practice*. Transparency is a 'regime' that involves particular technologies of observation, inspection, etc., implying a particular organization of observers and observed who are guided by particular institutionalized rules (Power 1994, 1997, Knorr Cetina & Bruegger 2002).

Paradoxically, a transparency regime of this kind may produce exactly the opposite of what it promises to deliver, that is to say intransparency, inefficiency, oppression and mistrust. Vattimo (1992) suggests that the modern mass-media society where everything can become an object of communication, leads - while finally fulfilling modernist dreams of transparency - also to something quite different, namely to an overwhelming multiplicity of voices and the absence of unifying perspectives that together undermine the liberating potential of transparency and create new and dangerous forms of nostalgia and closure (see also Christensen 2002). Tsoukas (1997) refers to the 'tyranny of light' in a critical discussion of the 'information society', claiming that the radical explosion of all-embracing information that is believed to result in transparency and social improvement, may in fact reduce understanding, undermine trust and lower the potential for rational government. Similarly Power has identified a spiral of distrust as one of the main drivers of the 'audit explosion'. Paradoxically, while the extension of monitoring and auditing activities has been motivated by a reference to decline in trust and the belief that such activities will re-build trust by creating transparency, they seem to in fact undermine trust even more and lead to yet more requests for auditing and monitoring (Power 1997, 2003, Hood et al. 1999, Moran 2002). Strathern (2000) examines the 'tyranny of transparency' and declares that 'the appeal to a benevolent or moral visibility is all too easily shown to have a tyrannous side – there is nothing innocent about making the invisible visible' (p. 309), and that the question is really '*What does visibility conceal?*' (p. 310, italics in the original). Finally, Mathiesen (1997) claims that we have entered upon a form of social organization that cannot be characterized solely in terms of the panopticon model (see Foucault 1977) in which the few see the many, but that implies a synoptic society in which 'the many see and contemplate the few'. With the expansion of the modern news-oriented mass media, decision-makers are now visible to large audiences. However, the synopticon does not entail the absence of power. Rather, power now resides with the institutional elites that control agenda-setting and framing processes in and around the media. Mathiesen then concludes that 'things are much *worse*' (p. 232) than Foucault invisaged, because the surveillance and discipline of panopticon technologies are now supplemented by new forms of social control installed by the synopticon.

These critical contributions have paved the way for a sociological debate on transparency as an institutionalized practice and regime. People are beginning to look at the way in which transparency is being produced, at the selectivity of particular arrangements for transparency, and at what transparency does – in other words at the consequences of the diffusion and institutionalization of transparency practices.

Following the pointers suggested by these critical studies of transparency we will now turn to the technological, organizational and institutional aspects of transparency practices, and to some of their possible organizational implications. We proceed from our fundamental assumption that media transparency can, and is to be, regarded as a particular social practice within a broader institutionalized field of knowledge.

Technological, Organizational and Institutional Aspects of Transparency

In this section we review the evolving practices of transparency and identify the position of business news, business journalism and the business press in relation to these. As transparency practices are regarded as part of a transparency regime, we will first consider three aspects of the regime concerned, namely technological aspects referring to particular transparency-creating technologies, organizational aspects connected with actors and organizations engaged in the creation of transparency, and institutional aspects attaching to wider institutional forces that in turn are concerned with transparency. The order in which we address these - from the most immediate and on to the most general or abstract – implies no particular order or dynamic in the practices of transparency discussed. On the contrary, as will become apparent below, we find that institutional, organizational and technological changes often involve dynamics of a mutually reinforcing kind.

Visualizing Technologies

Having established that the creation of transparency is not only – or even primarily - a question of removing obstacles or barriers that are concealing whatever is to be made transparent, but that it also involves the active creation of visibility, we now have to consider how this last is to be achieved. To begin with we can identify a set of technologies that are already being used to make corporate practices visible, together with their related consequences.

We have already mentioned the increase in auditing. Auditing is a form of *monitoring* – a way of scrutinizing actors and activities. Monitoring is undertaken by an impartial actor and is concerned with things that have already happened. Evaluation and inspection are forms related to monitoring and scrutiny. News coverage by the media can be regarded as a monitoring technology, and, as we have seen, one of the justifications for expanding the media coverage of business corporations is to enable the necessary public scrutiny of corporate affairs. Unlike audits, evaluations and inspections, the selection criteria of news reporting emphasize 'news value', such as novelty, conflict, and identification (Luhmann 2000, Schultz 2005) rather than more formal, efficiency-oriented or political selection criteria. In the case of business news, the news monitoring is also highly routinized (Tuchman 1978), so that specialized news media scrutinize particular types of firms (large publicly traded corporations) and particular types of corporate events (e.g. annual or quarterly reports) that are regarded auto-matically as newsworthy and relevant (Grafström et al. 2006).

The increase in monitoring is accompanied by an increase in the production of *accounts*. Like monitoring, the producing of accounts or reports occurs on a regular basis and according to clearly pre-structured forms. Media news reports, in this perspective, constitutes a particular type of account, structured according to particular technical and narrative formats, such as the 'inverted pyramid' that displays in-formation in a declining order of importance, or as narratives of con-flict, responsibility and action (Cook 1998: 98ff). However, like audits, inspections and evaluations, news reports are usually produced in in-teraction between the observer and the observed, in the sense that all monitoring and accounting technologies require some degree of active participation on the part of the organization being monitored (see also Grafström & Pallas in the present volume).

Monitoring and accounting technologies are interrelated, so that with more monitoring we also get an increase in accounts, and the pro-duction of more accounts in turn makes it easier to do the monitoring in more structured forms. It is these mutually reinforcing developments that Power refers to in discussing the emergent 'audit society'.

There is a third technology involved in those expanding spiral, namely *regulation*. Despite much talk of deregulation, most contempo-rary societies seem in fact to be characterized by a growing range of regulations. Expressions such as the 'golden era of regulation' (Levi-Faur & Jordana 2005), 'a regulatory explosion' (Ahrne & Brunsson 2005) or 'regulatory activism' (Djelic & Sahlin-Andersson 2006) have been coined to signal what is happening. The rules concerned tend to be of the 'softer' kind (Mörth 2004). They are voluntary and are aimed mainly at structuring organizational self-representations, accounts and monitoring activities (Hedmo et al. 2005). Thus they represent tech-nologies for structuring and ordering that which is to be made visible. At the same time they serve to classify and categorize activities, rela-tions and accounts (cf. Bowker & Star 1999). It seems that on one hand business news involves noticeably less regulation than financial audits or accreditation schemes, for example. On the other hand, how-ever, firms are being increasingly subjected to regulatory demands re-garding the publication of specific types of information. Stock ex-changes are thus subject to rigorous demands as to when and how cor-porate information is to be released to the public (including the media), for instance as quarterly financial statements.

The escalation of these three interrelated visualization technologies is supported in turn by other technologies conducive to large-scale monitoring and scrutinizing – exploiting data bases, for example, and the recording, storing and disseminating of large complex data sets. Recent developments in global information infrastructures such as on-line data bases have also tended to boost practices of transparency even more (Knorr Cetina & Bruegger 2002, Boyd-Barrett & Rantanen 1998).

Organizing for Transparency

Typically then, the visualizing technologies are directed at organizations. They are also developed and used by organizations, which means that the links between organizational practices and transparency-creation deserve some attention. As noted elsewhere in the present volume, the corporate environment includes a large population of transparency-producing organizations (see also Sahlin-Andersson & Engwall 2002).

On the one hand there are the *monitors and reporters* that is to say the many organizations that monitor corporate activities and report on them. This has spawned a number of organizational fields, such as the evaluation field with its consultancies, educational institutions, data bases, etc., or the environmental management field that comprises NGOs, consultants and public advisory bodies – all of which intersect and overlap with one another. The field of business news journalism - which comprises the business press, financial analysts, news bureaus and communication consultants – is not only a sub-field in its own right, but it also links and reinforces activities in several related fields in that it reports on the monitoring and reporting undertaken by other organizations (Grafström et al. 2006, Grafström 2006).

On the other hand, alongside the organizations involved in direct monitoring and reporting, we find the *regulators*, which include not only the rule-setting and more formally scrutinizing bodies such as the legal system, auditors, scrutinizing units connected with the stock exchange, corporate governance codes, etc., but also the standardizing and ranking bodies of various kinds that assess many aspects of the corporate world.

This population of transparency-producing organizations is thus multiplying and becoming increasingly complex. The escalation in the organizational world is accompanied by greater activity, more interaction, and enhanced competition among the numerous organizations involved. While some of these are supported by legal or other obviously legitimate systems, others are developing in response to transparency-producing activities and organizations that already exist. At the same time, certain non-state, voluntary regulations have begun to overlap or be combined with state regulations. In this context some representatives of the state have shown an interest in reshaping their own regulatory systems in line with the voluntary counterparts, and have sought to imitate certain aspects of these. A mechanism thus arose whereby increased regulation led to requests for even more new (complementary or competing) regulation, so that the many organizations whose existence depends on their transparency-producing activities are all striving for positions, legitimacy, resources and survival (cf. Hedmo et al. 2006) . We could in fact speak of a *transparency market*, in which organizations compete among themselves in developing and disseminating their visualizing technologies and activities, and in drawing attention to them (cf. Djelic & Sahlin-Andersson 2006). This dynamism among the transparency-producing organizations is part of a more general escalation of formal organizations, and in particular of the transnational kind (Boli & Thomas 1999), whose main task is often to monitor, regulate and report on their peers. In an increasingly densely populated landscape these organizations are competing for resources, attention and legitimacy, and in so doing are adding to escalation of visualizing technologies and activities.

Added to all this, the *organizations that are being monitored and regulated* may react in the same coin, with corporations organizing themselves to produce visibility, expanding information departments, organizing road shows, producing accounting and reporting material and so on. The arrival of observers and scrutinizers in corporate fields has been accompanied by a growing emphasis on self-presentation (see Engwall & Sahlin in the present volume). Thus, at an organizational level too, the manifest organizing and self-presentation support the practices of transparency and give them structure.

Up to now we have been seeking to show that transparency does not only mean removing barriers or veils. On the contrary, the practices of transparency also involve specific technologies and actors – or organizations. This also means that transparency looks different depending on the organizational setup of the organizations being scrutinized and of those making the scrutiny. Thus while we argue that even news reporting should be regarded as a scrutinizing technology and media organizations as part of a transparency market, it is important to take into account differences between the various technologies and organizations or actors involved.

Institutional Aspects of Transparency

We have suggested not only that the development of practices of transparency is contingent on the recent development of visualizing technologies and organizations, but also that these technologies and organizations display a self-reinforcing dynamic. First we showed how the three visualizing technologies – monitoring, accounting and regulation – were feeding and driving each other. Second, it appears that the organizations created around these technologies operate according to a dynamic usually to be found in organizations. In other words they seek survival, legitimacy, expansion and control (Pfeffer & Salancik 1978) which means in turn that they seek to uphold, expand and disseminate transparency technologies.

These widespread technologies and organizing efforts have been analyzed in an audit society perspective (Power 1997) or in an audit culture perspective (Strathern 2000, Shore & Wright 2000). These last concepts suggest that the quest for transparency is now an institutionalized aspect of our modern societies – and it could be claimed that in a more general way they have become an important aspect of the modern project.

We will not expatiate these historical trends and parallels, but will call attention instead to a number of current institutional aspects of the contemporary pursuit of transparency. At an institutional level, the pursuit of transparency has often been associated with the spread of neo-liberal ideologies and reforms – as captured by concepts such as shareholder value, new public management, etc., and indeed by several of the rationales of transparency reviewed above. However, while neo-liberalism and transparency certainly coincide, we find that practices of transparency are involved in several institutional transformations that, while including neo-liberalism, also transcend it. Inspired by Djelic and Sahlin-Andersson's (2006) search for a contemporary institutional dynamic to explain the expansion and development of transnational governance, we will consider the dominant institutional forces that, taken together, frame and drive transparency-seeking activities today.

Transnational governance consists largely of expansive and complex fields of monitoring and regulation (Jacobsson & Sahlin-Andersson 2006) – that is to say, of the visualizing technologies indicated above, and we thus believe that the analysis of transnational governance is also relevant to the interpretation of the institutional development of transparency. We will look in particular at five institutional forces that contribute to the expansion of a regime of transparency, in the sense that, in conjunction with particular technologies and organizing practices, they lay open certain aspects of society for scrutiny, representation and regulation in particular ways.

First, practices of transparency are structured and framed by the rise, expansion and influence of *scientific discourse* throughout the world (Drori et al. 2003, Drori & Meyer 2006). Actors, activities and settings are largely shaped and authorized in the name of science. As Max Weber has already pointed out this induces a drive for transparency:

> *The increasing intellectualization and rationalization do not, therefore, indicate an increased and general knowledge of the conditions under which one lives. It means something else, namely, the knowledge or belief that if one but wished one could learn it at any time. Hence, it means that principally there are no mysterious incalculable forces that come into play, but rather that one can, in principle, master all things by calculation. This means that the world is disenchanted. One need no longer have recourse to magical means in order to master or implore the spirits, as did the savage, for whom such mysterious powers existed. Technical means and calculations perform the service. This above all is what intellectualization means. This process of disenchantment, which has continued to exist in Occidental culture for millennia, and, in general, this 'progress,' to which science belongs as a link and motive force* (Weber 1919/1946).

The business press, in this context, embodies the ideal of rational calculation. The notion that the role of the business press is to supply information to economic decision-makers rests on the belief that economic actors make decisions on the basis of a rational choice between alternatives that can be evaluated by the collection of information about possible outcomes. While journalists also endorse other and more romantic or charismatic conceptions of management (Meindl et al. 1985), the ideal of rational calculation as a key trait of management remains central among journalists and is routinely used to evaluate and legitimate organizational practices (Vaara & Tienari 2002).

A second institutional force is of a later date, and is more clearly or directly tied to neo-liberal trends. Western societies, at least, are being *marketized* to the extent that not only are markets framed as superior arrangements for the allocation of goods and resources in every sphere of economic, social or even cultural and moral life, but they are also increasingly defined and perceived as the 'natural' way to organize and structure human interactions (Djelic 2006). As noted above, a common argument for maintaining transparency is that, in order to function well, markets demand transparency. Although business journalists are sometimes critical of concrete decisions or activities, they rarely question the idea that markets constitute an optimal allocation mechanism (see also Parsons 1989), and criticism is consequently more often directed at attempts to circumvent market forces by withholding information from the market (Lund 2002: 82), or by economic actors engaging in collusive arrangements behind the scenes (Kjær & Langer 2004).

Organizing is a third institutional force in this context. Organizing - which here is defined as the almost universal reliance on formal organizational structure for ordering social relations, achieving particular goals or solving particular problems - has resulted in what may be termed the organized society (Perrow 1991, 2002), a society in which formal organizations become the key vehicles for governance and social order (see also Ahrne & Brunsson 2004). The prevailing ideal of organizing is to order by making tasks, roles and relations explicit and subject to formal description – i.e. transparent. While business journalism has displayed an occasional interest in more fluid or network forms of organization (e.g. Morsing 1999), the standard perception of the business enterprise is usually that of the corporate hierarchy as represented by the organization chart. Thus journalists routinely turn to CEOs as an authoritative source regarding business events (Grafström et al. 2006), while sources and voices outside the corporate hierarchy rarely gain access to the news.

A fourth institutional force is what Djelic and Sahlin-Andersson term *moral rationalization* (Boli 2006); the widespread assessment and celebration of what is good and bad, excellent or insufficient – usually based on moral judgments and expressed in ranking lists, prizes, records, credentials and celebrations, published naming and shaming and the like and backed up by a rationalized moral order that assumes basic cognitive and normative judgment criteria. Here the business press plays a key role by publicizing, and sometimes even engaging in, the production of performance and status evaluations in relation to business activity. Evaluations of top CEOs, rankings of educational institutions, and the celebration of business plans are all part and parcel of contemporary business journalism (Elsbach & Kramer 1996, Hayward, Rindova & Pollock 2004).

Finally there is the urge toward *reinventing democracy*. As Mörth (2006) has convincingly argued, a view of democracy that emphasizes dialogue, deliberation and individual autonomy is gaining ground in our world, triggering a widespread demand for information upon which those taking part can base their actions and their contributions to the relevant dialogues. This institutional development not only encourages a more intensive pursuit of information on business developments and other aspects of society, but – if a meaningful dialogue is to emerge – it also calls for a critical and multifarious scrutiny of these developments. Business journalists often challenge the idea that key decisions should be made by democratic political institutions applauding instead the autonomy and decision-making capacity of business managers and investors. At the same time, the role of the business press also coincides with new ideas regarding shareholder democracy, corporate governance and consumerism that are rearticulating democratic ideals within a market context.

These technological, organizational and institutional practices thus come together in an unremitting pursuit of transparency. A transparency regime has emerged that affects not only the way people, associations, organizations and groups account for their activities but also the way they perceive and perform them. In society today, operations are being planned and performed in a way that allows them to be monitored, reported and visualized. Transparency thus needs to be understood not only as an external demand on organizations, individuals and groups. It is often also a case of individuals, groups and organizations that want to make their settings and operations visible and to present themselves in a positive light. Thus once again we find that transparency is driven by reciprocal and mutually einforcing interests.

Discussion: Living with Transparency

In this chapter we have interpreted the expansion of business news as part of an 'audit explosion'. Business news can then be regarded as part of a transparency regime – and not just as 'information circulation' or a special - and problematic version - of political news coverage. We have accordingly described the different rationales for transparency and suggested that transparency should be regarded as a regime with a particular set of technological, organizational and institutional practices. Thus, rather than comparing business news with political news, we should start comparing it with other monitoring, accounting and regulatory technologies. Rather than regarding the business press as a special offshoot of the general conventional media, we should think of it as part of a transparency market. Finally, rather than regarding the expansion of business journalism simply as an expression of dynamics in the media system, we should think of it as the out-come of wider transparency-enhancing institutional forces that func-tion on a global scale. Essentially, then we should begin to conceive the effects of the expansion of business news as part of broader con-temporary governance systems and regimes that center on practices of transparency.

Interpreting the role of business news as part of a transparency re-gime raises at least two important questions. First, what does it mean for organizations to live with mass media transparency and what are the intended or unintended organizational consequences of such trans-parency? Second, what exactly is the role of the business press as a governance institution, and what particular responsibilities may attach to its participation in a transparency regime?

The effects of transparency at the organizational level are only just beginning to be explored, and most studies so far have concentrated on the implications of the growth in auditing rather than the spread of me-dia transparency. Nonetheless, at least three types of effect have been looked at, namely structural, cultural (identity) and governance effects.

Transparency practices have consequences for *organizational struc-ture*. The pursuit of transparency involves systematic attempts to estab-lish or increase the visibility of organizational activities and outcomes. Organizational self-descriptions provide one way of achieving this, as organizations engage in producing and editing presentations of them-selves and their performance in light of various standard criteria for evaluation and description (Corvellec 1997). The formal structuring of activities provides another way for organizations to present themselves in an apparently transparent way, formally describing their activities, responsibilities and procedures, and enacting institutionalized ideals of the rationality and transparency of organizational practices (Meyer & Rowan 1977, DiMaggio & Powell 1991, Brunsson 1989). Finally, or-ganizations may become increasingly differentiated, creating particular organizational functions or units such as departments for quality, communications or investor relations dedicated to the on-going moni-toring, standardization and presentation of organizational performance (Engwall and Sahlin in the present volume). However, as several criti-cal analysts have pointed out, the outcome of transparency practices at the organization level is either a very particular form of transparency, i.e. one that is enacted by way of standard-setting and formalization, or a highly managed form of transparency designed to ensure that organ-izational operations can be effected under conditions of transparency. In this context, media transparency may thus lead not only to bureaucratization but also to a redistribution of the decision-making power in the organization – perhaps from operators to information managers or from low-level or middle managers to top managers eager to command corporate visibility when the organization is being scrutinized.

Transparency practices can also make an impact on *organizational culture and identity*. A number of studies associated with organizational culture and marketing research have especially noted the breakdown of the boundary between the 'inside' and 'outside' of organizations (Dutton & Dukerich 1991, Hatch & Schultz 1997, 2000). The (external) social legitimacy or reputation of an organization may have major consequences for its (internal) organizational identity, and thus for the ways its members perceive themselves and others. This breakdown is sometimes thought to be the outcome of subtle changes in occupational roles, but can also perhaps be reinforced by the technological, organizational and institutional dynamics outlined above, i.e. as an outcome of transparency practices (see also Christensen 2002). Hatch and Schultz (2000) emphasize how cultural processes within organizations become contingent upon the meanings associated with the organization in the broader environment, e.g. in the media. Morsing (1999) shows how media transparency may boost the redefinition of organizational identities in periods of intense media coverage, while Kjærgaard and Morsing (2006) show how media representations of organizational activities may create disjointed identities, such that organization members cannot link their external and internal 'selves'. Finally, several researchers, including Christensen and Cheney (2000), Christensen (2002), Hayward, Pollock and Rindova (2004), Rindova, Pollock and Hayward (2006), have discussed how various types of technologically enhanced transparency can create a new dynamic of organizational identity-formation, which in turn may lead to organizational narcissism and/or unrealistic perceptions of the importance of leadership.

Finally, practices of transparency have *governance* effects, i.e. effects on the way activities are governed within and between organizations (see Engwall & Sahlin in the present volume, Tsoukas 1999, Backer 1999). Thus in critical management studies, practices of auditing and accounting have been examined as examples of how a new 'governmentality' is manifested in concrete work practices. Miller and Rose (1990), working within a Foucauldian framework, have shown how knowledge and power are closely intertwined in the field of management and organization, and how the early development of practices of knowledge production and dissemination concerning work was intrinsically linked to the project of creating 'governable persons', i.e. transparency and power have always been two sides of the same coin. Power (1994, 1997) has suggested how the audit explosion has produced both auditees and auditors, i.e. how audit practices tend to produce what they observe, namely auditable actors in the sense that the 'victims' of audits are induced to present themselves and their activities in ways that render them accessible to external observation and description – in specific terms. Finally, Christensen and Morsing (2005), in a critical study of ideals of 'corporate communication', have emphasized how ideas of integrated communication management in which organization members at all levels are 'communicators', entail new forms of control and discipline directed towards the communicative conduct of individuals in organizations (Christensen & Morsing 2005: 92ff).

The second question, the question of the responsibility of the business press within the transparency regime can only be addressed as some of the possible outcomes of the regime begin to be investigated more thoroughly. Even then, the concrete role of the press may be quite difficult to pinpoint, because transparency practices are continuous, dispersed and discrete – and involve a host of actors beyond the media themselves. While it may be premature to formulate particular demands on the media as agents of transparency, a few themes can already be identified. First, it becomes relevant to evaluate journalistic practices as technologies of transparency, and to consider what aspects of business are rendered visible or invisible by particular types of scrutiny or reporting, i.e. reporting that emphasizes individual action rather than organizational context, or reporting that emphasizes financial performance rather than environmental performance or employment. Second, it becomes relevant to consider the role of media organizations in the transparency market, and especially the ways in which the media become dependent not only on company sources but also on a host of other monitors, reporters and regulators in the field, whose status is rarely evaluated. A case in point could be securities analysts whose observations and evaluations are widely and often uncritically reproduced by the media. Third, it becomes relevant to consider how the business media reflect broader institutionalized frames of meaning that involve ideals of knowledge, markets, democracy, organization etc., but that also entail particular interpretations or translations of these ideals on the part of media professionals.

Perhaps the issue here is not the particular responsibilities that researchers and others may envision for the media under a transparency regime, but rather that it should be demanded of journalists, editors and other media professionals that they begin to reflect more explicitly and openly on the practices, in which they are involved. In this sense, although our perspective on transparency has been a skeptical one, we also believe that the only way to handle the issue of transparency is through transparency – not just by making the objects of monitoring and accounting visible and their activities transparent, but also by asking the same of the monitors.

Bibliography

Ahrne, G. & N. Brunsson (Eds.) (2004) *Regelexplosionen*. Stockholm: EFI. Stockholm School of Economics.

Babe, R. E. (1995) Communication and the Transformation of Economics. *Essays in Information, Public Policy, and Political Economy*. Bouder: Westview.

Backer, L. (2001) The Mediated Transparent Society. *Corporate Reputation Review* Vol. 4 (3): 235-251.

Barnstone, D. A. (2005) *The Transparent State: Architecture and politics in postwar Germany*. London, New York: Routledge.

Boli, J. & G. M. Thomas (Eds.) (1999) *Constructing World Culture: International Nongovernmental Organizations since 1875*. Stanford: Stanford University Press.

Boli, J. (2006) The rationalization of virtue and virtuosity in world society. In Djelic, M.-L. & Sahlin-Andersson, K. (Eds.) *Transnational Governance: Institutional Dynamics of Regulation*. Cambridge University Press.

Boud, D. & J. Garrick (Eds.) (1999) *Understanding Learning at Work*. London: Routledge.

Bowker, G. C. & S. L. Star (1999) *Sorting Things Out*. Cambridge, MA: MIT Press.

Boyd-Barrett, O. & T. Rantanen (Eds.) (1998) *The Globalization of News*. London: Sage.

Brown, J. S. & P. Duguid (1991) Organizational Learning and Communities-of-Practice: Toward a Unified View of Working, Learning, and Innovation. *Organization Science* Vol. 2 (1): 40-57.

Brunsson, N. (1989) *The organization of hypocrisy: Talk, decisions and actions in organizations*. Chichester: Wiley.

Christensen, L. T. (2002) Corporate Communication: The Challenge of Transparency. *Corporate Communication: An International Journal*. Vol. 7 (3): 162-168.

Christensen, L. T. & G. Cheney (2000) Self-Absorption and Self-Seduction in the Corporate Identity Game. In Schultz, M., M. J. Hatch & M. H. Larsen (Eds.) *The Expressive Organization. Linking Identity, Reputation and the Corporate Brand*. Oxford: Oxford University Press.

Christensen, L. T. & Morsing, M. (2005) *Bagom Corporate Communication.* Copenhagen: Samfundslitteratur.

Clarke, T. (Ed.) (2004) *Theories of Corporate Governance: The Philosophical Foundations of Corporate Governance.* London and New York: Routledge.

Cook, T. (1998) *Governing with the News: The News Media as a Political Institution.* Chicago: University of Chicago Press.

Corvellec, H. (1997) *Stories of Achievements: Narrative Features of Organizational Performance.* New Brunswick: Transaction Publishers.

DiMaggio, P. J. & W. W. Powell (1991) [1983] The Iron Cage Revisited - Institutional Isomorphism and Collective Rationality in Organizational Fields. In Powell, W. W. & P. J. DiMaggio (Eds.) *The New Institutionalism in Organizational Analysis.* Chicago: Chicago University Press.

Djelic, M.-L. (2006) Marketization: From intellectual agenda to global policy making. In Djelic, M.-L. & K. Sahlin-Andersson (Eds.) *Transnational Governance: Institutional Dynamics of Regulation.* Cambridge: Cambridge University Press.

Djelic, M.-L. & K. Sahlin-Andersson (Eds.) (2006) *Transnational Governance: Institutional Dynamics of Regulation.* Cambridge: Cambridge University Press.

Drori, G., J. Meyer, F. Ramirez & E. Schofer (2003) *Science in the Modern World Polity.* Stanford: Stanford University Press.

Drori, G. S. & J. W. Meyer (2006) Scientizaton: Making a world safe for organizing. In Djelic, M.-L. & K. Sahlin-Andersson (Eds.) *Transnational Governance: Institutional Dynamics of Regulation.* Cambridge: Cambridge University Press.

Dutton, J. E. & J. M. Dukerich (1991) Keeping an Eye on the Mirror: Image and Identity in Organizational Adaptation. *Academy of Management Journal* Vol. 34 (3): 517-554.

Elsbach, K. D. & Kramer R. M. (1996) Members' Responses to Organizational Identity Threats: Encountering and Countering the Business Week Rankings. *Administrative Science Quarterly* Vol. 41: 442-476.

Eriksen, E. O. (1999) *Kommunikativ ledelse: om verdier og styring i offentlig sektor.* Bergen: Fagbokforlaget.

Foucault, M. (1991) *Discipline and Punish. The Birth of the Prison.* London: Penguin Books.

Grafström, M. (2006) *The Development of Swedish Business Journalism. Historical Roots of an Organisational Field.* Doctoral Thesis No. 121. Department of Business Studies, Uppsala University.

Grafström, M., J. Grünberg, J. Pallas & K. Windell (2006) *Ekonominyhetens väg: Från kvartalsrapporter till ekonominyheter.* Stockholm: SNS Medieforum.

Habermas, J. (1991) *The Structural Transformation of the Public Sphere: An Inquiry Into a Category of Bourgeois Society.* Cambridge MA: MIT Press.

Hatch, M. J. & M. Schultz (2000) Scaling the Tower of Babel: Relational Differences between Identity, Image, and Culture in Organizations. In Schultz, M., M. J. Hatch & M. H. Larsen (Eds.) *The Expressive Organi-*

zation. Linking Identity, Reputation and the Corporate Brand. Oxford: Oxford University Press.

Hatch, M. J. & M. Schultz (1997) Relations between Organizational Culture, Identity and Image. *European Journal of Marketing* Vol. 31 (5): 356-365.

Hayward, M. L. A., V. P. Rindova & T. G. Pollock (2004) Believing One's Own Press: The Causes and Consequences of CEO Celebrity. *Strategic Management Journal* Vol. 25(7): 637-653.

Hedmo, T., K. Sahlin-Andersson & L. Wedlin (2005) Fields of Imitation: The Global Expansion of Management Education. In Czarniawska, B. & G. Sevón (Eds.) *Global Ideas: How Ideas, Objects and Practices Travel in the Global Economy.* Malmö & Copenhagen: Liber & Copenhagen Business Press.

Hedmo, T., K. Sahlin-Andersson & L. Wedlin (2006) The Emergence of a Europan Regulatory Field of Managment Education. In Djelic, M.-L. & K. Sahlin-Andersson (Eds.) *Transnational Governance: Institutional Dynamics of Regulation.* Cambridge: Cambridge University Press.

Henriques, D. B. (2000) What Journalists Should Be Doing about Business Coverage-But Aren't. *The Harvard International Journal of Press/Politics* Vol. 5 (2): 118-121.

Hood, C., C. Scott, O. James, G. Jones & T. Travers (1999) *Regulation Inside Government.* Oxford: Oxford University Press.

Jacobsson, B. & K. Sahlin-Andersson(2006) Dynamics of Soft Regulations. In Djelic, M.-L. & K. Sahlin-Andersson (Eds.) *Transnational Governance: Institutional Dynamics of Regulation.* Cambridge: Cambridge University Press.

Kjær, P. & R. Langer (2004) Virksomhed og politik i en mediestorm. En analyse af SAS-Mærsk kartelsagen. In Frankel, C. (Ed.) *Den politiske virksomhed.* Frederiksberg: Samfundslitteratur.

Kjærgaard, A. & M. Morsing (2006) Captured by the image in the mirror: A longitudinal analysis of the dynamics of corporate and organisational identity. Paper presented at the European Group on Organization Studies (EGOS), Bergen, July 6-8 2006.

Knorr Cetina, K. & U. Bruegger (2002) Global Microstructures: The Virtual Societies of Financial Markets. *American Journal of Sociology* Vol. 107 (4): 905-950.

Levi-Faur, D. & Jordana, J. (Eds.) (2005) *The Rise of Regulatory Capitalism: the Global Diffusion of a New Regulatory Order.* The Annals of the Americal Academy of Political and Social Science. Vol. 598. London: Sage.

Luhmann, N. (2000) *The Reality of the Mass Media.* Cambridge: Polity Press.

Lund, A. B. (2002) *Den redigerende magt – nyhedsinstitutionens politiske indflydelse.* Aarhus: Aarhus Universitetsforlag.

Mathiesen, T. (1997) The viewer society. Michel Foucault's 'Panopticon' revisited. *Theoretical Criminology* Vol. 1 (2): 215-234.

Meindl, J. R., S. B. Ehrlich & J. M. Dukerich (1985) The Romance of Leadership. *Administrative Science Quarterly* Vol. 30 (2): 78-102.

Meyer, J. W. & B. Rowan (1977) Institutionalized Organizations: Formal Structure as Myth and Ceremony. *American Journal of Sociology* Vol. 83 (2): 364-385.
Miller, P. & T. O'Leary (1987) Acounting and the Construction of the Governable Person. *Accounting, Organizations and Society* Vol. 12 (3): 235–265.
Miller, P. & N. Rose (1990) Governing Economic Life. *Economy and Society* Vol. 19 (1): 1-31.
Monks, Robert A. G. & Nell Minow (1995) *Corporate Governance*. Oxford: Blackwell Business.
Moran, M. (2002) Understanding the Regulatory State. *British Journal of Political Science* Vol. 32 (2): 391–413.
Morsing, M. (1999) The Media Boomerang: The Media's Role in Changing Identity by Changing Image. *Corporate Reputation Review* Vol. 2 (2): 116-136.
Mörth, U. (Ed.) (2004) *Soft Law in Governance and Regulation*. Cheltenham: Edward Elgar.
Mörth, U. (2006) Soft Regulation and Global Democracy. In Djelic, M.-L. & K. Sahlin-Andersson (Eds.) *Transnational Governance: Institutional Dynamics of Regulation*. Cambridge University Press.
North, D. C. (1990) *Institutions, Institutional Change and Economic Performance*. New York: Cambridge University Press.
Parsons, W. D. (1989) *The Power of the Financial Press. Journalism and Economic Opinion in Britain and America*. Aldershot: Edward Elgar Press.
Perrow, C. (1991) A society of organizations. *Theory and society* Vol. 20 (6): 725-762.
Perrow, C. (2002) *Organizing America: Wealth, Power, and the Origins of Corporate Capitalism*. New Jersey: University Presses of California, Columbia and Princeton.
Pfeffer, J. & G. R. Salancik (1978) *The External Control of Organizations. A Resource Dependence Perspective*. New York: Harper & Row Publishers.
Power, M. (1994) The Audit Society. In Hopwood, A. G. & P. Miller (Eds.) *Accounting and Social and Institutional Practice*. Cambridge: Cambridge University Press.
Power, M. (1997) *The Audit Society*. Oxford: Oxford University Press.
Power, M. (2003) Evaluating the Audit Explosion. *Law & Policy* Vol. 25 (3): 115-202.
Rindova, V. P., T. G. Pollock & M. L. A. Hayward (2006) Celebrity Firms: The Social Construction of Market Popularity. *Academy of Management Review* Vol. 31 (1): 50-71.
Rosenberg, J. M. (1982) *Inside the Wall Street Journal. The History and the Power of Dow Jones and Company and America's Most Influential Newspaper*. New York: MacMillan.
Sahlin-Andersson, K. & L. Engwall (2002) *The expansion of management knowledge. Carriers, flows, and sources*. Palo Alto: Stanford University Press.
Schultz, I. (2006) *Bag nyhederne*. Fredriksberg: Forlaget Samfundslitteratur.

Shore, C. & S. Wright (2000) Coercive Accountability. The Rise of Audit Culture in Higher Education. In Strathern, M. (Ed.) *Audit Cultures*. London: Routledge.

Strathern, M. (2000) The Tyranny of Transparency. *British Educational Research Journal* Vol. 26 (3): 309–321.

Tsoukas, H. (1999) David and Goliath in the Risk Society. Making Sense of the Conflict Between Shell and Greenpeace in the North Sea. *Organization* Vol. 6 (1): 499-528.

Tsoukas, H. (1997) The Tyranny of Light. The Temptations and Paradoxes of the Information Society. *Futures* Vol. 29 (9): 827-843.

Tuchman, G. (1978) *Making News*. New York: The Free Press.

Vaara, E. & J. Tienari (2002) Justification, Legitimization and Naturalization of Mergers and Acquisitions: A Critical Discourse Analysis of Media Texts. *Organization* Vol. 9 (2): 275-303.

Vattimo, G. (1992) *The Tranparent Society*. Cambridge: Polity Press.

Weber, M. (1919/1946) Science as a vocation. In Gerth, H.H. & C. Wright Mills (Eds.) *From Max Weber. Essays in Sociology*. New York: Oxford University Press.

Wenger, E. (2000) Communities of Practice and Social Learning Systems. *Organization* Vol. 7 (2): 225-246.